RELIGIOUS CONVICTIONS
AND POLITICAL CHOICE

RELIGIOUS CONVICTIONS

AND POLITICAL CHOICE

Kent Greenawalt

Columbia University

BIP87
New York   *   Oxford
OXFORD UNIVERSITY PRESS
1988

Oxford University Press

Oxford   New York   Toronto
Delhi   Bombay   Calcutta   Madras   Karachi
Petaling Jaya   Singapore   Hong Kong   Tokyo
Nairobi   Dar es Salaam   Cape Town
Melbourne   Auckland

and associated companies in

Beirut   Berlin   Ibadan   Nicosia

Library of Congress Cataloging-in-Publication Data
Greenawalt, R. Kent, 1936-
Religious convictions and political choice.
Includes index.
1. Religion and politics—United States.   2. Religion
and state—United States.   3. United States—Religion.
I. Title.
BL65.P7G73   1988   320′.01′9   87-12456
ISBN 0-19-504913-6

2 4 6 8 10 9 7 5 3 1

Printed in the United States of America
on acid-free paper

To Robert,
With a parent's love and pride

PREFACE

This book is concerned with the extent to which citizens and officials in this liberal democracy properly rely on their religious convictions when they decide what political actions to take. Although the immediate generation of my work on this topic was an invitation to deliver the 1986 Cooley lectures at the University of Michigan Law School, the subject reflects themes of much longer standing in my personal and intellectual life.

I was raised in a family in which both religion and the values of liberal democracy were seriously regarded. My father was long head of the board of trustees of the Plymouth Church of the Pilgrims, Henry Ward Beecher's old church, and as a child I went there as well as to the local community church in which I was confirmed. During my youth, I took it for granted that one's religious commitments and understandings would matter for one's life, including one's life as a citizen, and that liberal democracy was a system of governance that warranted support. At Swarthmore College, where I took political science as a major and religion as a minor, most of what I believed was in one way or another subjected to challenge, but my belief that taking religion as a serious matter did not compromise one's efforts to be a liberal citizen remained assumed and unexamined. I was much influenced by the writings of Reinhold Niebuhr, who then, and subsequently, struck me as fully committed to democratic values while relying on a Christian perspective to inform his understanding of politics and of right political action. A summer spent in East Harlem working under Norman Eddy in the East Harlem Protestant Parish provided some personal confirmation of the appropriateness of relating one's religious life to one's political involvement.

My views about the positive relation between religious convictions and political action did not alter during years of studying political philosophy at Oxford and law at Columbia, or indeed for most of my career as a legal academic. During my first year of law school, the question of religion and politics was raised during John F. Kennedy's presidential campaign, but I took the issue then as being whether Kennedy would adhere to American law and political institutions if these somehow came into conflict with Roman Catholic directives or premises, not as whether his views on the wide range of political issues would be unaffected by his religious faith. As editor-in-chief of the Columbia Law Review, I read Louis Henkin's well-known article on obscenity as sin very closely during the editing process, but some of its possible broader implications for secularizing political decisions escaped me at the time. Similarly when I read and admired John Rawls' *A Theory of Justice*, I did not realize the extent to which acceptance of its basic premises would exclude religious perceptions from the political sphere.

My comfortable acceptance of the idea that one's religious convictions may affect one's political judgment has no doubt been reinforced by the fact that two of my oldest and closest friends, James Miller and Bruce Hanson, my brother-in-law, William Abernethy, and my sister, Ann Green-awalt Abernethy, are all ministers for whom questions of social justice have loomed as very important. Though in my adult life I have been only an occasional churchgoer, these close associations have helped confirm my continuing belief in the importance of religious understanding.

My focused intellectual interest in this topic began when debate over abortion produced frequent arguments that people were trying to impose their religious views on others. Bruce Ackerman's book, *Social Justice and the Liberal State*, which contends for the exclusion of religious premises with a novel starkness and clarity, persuaded me that this was a subject that warranted the most careful consideration. The invitation to deliver the Cooley lectures provided the needed spark for me to marshall my resources to make that effort.

Since the late fall of 1984, when I began work on the subject, I have benefited greatly from comments of members of groups before whom I have presented parts of my work, from individuals who have criticized drafts, and from institutions whose financial support has freed my time for research. Roughly in order, the work has been discussed by the faculty of the Campbell University School of Law, the faculty of the Marshall-Wythe School of Law, College of William and Mary, a symposium on Perspectives on the Religion Clauses of the First Amendment, at the J. Reuben Clark Law School, Brigham Young University, the Law and Philosophy colloqium of New York University, students and faculty of the University of Michigan Law School, a symposium on Religion and the State sponsored by the Institute of Bill of Rights Law, at the Marshall-Wythe School of Law, the faculty of Columbia Law School, the students and faculty of Cleveland-Marshall School of the Law, and a workshop of the Faculty of the University of California at Berkeley Law School. The comments on my paper at the Brigham Young symposium by Cole Durham, and the comments on my paper at the Marshall-Wythe symposium by Michael Perry, Frederick Schauer, Michael Smith, and Diane Zimmerman were of great value. The richly rewarding three days I spent delivering the lectures at Michigan were capped by a dinner on the final evening at which my fundamental ideas were subjected to a searching examination that required many revisions in this final version. In addition to these discrete occasions for comment, I have also learned from students in seminars on Law, Religion, and Politics at the Marshall-Wythe School of Law and at Columbia.

Meir Dan-Cohen, Herbert Deane, Louis Henkin, Henry Monaghan, Gene R. Nichol, and William F. Young read all or much of the manuscript in an earlier draft and gave me very helpful suggestions. At a number of points in the process, Bruce Ackerman has given generously of his time. I have been much encouraged by how fruitful conversation can be even when views are as sharply opposed as are ours on this topic, and my sensitivity to a major position I reject would be much less if this dialogue had not occurred.

The honorarium that the Cooley lectures carry has been one source of financial support. During the summers of 1985 and 1986 my work has been aided by a grant from Columbia Law School's Samuel Rubin Program for the Advancement of Liberty and Equality through Law. A Distinguished Lee Visiting Professorship at the Marshall-Wythe School of Law during the autumn of 1985 made available a great deal of time for research and writing.

My work on the book has been aided considerably by the research assistance and comments of Joseph Nisa, Maureen Carroll, and Daniel Alter. Steven Walt has devoted much time and effort helping me through drafts of the manuscript, has offered trenchant criticisms of aspects of the analysis, and has prepared the index. Krista Page, at Columbia, and Millie Arthur, at William and Mary, typed early drafts with great efficiency and patience. From the spring of 1986 Rhonda Callison has accommodated my successive changes despite problems of transposition from one system to another. Their good spirits in the face of insistent time pressures have been a source of much reassurance.

Parts of earlier drafts of the book have been published in law reviews. The much more summary lectures are printed, nearly as delivered, as

"Religious Convictions and Lawmaking" in the *Michigan Law Review* (vol. 84, pp. 352–404 [1985]). An article entitled "Religiously Based Premises and Laws Restrictive of Liberty" appears in the *Brigham Young Law Review* (vol. 1986, pp. 245–97) and "The Limits of Rationality and the Place of Religious Convictions: Protecting Animals and the Environment" is in the *William and Mary Law Review* (vol. 27, pp. 1011–65 [1986]).

The importance of thought about religion and liberal democracy is continually brought home to all of us by events in the political arena. A more personal reminder for me during the past two years has been the development in my two older sons, Robert, 16, and Sasha 15, of distinctive religious and political convictions that owe relatively little to parental influence. Seeing the ways in which their deepening religious faith affects their opinions about political subjects reemphasizes for me the centrality of the question whether such an effect is somehow in tension with liberal democracy.

That is what this book is about. I hope it will illuminate how religious convictions figure in political judgments for those who already have fairly developed positions; I also hope it will be of some help for those who are trying to sort out in their own lives the appropriate domains of religion and politics.

New York City   K. G.
April 1987

CONTENTS

III. Dialogue, Official Action, and Constitutionality

I

LIBERAL DEMOCRACY AND PUBLICLY ACCESSIBLE REASONS

1

The Aim and Scope of the Inquiry

The Underlying Question

This book concentrates on one facet of the uneasy and complicated relationships between religion and government in the United States, the connection between peoples' religious convictions and their political choices.

I can best introduce the basic underlying issue by illustrations in some practical contexts.

Jean is a legislator deciding whether she should vote for stringent protections to prevent obscure species of fish from becoming extinct. She decides that neither present nor future human interests warrant the strict protection that has been proposed. But she also believes that the natural environment was created by God and that people should not alter it irrevocably if they can avoid doing so.

George is a voter deciding which candidate for president to support. He believes that the economic programs of the Republican candidate would create more general prosperity at the expense of the poor; the programs of the Democrat would help the poor but be less conducive to general welfare. George belongs to a religious group that teaches that aiding the poor is the first obligation of society.

Doris is a prominent lawyer who is asked to lend her support to a proposal that imprisonment be radically increased in comparison with probation and parole. Doris recognizes that the new regime would involve much pain and unhappiness, but she has a religiously informed pessimism about human sinfulness. The need she perceives to repress people's selfish inclinations leads her to think we need more imprisonment than we now have.

The central question I want to address is whether people like Jean, George, and Doris properly rely on their religious convictions in deciding what public laws and policies to support.

What do I mean when I say "properly rely?" Certainly no citizen violates any law by relying on his or her religious views when adopting political positions. Indeed, any law that attempted to restrict such behavior would infringe constitutional guarantees of the free exercise of religion and of free speech. The most that might be urged about similar reliance on religious views by a public official is that it affects the constitutional validity of his or her actions. Though my final chapter considers the question whether laws that derive from religious convictions may be unconstitutional, that subject is subsidiary to my major concern. I am not talking mainly about legal propriety.

I also am not asking whether reliance on religious convictions is best overall. Suppose that George believes God *insists* that we support candidates who give priority to the welfare of the poor. To say that George would be wrong overall to rely on that religious conviction, one would have to find reasons why his religious judgment itself was incorrect. I try hard to avoid direct claims about theological truth.

My perspectives for evaluation are the premises of our particular liberal democratic polity, supplemented by judgments about how people make (and can be expected to make) moral evaluations. When I ask whether Jean, George, and Doris properly rely on their religious convictions, I mean to raise a question about the implications of membership in this liberal society. Would a good member of our liberal democracy rely on his or her religious convictions?

Even here, I need to be careful. A central feature of liberal democracy is its tolerance of people who use illiberal political programs or rely on illiberal reasons. At least so long as these people accept legal mechanisms for change, they are not *bad* citizens, to be *condemned* by the rest of us. So when I ask if people "properly rely" on their religious convictions, I do not mean that all *improper* reliance deserves condemnation. Rather, I am asking about a kind of model of good liberal citizenship.

Why the Question Matters

The question regarding reliance on religious convictions has intense contemporary relevance, in both the political arena and academic discourse, yet neither its full dimensions nor the complexity of how it relates to other church-state problems is adequately understood.

The 1984 presidential campaign amply shows the topic's present public importance and the confusion surrounding it. President Reagan's close association with right wing fundamentalist leaders caused some worry, but the more enduring concerns about church and state involved the emotional issues of abortion, school prayer, and public aid to private religious education. During one televised national debate, Walter Mondale claimed that the Republican platform, in demanding that prospective judges have a "prolife" position on abortion, had set a religious test for judges.[1] President Reagan responded that abortion was a constitutional, not a religious issue.[2] These rhetorical thrusts, in capsule form, exemplified the powerful tendency to oversimplify the question whether it is appropriate to base a political standard on moral premises that are somehow derived from religious beliefs.

The evident importance of this problem for political philosophy partly results from the advent of modern comprehensive theories of justice.[3] If liberal democracy is seen primarily as a set of institutions for accommodating conflicting interests and desires, the manner in which people ground their claims to satisfaction is not of primary importance; but when the ideal aim of citizens and officials in their political lives is understood as achieving justice, what considerations count as relevant to justice becomes critical. From *this* vantage point, the place of religious convictions is related to the place of conceptions of the good and other "fundamental" beliefs about human existence.[4] The appropriate place of all these sorts of grounds turns partly on the possibility of resolving political problems on the basis of shared premises of justice and shared criteria for determining truth.

My own interest in this subject derives from my outlook and experiences. With some uncertainty and tentativeness, I hold religious convictions, but I find myself in a pervasively secular discipline. My convictions tell me that no aspect of life should be wholly untouched by the transcendent reality in which I believe, yet a basic premise of common legal argument is that any reference to such a perspective is out of bounds. This personal and professional dilemma helps explain my concern with the place of religious convictions in the process by which laws are made.

The thread of my argument, however, is general. I am not relating a personal search for accommodation or explaining where one peculiar set of religious convictions leads. If what I say in this book is sound, my own philosophical views will certainly not have escaped influence by my religious beliefs, but the analysis and conclusions I offer do not depend on the truth or falsity of particular religious positions; they lay claim to a broader persuasiveness.

Why should others be interested in this discussion? Many readers may face on a personal level questions similar to mine about how their religious beliefs bear on their involvement in some secular vocation that involves working toward a better social and legal order. The endeavor to find the place of religious convictions should have immediate appeal for them. Others will have religious convictions whose import for political activities is quite clear. Knowing what those convictions demand of them in their political life, they may feel impatient with any efforts to classify those actions as within or without the boundaries of principles that underlie liberal democracy. But such impatience would be misconceived. They must deal with people who think that religious convictions have little or no proper place in the political life of our country, and they would do well to understand how far their own positions are fairly grounded in our political traditions. If persuaded that some part of what they accept as proper actually is at odds with those traditions, they might reconsider what their religious convictions really demand in this society.

Finally, many readers will hold no religious beliefs at all or will think that the beliefs they do hold are irrelevant to their political choices. This group may well include the majority of faculty members in law schools and philosophy and political science departments of leading universities. A good many professors and other intellectuals display a hostility or skeptical indifference to religion that amounts to a thinly disguised contempt for belief in any reality beyond that discoverable by scientific inquiry and ordinary human experience.

Those who view religious convictions as foolish superstitions whose impact on our social life should be minimized as far as possible may find discussions of the place of religious convictions a most unappetizing theme. Yet this very group is the one at which my comments are mainly addressed. Since these skeptics live in a country in which many people are seriously religious, they need to understand how far their wish to minimize the place of religion in our political life may fairly be based on claims about the premises of liberal democracy and how far that wish must rest on the intrinsic foolishness of religion, a foolishness many skeptics are more comfortable accepting than trying to demonstrate.

My primary aim is normative, to say something about what people should or may do, rather than to describe what people do or have done. My main perspective for normative evaluation is the moral and political philosophy that undergirds our law and government. Without making a systematic defense of my views, I indicate in Chapter 2 what I take to be dominant features of that philosophy. This account both brings into sharp focus how the proper place of religious convictions differs from other church-state problems and provides some standards against which to measure reliance on religious convictions.

Among the important issues about religion and government familiar to American lawyers and students of government are the closeness of relations between political and religious organizations, the degree of permissible public support to religiously sponsored endeavors, the legitimacy of government-sponsored positions on religious subjects, the scope of freedom for religious expression and worship, and the appropriateness of exemptions from ordinary rules for those with objections based on religious conscience. Accommodations regarding these issues are a continuing source of adjustment and bitterness in the political process, and they generate controversial interpretations of federal and state constitutional provisions on religion.

At a deeper level lie two more abstract and philosophical questions about religion and a liberal polity. The first is about the justification of political institutions: can the authority of government and the obligation to obey its directives be persuasively defended in purely secular terms or is a religious underpinning required? The second, related, question concerns the conditions of civic virtue: can liberal government survive and prosper if its citizens do not understand its authority and law from a religious perspective?

My analysis shows why, contrary to frequently made assumptions, the topic of religious convictions and political choice is not simply a subdivision of one of the other subjects involving religion and government. Though I start with assumptions about some of these other issues and state or imply some conclusions about others, my aim is not to contribute directly to their understanding and resolution. My focus differs from that of recent authors, notably Harold Berman[5] and Richard John Neuhaus,[6] who have asked whether a politics devoid of religion will lack coherence, will undermine the moral character of our people, or will open the door to secular totalitarian movements. I am mainly interested in what one can fairly expect of religious citizens if one accepts the premises that underlie our political institutions.

Because the term "unconstitutional" comes up a lot in debates about religion and politics and because the topic of religious convictions and political choice has profound importance for our legal culture, it may help avoid confusion to clarify at this preliminary stage three relevant senses of unconstitutionality as they apply here.

The strongest sense of unconstitutionality is that some law or government action will be (or would be if challenged) struck down by courts as in conflict with provisions of our written Constitution. That sense is relevant to this study only insofar as reliance on religious convictions might render laws or government programs invalid.

Another, more subtle, sense of unconstitutionality lies fairly close to this standard one. The Constitution may actually prohibit certain actions that courts will not declare to be unconstitutional. The point is most obvious in relation to actions that courts deem to be within what is left of the political question doctrine.[7] A government act within the range of that doctrine may be unconstitutional, though immune from judicial invalidation because the subject matter is not apt for courts. The political question doctrine is explicit and straightforward in this respect, but other judicial standards for declarations of unconstitutionality may have a similar import. One way of looking at the extreme latitude courts ordinarily give legislatures to decide what regulations will serve public welfare[8] is that courts accept some enactments that actually violate constitutional demands of nonarbitrariness because the arbitrariness of legislative action is not demonstrable.

One of the more bizarre charges of the 1984 election was that President Reagan had told Rev. Jerry Falwell that he could pick two Supreme Court justices in a second Reagan term. Without doubt, a president can seek advice from private citizens, including clerics, about appointments. Without doubt, any formal law that authorized clergy to select secular judges would be an unconstitutional establishment of religion. If a president actually promised to allow a cleric to select a Supreme Court justice and stuck to his promise, he would almost certainly be acting in an unconstitutional manner.[9] But if a president offered the appointment as his own and it was approved by the Senate, the appointment would be beyond effective judicial scrutiny.

This second sense of unconstitutionality may be raised by our topic when individual legislators rely inappropriately on religious bases of judgment. Arguably, such reliance is itself at odds with constitutional premises whether or not it is discoverable by courts and whether or not the grounds on which individual legislators vote infect the validity of adopted statutes.

Beyond these legal senses of unconstitutionality stands a looser and more metaphorical sense, the idea that a practice violates basic principles of our constitutional order. Suppose that a Roman Catholic bishop directs each parish priest to read in church a letter that urges all Catholics to vote against any candidate who supports permissive abortion laws. One thing that is certain is that the bishop's act is not unconstitutional in any technical legal way. With the exception of the prohibition of slavery and involuntary servitude, the Constitution, including the clause of the First Amendment that bars an "establishment" of religion, reaches only acts that are done by the government, in cooperation with the government, or in lieu of ordinary government authority. The bishop's directive falls in none of the relevant categories, and indeed is itself constitutionally protected under the clauses of the First Amendment that protect freedom of speech and the free exercise of religion. What is not so clear, however, is whether the bishop's directive respects the appropriate spheres of government and religion in our political order. From that perspective his directive may be argued to be unconstitutional. Arguments that some practice is unconstitutional in this broad sense amount to claims that the practice is at odds with the theory and tradition of our institutions. It is just such claims that I mainly address, and the model of liberal democracy that I suggest in the next chapter is the standard against which I evaluate these claims.

The Strategy of Exposition

The main questions I consider are the following. How far are private citizens appropriately guided by religious perspectives in their political decisions? How far are the reasons they put forward for their actions appropriately religious? How far should religious leaders and members of religious organizations use these organizations as vehicles for presenting and promoting their views on political matters? How far are officials and candidates for office appropriately guided in their decisions by their own religious perspectives or those of their constituents? How far can they appropriately put forward religious reasons for their decisions? Do judges differ in these respects from other officials? When, if ever, does reliance on religious convictions render legislation unconstitutional? In the course of dealing with these questions, I also address similar questions about "fundamental" nonreligious beliefs.

Any attempt to answer these immense questions must draw from a variety of disciplines, including moral philosophy, political philosophy, political science, religious ethics, American history, and constitutional law. No one can hope to answer all these questions satisfactorily in a short compass, and I am far from a master of all the needed disciplines. Why then have I cast such a broad net? The reason is that the answer to each of most of the questions is intertwined with the answers to others. Anything that aspires to be at all systematic in its analysis of the place of religion in politics and law must come to grips with the range of these questions and deal, however inadequately, with all these disciplines. Even a stumbling and tentative effort of this sort is preferable to myopic appraisal from a single point of view.

I begin in Chapter 2 with a broad account of what I understand to be the basic premises of our liberal democracy. Next I discuss religious convictions and how they may influence political views. Following is a general comparison between socially shared grounds of decision and grounds based on religious convictions, a comparison that focuses on the claim that only the former grounds are appropriately relied upon in a liberal democracy.

The chapters in Part II deal with a number of particular political issues, showing how religious convictions might matter to a citizen making a decision about each of them and inquiring whether reliance on those convictions is proper, given liberal democratic premises. In the course of these discussions, I critically examine the claim that citizens should rely exclusively on shared bases of appraisal, considering the imperfect capacities of actual human beings. This examination touches on the place of nonreligious fundamental premises that some theorists have wished to exclude, along with religious premises, from political decisions and discourse. I treat briefly the particularly thorny problem of religious convictions that are at odds with generally shared bases for judgment.

Though the significance of political discourse figures to some degree in the discussion up to that point, I next address such discourse as a special question, suggesting how my conclusions imply limits to any ideal democratic dialogue. Only after that do I consider official actions and religious conviction. Finally, I analyze the borders of unconstitutionality in the legal sense.

As this summary suggests, much of my discussion is devoted to the implications of citizenship in a liberal democratic state. Focus on the proper attitudes of private members of society may initially seem much less productive than addressing the actions of officials. After all, what officials do determines what gets to be law and officials as a group may seem more amenable to persuasion about what they should or should not take into account than the vast body of the citizenry. A theory of government may bear much more heavily on the actions of officials than on the occasional involvements of ordinary people in the political process. Moreover, if officials limit themselves to proper considerations, perhaps it does not matter much what grounds motivate citizens pressing claims on the officials. Certainly if a law is actually to be challenged as an unconstitutional promotion of religion, the aims of those who adopted it will count for more than the perspectives of citizens who favored it.

Yet I want to insist that the implications of good citizenship for individuals is the right place to start. Although citizens are not usually in the position of voting directly on particular political issues, their views on issues affect their votes for candidates, and the more active among them urge positions upon officials and upon their fellow citizens. Further, votes on referenda and state constitutional amendments do afford citizens occasional opportunities to vote directly on issues. Liberal democracy does bear on how citizens as well as officials think about issues and conduct themselves.

We can see this point clearly if we attend to the possible position that religious convictions are acceptable bases for judgment for citizens in a liberal democracy because any bases for judgment are acceptable. This position, which boils down to the view that liberal democracy is a set of procedures for making political decisions—with some understood limits on what the majority can do to the minority, suggests that the premises of liberal democracy have nothing to say about *why* citizens support the political positions they do.

Stated so absolutely, the view is clearly wrong, because linked to premises about how liberal political institutions should operate are premises about a liberal citizenry. Within a liberal democracy people are *permitted* to support outcomes, such as the legal subjugation of one race by another, that are plainly unjust under liberal democratic conceptions, but a model liberal citizen does not support such outcomes. So much is obvious. But if the liberal citizen does not support outcomes that are unjust from the liberal point of view, there must also be a limit on the reasons he uses to support acceptable outcomes. Suppose that alternative outcomes are both within the range of liberal positions and each is supported by substantial liberal arguments. I believe this is true about the present debate over preferential treatment of minorities. Opposing preferences because one thinks any racial classifications are unjust or reinforce racist attitudes is not illiberal. But opposing preferences because one hopes to perpetuate the social inferiority of racial minorities is illiberal. This conclusion establishes that premises of liberal democracy do have *something* to say about acceptable *bases* for the political positions of citizens as well as about acceptable political outcomes.

If we put aside motivations to attain ultimate results that are themselves at odds with liberal democratic premises, are not people free to decide on any other bases? Isn't liberal democracy *otherwise* indifferent about the bases of personal preferences? This question is somewhat more troublesome and all I shall do is state my own view succinctly. Some issues properly turn on personal preferences. Were a vote taken, for example, whether a bear or a fox were to become the state symbol, people could rightly vote in terms of pure preferences. For such issues, any mode of deriving a preference is appropriate, including a religiously based view that the bear is a loftier creature. On some other issues, however, a good citizen has a responsibility to decide what is right, not simply to vote his or her preference. I assume that a model citizen should decide in this way about such matters as abortion, treatment of animals, capital punishment, and foreign affairs. A woman would not be justified in supporting capital punishment just because she finds the practice emotionally satisfying or because she profits from executions as the publisher of a sensational newspaper.[10] We expect something more of the good citizen than these inadequate reasons. As to issues of this sort, the appropriateness of relying on religious convictions needs to be examined. Such reliance cannot simply be lumped together with other bases of personal preference and justified on the theory that people can vote their preferences.

Unless we are clear about the right perspectives for ordinary citizens to adopt, we can hardly assess what officials should consider. Were it really proper for citizens to rely on any grounds whatsoever, serious incongruity would arise if officials were expected to disregard some grounds in favor of others. One should hope for a theory under which what citizens may rely upon is compatible with proper perspectives for officials. Once one answers the questions about individual responsibilities, the worries about official roles become more tractable.

Since my analysis at stages becomes rather complex and my conclusions are punctuated by doubts and qualifications, I here state my main conclusions: Legislation must be justified in terms of secular objectives, but when people reasonably think that shared premises of justice and criteria for determining truth cannot resolve critical questions of fact, fundamental questions of value, or the weighing of competing benefits and harms, they do appropriately rely on religious convictions that help them answer these questions. Not only is such reliance appropriate for ordinary citizens, legislators in similar instances may also rely on their own religious convictions and those of their constitutents, and occasionally such reliance is warranted even for judges. Though reliance on religious convictions may be appropriate in these settings, argument in religious terms is often an inapt form of public dialogue. Appropriate reliance on many nonreligious "fundamental" beliefs is as broad as appropriate reliance on religious convictions, and public arguments based on some of these are not subject to objections of the same force as those that apply to religious arguments. Even were people ideally motivated and political institutions ideally constituted, shared standards of decision would be incapable of resolving many political issues.

Notes

1. "The Candidates Debate: Religion, Abortion and the Quality of Life," *New York Times*, Oct. 8, 1984, p. B5, col. 2.

2. Id., col. 3.

3. See, e.g., J. Rawls, *A Theory of Justice* (Cambridge, Mass., Harvard Univ. Pr. 1971); B. Ackerman, *Social Justice in the Liberal State* (New Haven, Conn., Yale Univ. Pr. 1980).

4. What I mean to include by other fundamental beliefs will become clearer in subsequent chapters.

5. H. Berman, *The Interaction of Law and Religion* (Nashville, Tenn., Abingdon Pr. 1974).

6. R. J. Neuhaus, *The Naked Public Square*, pp. 21, 51, 60, 82–86 (Grand Rapids, Mich., William B. Eerdmans Pub. Co. 1984).

7. Baker v. Carr, 369 U.S. 186 (1962); Powell v. McCormack, 395 U.S. 486 (1969). In some cases, the term "political question" is used to indicate that any decision on a subject by the executive or legislative branch is constitutionally permissible; however, according to the narrower political question doctrine referred to in the text, courts will not determine whether a challenged act of a coordinate branch violates the Constitution. See L. Henkin, "Is There a Political Question Doctrine?" 85 *Yale Law Journal*, pp. 597–625 (1976). When a court says recognition of a foreign government is a political question, it means that the executive under the constitution is free to do whatever it wants; when courts said the legality of the Vietnam War was a political question, they meant that judges would not decide if the executive had acted unconstitutionally.

8. I refer here to the relaxed "rational basis" standards courts use for "ordinary" substantive due process and equal protection cases. An ordinary economic regulation, say of coal mining practices, may be challenged as involving an arbitrary deprivation of liberty or property without due process or as involving an arbitrary classification (as between coal mining and some other mining) that denies equal protection. In response to challenges of this sort, federal courts almost never declare regulations unconstitutional, accepting legislative judgments if any reasonable basis for them can be conceived. Judicial review of legislation is much more stringent if fundamental rights, such as procreative rights, or suspect classifications, such as racial classifications, are in question.

9. Allowing a cleric to veto prospects would present a more troublesome constitutional question.

10. As Carl Henry put it, "Failure to cast one's vote in a political society such as ours is nonperformance of duty, but so likewise is voting merely on the basis of selfish interest or political prejudice" (*Aspects of Christian Social Ethics*, p. 131 [Grand Rapids, Mich., William B. Eerdmans Pub. Co. 1964]).

2

Premises of Liberal Democracy and the Place of Religion

In this chapter I develop a partial model of liberal democracy, addressing aspects that are relevant for my inquiry about the place of religious convictions in the late-twentieth-century United States. Much of the rest of the book can be understood as an effort to see how far the implications of that model reach.

Though all agree that we live in a liberal democracy, exactly what that means is not so simple, and this preliminary exercise is both important and difficult. What one includes in a model concerning relations of religion and the state may, of course, affect conclusions about the place of religious convictions in political choice; and since controversial conclusions do not gain in cogency by being imported into an initially innocuous-looking model, I need to explain my purposes and methodology carefully.

One critical aim is to show that no straightforward conclusion about reliance on religious convictions follows ineluctably, as some may have thought, from common assumptions about liberal democracy. The discussion here begins to suggest how much more complicated the problem is. Part of the argument of the book as a whole is that a substantially secular and separationist model of liberal democracy does not establish that people should always eschew their religious convictions in making political choices.

A second purpose of my model is to provide a base, one that presently enjoys reasonably wide acceptance, against which conclusions about specific issues can be judged. I do not claim that all my conclusions *follow from* this initial model. The model does provide arguments for many of them,

14

but other arguments rest on independent considerations. Perhaps my most important claim about the model is that it does not *require* any conclusions that are contrary to the ones I draw.

My model has not been chosen with blind disregard of what it would allow and disallow. The model and my judgments about acceptable practices have developed together,[1] and the model reflects that process of evaluation. Though the model helps clarify my judgments, its presence need not impel consent from those inclined to reject the judgments. A critic may dispute my claims about arguments drawn from the model or dissent from independent aspects of the analysis. As to practical conclusions that do flow clearly from the model, he may prefer some alternative model of liberal democracy that implies different conclusions. Finally, no model of liberal democracy can settle what are the best practices overall. A person who concedes that ideas underpinning liberal democracy yield a particular practical conclusion may always contend that the ideas of liberal democracy should be rejected outright or sharply qualified. Although a partial model of liberal democracy may assist thought about religious convictions and political choice, crucial steps must be taken from the model to any judgments about what really is best in our society.

The model, as I have said, is partial. Some of the important features of a theory of liberal democracy that it does not touch, such as a theory of representation, are dealt with as they become relevant in later parts of the book.

What criteria should one use to develop a model of liberal democracy for the United States? The most basic standards involve the minimal conditions for application of the concept of liberal democracy; a model's features cannot be at odds with the meaning of that concept.[2] Other standards may be derived from the clear foundations of this particular liberal democracy, though not essential for liberal democracies generally. Since liberal democracy rests on an assumption that the government should deal fairly with all citizens,[3] a model should not include features that are unfair to some members of the society.[4] Nor should a model for the United States have features that are plainly inapt for American society; evident fitness for this society is another relevant criterion. Finally, other criteria of preferability may be needed, ones that include features in preference to alternatives because the features are intrinsically superior or will work better. With the use of these last criteria, the danger of smuggling one's desired practical conclusions into the model's premises is most acute. When a choice is made between two alternatives, both of which would be fair, fit for the society, and consonant with the concept of liberal democracy, the choice requires articulate defense.

Democratic Governance and Individual Liberty

Some central elements of liberal democracy are easily identified. Political power is largely dispersed. Ordinary citizens have the right to express themselves in the process of governance and have, formally at least, ultimate political authority since they decide in elections which persons will become legislators and chief executives. Either by written constitution or by tradition, government power over individuals' lives is limited. People are free to develop their own values and, at least within limits, styles of life; they are free to express their views not only about political questions but about other human concerns; and they are free to develop a wide variety of religious perspectives and practices.

These features of indirect democratic governance and personal liberty are indisputable aspects of liberal democracy and of our own political traditions. Though at the time of our Constitution a more conservative republican polity was consciously preferred to fully democratic institutions, extension of suffrage and the eroding significance of indirect elections have made us more democratic. Democratic governance and personal liberty have long characterized political life in this country, and people of highly diverse political opinions take them as unquestioned premises. Any country that failed to exhibit these features in its political life would not be a liberal democracy.

Government That Rests on Secular Justifications and Does Not Support Religion

Although relations between government and religion in a liberal democracy cannot be disposed of so easily, one consistent aspect of liberal democratic political theory has been a secular justification for the state. The dominant theory has been social contract. According to the version of that theory that has been elaborated in our political tradition, government is justified by the consent of the governed and by its protection of natural rights. These rights, whether life, liberty, and property as in Locke's formulation,[5] or life, liberty, and the pursuit of happiness as in the Declaration of Independence,[6] can be understood in nonreligious terms, and the interests they protect are not distinctly religious. This liberal social contract theory thus provides a justification for the government and its powers, and an explanation for the citizen's duty to obey, that does not depend on religious truth. Similar in these respects is utilitarianism in its various forms, the most prominent liberal competitor to social contract theory.[7] For utilitarians, a government is justified by its capacity to promote human welfare or the satisfaction of people's preferences.

To say that a liberal government rests on secular justification is not necessarily to deny that government generally, or liberal government in particular, may also be ordained by God. Supplemental justifications accepted by religious believers need not be at odds with unifying justifications that can be accepted by citizens regardless of their religious beliefs. It may even be true, as Harold Berman has eloquently argued,[8] that a society will be stronger if most citizens believe that its government and law enjoy some form of divine support.

For the subject of this essay, the theory of a government's justification is much less important than the proper purposes of government. These must be addressed independently. A person who thinks that government is ordained by God as a consequence of human sin may nevertheless believe that the government under which true religion flourishes best is one that does not take a position on religious truth. And a person who thinks that government rests on basic secular justifications may suppose that its promotion of religious positions is warranted. Since liberal democracy has traditionally been linked to secular justifications, this latter possibility is the one that requires our attention.

One might support government sponsorship of religious truth because it helps make citizens manifest civic virtues. Henry May has written of the New England High Federalists of the 1790s that, despite religious views ranging from deism to evangelical Christianity, all "believed morality essential to republics, and some sort of religion essential to morality."[9] This view, that civic virtue and respect for law and government depend on a religiously based morality, has, of course, been much more widely shared, and only a modest step from it is needed to reach the conclusion that the government may, for secular reasons, promote religion.[10]

Apart from the connection to civic virtue, promotion of religion might be regarded as an independently worthwhile venture for government. Suppose one believes that the essential purpose of government is to curtail aggressive rapaciousness, as did St. Augustine,[11] or to promote the common good and create conditions for human flourishing, as did St. Thomas Aquinas.[12] These purposes can be understood in nonreligious terms, and both Augustine and Aquinas conceived of non-Christian governments.[13] Nevertheless, if those who happen to control the government also understand what is true religion, why should they not contribute to human welfare in a supplemental way, using public power to promote religious truth in cooperation with the church, the dominant institutional representative of that truth? The Gelasian doctrine of the Two Swords,[14] which dominated the medieval period, envisioned just such cooperation, and it is not obviously foreclosed by a secular conception of the basic justifications of the state. Even if religious diversity makes inadvisable any close union between the government and a single organized church, more tenuous ties or general support for religion (or, specifically, Christianity) might be thought apt. Many European countries that qualify as liberal democracies, including Great Britain, retain established churches and sponsor religion in various ways. And, at present, a good many American citizens would regard[15] a self-conscious failure by the government to take any position on religious truth as an unacceptable abdication from matters vital to human welfare in the deepest sense.

If, as I have suggested, religious liberty is a defining feature of liberal democracy, some obvious constraints are set on the government's promotion of religious truth, and local conditions may further limit possible approaches. Burning heretics, compelled worship, and many other forms of state "encouragement" are out of bounds for any liberal government. The Constitution, traditions, and present diversity of the United States also constrain the range of alternatives. That the federal government may not promote any particular religious denomination or its theological positions is clearly settled by the establishment clause of the First Amendment. Some state establishments survived adoption of the federal Constitution and its Bill of Rights, but these were abandoned within a few decades. The Supreme Court's unanimous assumption that the Fourteenth Amendment, which prohibits state denials of due process of law, makes the principle of no establishment applicable against the states[16] has been challenged as an exercise in constitutional interpretation, but no one recommends state endorsement of a particular denomination. The political theory of the United States plainly bars promoting particular religious positions in this narrow sense.

The serious issue for our society concerns government promotion of religion generally or theism, a Judeo-Christian perspective, or Christianity. The establishment clause has been read by the Supreme Court to bar such support as well; but Mark DeWolfe Howe has argued elegantly that this was not its historical import,[17] and many modern observers, including leading representatives of the Reagan administration, have challenged the Court's interpretations.[18]

One argument in favor of the appropriateness of government support rests on the acceptance by the vast majority of Americans of broadly Christian perspectives. Without more, an argument from common beliefs is incomplete, because it does not explain why support of these beliefs is a proper aim of the government, but the argument can be filled out with claims about civic virtue or the inherent value of spreading religious truth. Assumptions such as these animate those who assert that government policy should reflect our status as a Christian or religious nation. These people do not deny that liberal societies should tolerate individuals with pervasively secular attitudes, but they are likely to think that general adoption of such attitudes would endanger the social fabric. Against objections that any government sponsorship inevitably impairs the rights of the nonbelieving minority and the rights of those members of the majority who find the particular form of sponsorship unacceptable,[19] proponents of sponsorship rejoin that appropriate measures need not infringe any serious freedom of those who dissent from the positions promoted or the form promotion takes.

The competing position is that despite the undeniable importance of religious tenets,[20] their truth is best left to the private order. The argument for nonsponsorship is that government support for particular religious ideas, however broadly conceived, does impinge on the liberty and sense of respect of those who do not accept these positions or object to forms of sponsorship, and that civic virtue and decent respect for government may be adequately maintained by private religious morality and by the government promoting good civic attitudes in schools and elsewhere in terms that are nonreligious.

Although Howe's historical thesis that aid to religion generally was not meant to be barred by federal and state restrictions on establishment may be correct, the country has changed significantly in the meantime. Not only is there greater pluralism of religious beliefs, a greater number of people are agnostics or atheists. Even if general support for religion or Christianity represented a proper stance of neutrality in 1791, when the Bill of Rights was ratified, it may no longer do so today, given the present degree of diversity and nonbelief.[21] Whether it is or is not actually rooted in our written constitutions, the principle of nonsponsorship reflected in major Supreme Court decisions over the past few decades[22] represents one cogent account of proper relations between government and religion in a liberal state.

In this book, I accept the assumption that liberal democratic government in the United States should not promote religious truth. In my mind, that position represents the fullest working out of a sound principle of religious liberty, and it most adequately represents the country's tradition of religious tolerance and government separation from religion as applied to modern social conditions. Though the worry that a polity devoid of any religious grounding and support may lack cohesion and stability troubles me, I am skeptical that government promotion of religion is the way to supply whatever religious underpinnings may be necessary for a healthy civic order. A comparison between the United States and European countries with established churches suggests that, in this era at least, religion may remain more vital when it does not bear the imprimatur of government.[23]

The arguments on both sides of this debate have become familiar, and neither my summary enumeration of the positions nor my expression of acceptance of nonsponsorship is designed to persuade those of contrary view. Since much of my effort is to suggest how far religious views may count in political decisions even if one starts with the principle that the government should not promote religious views, my conclusions should have interest for those who reject that principle. They will be able to see more clearly which sorts of reliances on religious convictions depend on the controversial principle of permissible support that they accept and I and many others reject, and which reliances on religious conviction can be reasonably defend d as consonant with my model of nonpromotion, the model from which all those who favor an unabashedly secular polity begin.

Before proceeding further, I should clarify the scope of the principle that the government should not promote religious positions, that it "should know no religious truth." The government must, of course, adopt laws and policies; its officers must defend its actions and enforce the law against those who break it. Unless they deem religious beliefs wholly irrelevant to political decisions, legislators who vote to go to war and to integrate public facilities evidently do not believe in a god who demands pacifism or racial segregation. In this sense, government actions have implications for what is taken as religious truth as that truth relates to social life.[24] The public actions indicate that those who take them are not being guided by certain religious propositions. This weak, indirect, form of support for the propositions that compete with those that are implicitly rejected may be an unavoidable byproduct of any government action; such "support" is not barred by a principle of nonsponsorship. What the government may not do under that principle is directly aim at furthering belief in some religious positions at the expense of others.

Adding the principle of nonsponsorship to other appropriate features of church-state relations, we may conclude that political authority should not promote particular religious views, that church and state should be substantially separate, that government officials should not dictate the decisions of religious organizations and that religious authorities should not possess secular political authority by dint of their clerical positions. Further, laws adopted by the government should rest on some secular objective. By this I mean that laws should seek to promote some good that is comprehensible in nonreligious terms. These premises, alone or together, do not, as I shall show, establish the inappropriateness of reliance on religious convictions on many important political subjects.

Individualism and Rationalism

The partial model of liberal democracy developed thus far does not directly address two important features of liberalism more broadly understood: individualism and rationalism. I turn now to these crucial subjects.

Liberalism is often associated with a rejection of corporate authority in favor of individual autonomy and with a belief that important questions can be resolved by rational inquiry. What is called liberal religion, for example, is religion that emphasizes rationality and individual discovery of truth and downgrades emotional commitment, scriptural revelation, and hierarchical control. One may similarly talk about liberal psychology and liberal morality as individualist and rationalist.

Assumptions about these aspects of liberalism might relate to a model of liberal democracy in at least three significant ways. Before addressing the way that is of main interest for us, I briefly discuss the two other possibilities.

It may be that liberal democracy will work best in societies in which a substantial proportion of the people accept individualism and rationalism. The suggestion has often been made that there is a serious tension when a powerful nonliberal religious organization exists in a liberal democracy, the typical target prior to the Second Vatican Council being the Roman Catholic Church.[25] On the other hand, we know that liberal democracy can thrive in countries in which significant numbers of people do not accept broader liberal premises. Since I am not engaged in descriptive comparative sociology, I do not delve into the conditions requisite for liberal democracy to flourish. I do, however, try to identify certain attitudes and practices regarding religion that have been common in American society and do not conflict with the premises of our polity, and I assume that continuance of these attitudes and practices will not undermine the stability or character of our liberal democracy.

The second possible connection between liberal democracy and broader liberalism is that only people committed to individualism and rationalism could regard liberal democracy as the best, or a good, form of government. Any connection of this sort is implausible unless one assigns a very inclusive meaning to individualism and rationalism. Certainly one need not be an *unremitting* individualist or rationalist to believe that liberal democracy is a highly desirable form of government. One need only believe, first, that small nonresponsible elites are to be trusted less to determine the welfare of citizens than officials selected by a democratic process and, second, that even officials selected in that way cannot be fully trusted to safeguard identifiable minorities and nonconformists unless constrained by established guarantees of liberty, by political checks and balances, by strong social traditions, or by some combination of these.

Approval of liberal democracy does imply acceptance of a degree of individualism; a liberal democrat rejects compulsion of beliefs and patterns of life and regards informed individuals as a vital protection of a fair political process. But a liberal democrat need not deny that human beings are social creatures, that human character is socially formed, that the arrival at partial truth is achieved by a process of community dialogue, and that some of the most fulfilling aspects of human existence involve organic social units that have a kind of priority over the individuals within them. One could believe each of these things and still think that the government of a large state, rather than dictating patterns of life for its citizens, should allow those patterns to develop in spontaneous ways. Thus one might support a liberal polity precisely because, as Robert Nozick suggests,[26] it would allow a flowering of very different kinds of social units.

Our country's tradition has never included the notion that a justification for liberal democracy depends on extreme individualism. Though many of our country's founders were affected by the highly individualist political theory of John Locke, recent writers have emphasized the influence of the Scottish "common sense" thinkers, who offered a more social version of the development of understanding and of fruitful human interaction.[27] From the original settlements at Jamestown and Plymouth down to the present, forms of religion have flourished that stress the critical role of the church body, whether the local congregation or a much larger institutional church. Many social groups that have been antithetical to extreme individualism have joined in accepting the country's political institutions.

Unstinting rationalism is no more a required component of a justification for liberal democracy than unstinting individualism.[28] Though eighteenth century American thought was in many dimensions strongly rationalist, many vocal dissenters remained, especially among evangelical Protestants.[29] Conjecture about the opinions of ordinary people on such an abstract subject as the merits of rationalism is treacherous, but both the rationalist approach of natural religion[30] and the nonrationalist views of the evangelical sects claimed wide followings.[31] Our country has gone through more and less rationalist phases, and the defense of our political structures has not been thought to require strongly rationalist premises. We can easily understand why. A person can be extremely skeptical about what reason can discover and still distrust nonresponsible political elites. Acceptance of liberal democracy may presuppose an ability of people to work out most practical conflicts by some sort of reasoned process, but a liberal democrat's belief in rational capacities can fall far short of any assumption that all or most fundamental human problems have correct answers at which people can arrive by rational deliberation.

For our purposes the implications of a commitment to liberal democracy for how officials and citizens should act are much more important than either the conditions under which liberal democracy will work or the aspects of a theory of its justification. Is liberal democracy connected to individualism and rationalism in the sense that a sound model of liberal democracy includes an injunction on people to act upon individualist and rationalist premises in their public actions?

Although the principle that protects individual liberty does constrain officials and citizens in a liberal democracy, they need not aim to break the influence of organic forms of social existence, such as families and churches, over their members. Indeed the autonomy that liberal societies concede to families and other social organizations may be understood as approving acceptance of some nonindividualist social engagements.[32] Troublesome questions can arise when government must choose between acquiescing in the influence and authority of these units or enhancing the individual autonomy of some members of a unit who presently disagree, or potentially may disagree, with its dispositions. Should the state allow church members to "shun" a wayward fellow? Should it support parental decisions against competing wishes of children? Should it support parental decisions, such as withdrawal of children from school, that are presently accepted by the children but may foreclose future choices by the children?[33] Should it support the authority of Indian tribal government when some members of the tribe dissent? No sensible person supposes that a liberal government must disregard the social character of human beings and approach such issues with an unqualified individualist point of view.

For this book, how far liberal democracy is committed to some form of rationalism is more critical than the place for individualist premises. The centrality of this problem is evident once one understands that the argument against reliance on religious convictions often comes down to an argument *for* reliance on premises that are deemed rational in some way that excludes religious convictions.

In most parts of this book I talk about whether judgments are based on publicly accessible forms of reason, rather than whether they are rational, irrational (against reason), or nonrational (going beyond reason). Though the terms I do employ are themselves by no means free of difficulty, they at least avoid the immensely complex and controversial task of developing a concept of rationality. And they seem more apt for the job that needs to be done. As we shall see, for theories about political decisions in democracies, whether the decisions are backed by reasons whose relevance is generally acknowledged matters more than whether decisions are backed by reasons that may be defended as rational in some transcultural sense. Nevertheless, both because shared forms of reasoning in a society are likely to be very close to what members of society regard as rational bases for judgment and because much of the inquiry I do undertake is barely distinguishable from an inquiry about the place of rational bases of decision, I briefly set the framework for future discussion by indicating how a commitment to rationalism might be made a part of a model of liberal democracy.

In liberal theory, rationality may be contrasted with reliance on personal intuition, feeling, commitment, tradition, and authority as bases for judgment.[34] A commitment to rationalism could take stronger or weaker forms. The most robust form of rationalism would be one that demanded that citizens and officials alike seek to make political choices on exclusively rational grounds. Although a thoroughgoing rationalist might insist that all decisions should ideally be made rationally,[35] I assume that someone morally free to pursue selfish interests does not have a responsibility to others to pursue those interests rationally. Were it perfectly proper for citizens to advance their own narrow, selfish interests at the expense of others, they would owe no duty to fellow citizens to determine and implement their selfish interests in a rational way. Thus, a claim that citizens have a political responsibility to make choices on rational grounds makes sense only if the proper aim of citizens, as well as officials, is to determine what is rationally appropriate for society as a whole, or for some other unit larger than themselves.

A weaker commitment to rationalism might insist only that rational deliberation be one component of decisions, or require officials to decide rationally while leaving citizens free to decide on whatever grounds appeal to them, or permit some issues to be decided on the basis of whatever preferences people have but demand that others be resolved on rational grounds.[36]

On what basis might one posit that officials and perhaps citizens in a liberal democracy should be guided by rational principles of choice in their political decisions? A rationalist might, of course, suppose that only such principles bear relevantly on whatever problems require resolution. Roughly speaking, all other bases of choice would be illegitimate, as an attractive bribe would be, or would amount to nothing more than misguided superstition. Because only rational techniques would be intrinsically appropriate for deciding political issues, rationalism should reign, at least in any society that does not self-consciously endorse other techniques of decision.[37] Since liberal democracy plainly does not represent any *preference* for nonrational and irrational bases of choice over rational ones, the rationalist within a liberal democracy can rightly claim that if rational bases of decision are intrinsically superior to other bases, they should be preferred.

A claim based on the inherent superiority of rationalism as a method of decision, however, does not carry great appeal for those who think that undiluted rationalism of a characteristic liberal type represents an impoverished picture of human life and establishes utterly unrealistic aspirations for human choice. And a claim based on intrinsic superiority does not rest on anything special about liberal democracy that demands rationality of its citizens. When it is said that citizens or officials of a liberal democracy should decide on rational grounds, the usual intimation is that something special about that polity commits one to rational grounds of choice.

A claim that moves from liberal democracy to rationalism could be based on traditional understandings, on fairness, or on effectiveness. Any long-seated understanding that only rational principles of choice will be used is impossible to find for American society. Before the Revolution and in all intervening periods, great numbers of people have believed not only that the destiny of the country should be understood in religious terms[38] but also that Christian and Jewish revelation bear on proper political choices. Though these same people have often believed that revelation was consonant with what reason independently dictates, they have not regarded revelation as an illegitimate source of political guidance. Our country is not based on any historical or present consensus that reliance on any grounds beyond narrowly rational ones is simply out of bounds in politics.

Other possible bases for insisting on rationalism are fairness to fellow citizens and the effective working of a democratic polity. Bases of these sorts underlie the most plausible claims that citizens and officials in our society should not rely on religious convictions when making political choices. The strength of such bases is the subject of intensive investigation in the following chapters, which argue that though liberal democracy involves a limited commitment to publicly accessible reasons for decision, it does not entail for the political realm either exclusive reliance on such reasons or an unqualified acceptance of a narrow form of rationalism.

I have outlined a model of liberal democracy that includes indirect democratic governance, extensive individual liberty, separation of governmental and religious institutions, nonsponsorship of religion by government, and secular purposes for laws. I have suggested that liberal democratic principles may involve a commitment to qualified forms of individualism and rationalism, but they do not demand that the strongest versions of individualism and rationalism be accepted as theoretically correct or used as the operative standards for political decisions.

The remainder of the book is largely devoted to the relationship between the principles developed in this chapter and reliance on religious convictions in political decisions and discourse.

Notes

1. The process is like the common "reflective equilibrium" way of thinking about moral principles and particular outcomes, explicated in John Rawls's *A Theory of Justice* (Cambridge, Mass., Harvard Univ. Pr. 1971) and employed by Rawls to develop the stipulations of his original position.

2. I put aside here the possibility of including a feature that plainly conflicts with traditionally accepted ideas of liberal democracy but is argued to fit better with other indisputable features of liberal democracy than the traditionally accepted feature that it displaces. That sort of conscious alteration in a complex concept is certainly defensible on occasion, but it requires explanation and argument.

3. John Rawls, supra note 1, tries to build a comprehensive theory of justice out of notions of fairness.

4. Fairness is not necessarily a criterion for every political model.

5. See J. Locke, *Second Treatise of Civil Government*, in J. Locke, *Two Treatises of Government*, P. Laslett, ed. (Cambridge, Cambridge Univ. Pr. 1960). Roger Williams's view of the function of government was similar. See E.S. Morgan, *Roger Williams: The Church and the State*, pp. 116–27 (N.Y., Harcourt, Brace & World 1967).

6. For an explanation of Jefferson's choice of the language "pursuit of happiness" and an interpretation of the Declaration as a whole as reflecting Scottish "common sense" philosophy, see G. Wills, *Inventing America* (Garden City, N.Y., Doubleday & Co. 1978).

7. Although utilitarianism provides substantial reasons relating to general welfare for citizens to obey good government, in the simple version of act-utilitarianism (that a person should choose an act with the best consequences), it posits no general duty to obey. See K. Greenawalt, *Conflicts of Law and Morality*, pp. 99–104 (N.Y., Oxford Univ. Pr. 1987).

8. See H. Berman, *The Interaction of Law and Religion* (Nashville, Tenn., Abingdon Pr. 1974).

9. H.F. May, *The Enlightenment in America*, p. 257 (N.Y., Oxford Univ. Pr. 1976).

10. This idea is clearly seen in the notions of Rousseau and Robespierre that a state-sponsored religion should promote civil virtue. In one of the greatest defenses of religious toleration, John Locke's *Essay on Toleration* assumed that atheists could not be trusted, because they would break their word with impunity.

11. See H. Deane, *The Political and Social Ideas of St. Augustine*, pp. 7, 117 (N.Y., Columbia Univ. Pr. 1963).

12. St. Thomas Aquinas, "Treatise on Law," *Summa Theologica*, pp. 1–19 (Indiana: Regnery/Gateway Inc. 1963).

13. However, both Augustine and Aquinas viewed government as ordained by God. See Deane, supra note 11, at pp. 78–79.

14. See H. Berman, "Religious Foundations of Law in the West: An Historical Perspective," 1 *Journal of Law and Religion*, pp. 3, 15 (1983). Compare H. Deane, supra note 11, at pp. 148, 172–74, 195–96, 204–08.

15. These citizens may think either that the failure is already occurring or that it would occur if existing slender threads between government and religion were broken.

16. See Everson v. United States, 333 U.S. 1 (1947).

17. See M.D. Howe, *The Garden and the Wilderness* (Chicago, University of Chicago Pr. 1965). I disregard in the text the highly complicating factor that the original establishment clause had at least as much to do with federalism, the distribution of responsibilities between federal and state governments, as with proper relations between government and religion.

18. See, e.g., E. Meese III, "Address Before the American Bar Association," July 9, 1985, pp. 11–12 (Wash., D.C., Department of Justice).

19. One who accepts the beliefs that are sponsored may object in principle to government sponsorship or he may object to the ideas being cast in a general form that disregards what he takes as distinctive. Thus, some devout Christians might object to any sponsorship of the idea that God exists that would not also mention the divine character of Jesus Christ.

20. Strictly perhaps, the few people who think religious assertions are meaningless may not regard them as inherently important, though even they may concede their social importance. In the sense I use in the text, an ordinary atheist does regard religious tenets as important, believing that theists have mistaken views about questions of considerable significance for human life.

21. See Wallace v. Jaffree, 105 S. Ct. 2479, 2488 (1985), quoting Justice Story to the effect that the First Amendment was intended only to prevent rivalry among Christian sects, but declaring that the underlying principle of freedom of conscience has been more broadly applied. Compare the concurring opinion of Justice O'Connor, 105 S. Ct. at p. 2497.

22. See, e.g., Everson v. Board of Education, 330 U.S. 1 (1947); Engel v. Vitale,

370 U.S. 421 (1962); Aguilar v. Felton, 473 U.S. 402 (1985). For decisions that lie in some tension with this dominant approach, see Lynch v. Donnelly, 465 U.S. 668 (1984); Marsh v. Chambers, 463 U.S. 783 (1983).

23. Poland provides a powerful example of the flourishing of religious faith without state support.

24. See J. Mansfield, "The Religion Clauses of the First Amendment and the Philosophy of the Constitution," 72 *Calif. Law Review*, pp. 847, 857 (1984).

25. See, e.g., P. Blanshard, *American Freedom and Catholic Power* (Greenwood, Conn., Greenwood Pr. 1984).

26. R. Nozick, *Anarchy, State, and Utopia*, pp. 297–334 (N.Y., Basic Books 1974). See also B. Ackerman, *Social Justice in the Liberal State*, pp. 177–80 (New Haven, Conn., Yale Univ. Pr. 1980); M. Novak, *Confessions of a Catholic*, p. 192 (San Francisco, Harper & Row 1983).

27. See, e.g., G. Wills, *Inventing America*, pp. 184–91 (Garden City, N.Y., Doubleday & Company 1978); H.F. May, supra note 9, at pp. 33, 62.

28. Henry May considers the view that we understand nature and men best through the use of natural faculties as one aspect of the Enlightenment. He comments that this view excludes people like John Wesley and Jonathan Edwards who believed that revelation, tradition, or illumination are the surest guides for human beings; the view also "excludes many, probably most people who lived in America in the eighteenth and nineteenth centuries." H.F. May, supra note 9, at p. xiv.

29. See H.F. May, supra note 9, at pp. 42–65.

30. See W.W. Sweet, "Natural Religion and Religious Liberty in America," 25 *Journal of Religion*, pp. 45, 54 (1945).

31. See H.F. May, supra note 9, at pp. 42–65.

32. See M. Novak, supra note 26, at p. 192. When the basis of a social organization is individual consent, conceding autonomy to it might be fully compatible with extreme individualism, but some organizations, most frequently the family, are not wholly voluntary.

33. See Wisconsin v. Yoder, 406 U.S. 205 (1972) (choice of Amish parents not to send children to school past eighth grade).

34. See, e.g., M. Oakeshott, *Rationalism in Politics*, p. 1 (London, Methuen & Co., 1977).

35. I do not consider philosophical premises that might require people to act rationally even in pursuit of selfish interests, since such premises are not plausibly part of a model of liberal democracy.

36. John Rawls's theory of justice, discussed in Chapter 4, can be understood to demand that issues of justice, at least, be decided on rational grounds. J. Rawls, supra note 1. Though his later writing makes clear that his original position analysis is not intended to establish that one set of principles of justice is rationally superior to every other, see "Justice as Fairness: Political not Metaphysical," 14 *Philosophy and Public Affairs*, p. 223 (1985), the analysis remains a way in which principles of

justice, principles that participants in an ideal liberal society would use to resolve issues, are rationally derived from the value premises of liberal democracy.

37. A polity might be grounded in a clear understanding that other than rational principles will control. Imagine a group of people who self-consciously agreed that all decisions about law in their society will be based on the Islamic *sharia*. A rationalist who moved into this society or observed it from outside might concede that within the society political decisions could appropriately be made on other than rational bases, though he would regard the shared social understanding conferring legitimacy on those bases as regrettable.

38. See, e.g., R. Bellah, "Civil Religion in America," in D. Cutler, ed., *The Religious Situation*, p. 389 (Boston, Beacon Pr. 1968).

3

The Relevance
of Religious Convictions
for Political Choice

A simple sentence, self-evident to most seriously religious persons, sums up the gist of this chapter: Religious convictions of the sort familiar in this society bear pervasively on people's ethical choices, including choices about laws and government policies. This thought is a critical one for most of the rest of this book because, if it is true, a citizen's reliance on religious convictions is inapt only if (1) the religious convictions themselves are wrong, or (2) they merely replicate what is otherwise discoverable by means more consonant with notions of liberal democracy, or (3) they are disqualified by some aspect of liberal democracy or its underlying principles. Because the thought about the relevance of religious convictions is critical, I indicate something about the rich variety of ways that religious convictions can affect political choices.

Religious Sources of Guidance for Ethical and Political Decisions

I talk of religious convictions, perspectives, and bases of judgment. I need say relatively little about what beliefs and systems of beliefs count as religious, though that is itself a perplexing topic.[1] I focus in this book mainly on Christian and Jewish beliefs that are undoubtedly aspects of religious viewpoints. Like most other major religions, Judaism and Christianity involve belief in a transcendent reality, forms of worship and contemplation, experiences of the "Holy,"[2] ideas of sacred authority, myths and doctrines that interpret reality, and social institutions that embody the religion.[3] They try to make sense of the natural and social world, to offer a "deep understanding" of the place of human beings, and to provide guidance about the most worthwhile way to live.[4] More specifically, and more to the point for our purposes, Christianity and Judaism, like most religions, also embody ethical teachings. How many of these typical characteristics of religion are required to make a belief or practice religious is the troubling "definitional" question I largely avoid.[5] My own view is that there are no particular single features that are necessary to make a religion. Even belief in some form of transcendence is unnecessary if enough other features are present, as in the Ethical Culture Society. I do not count as religious, however, every moral conviction that is accepted as an "ultimate concern,"[6] nor do I include as being religious the beliefs about people and what they should do that derive from comprehensive social philosophies like Marxism.[7] My major theses would be unaffected by a broadening of what I treat as religious, but they would require some reformulation.

To say only that a religion embodies ethical teachings would be to obscure the various ways in which the connection between religious conviction and ethical conclusion can arise. I shall concentrate primarily on Christian points of view, the ones with which I am most familiar, but I am reasonably confident many similar observations could be made about Jewish perspectives. In seeking to understand the various strands of tradition in Christian ethics, one can roughly distinguish among sources of guidance and kinds of guidance given. Disagreements, or strong differences in emphasis, about these lead to sharply variant conceptions of the essential nature of Christian ethics.

Among sources of ethical guidance we can include sacred texts, authoritative statements by church organizations and religious leaders, consultation with the community of believers, and direct inspiration, usually through prayer or meditation. Although reason is omitted from this listing because I assume it does not count as a distinctly religious source, variations among believers over how far religious sources of guidance should be mediated by reason are highly important. While wide agreement may exist among Christians about the validity of all these sources of guidance, including reason, their respective importance is variously assessed.

The most obvious kind of guidance that religious sources can give is ethical prescription. In both the Jewish and Christian traditions, the Ten Commandments are a striking example of scriptual norms; various biblical formulations of the Golden Rule also announce a standard of behavior, though one that is much less precise. Statements by popes and other members of the church hierarchy cover a great many moral choices that

Roman Catholics face. Although few branches of Protestantism now undertake the kind of extensive regulation of the moral life sought to be achieved by our Puritan forebears in Massachusetts, statements of denominational bodies and of individual ministers still recommend some actions and condemn others. It has been said that a religious ethics is "essentially authoritative";[8] certainly belief that scripture or church leaders can articulate binding or highly persuasive ethical norms constitutes one kind of authoritative ethics.

Rather than prescribing behavior, religious sources may recommend attitudes of heart and mind, such as injunctions to love one's neighbor or one's enemies, or they may indicate whether what many people regard as goods really are worth attaining. More generally, as I have already suggested, religious sources incorporate broad perspectives on the nature of human beings and society. These perspectives include not only what are essentially factual appraisals, such as whether people are intrinsically self-centered, but also a vision about the "ultimate meaning" of human life and the place of humankind in the universe. Understandings about these matters color one's view of what an ideal human life might be like and affect more mundane ethical judgments about how we should govern our own lives and deal with others.[9]

Yet another kind of ethical guidance involves conceptions of the nature of the religious object one worships and of the role one properly occupies in relation to that object. A person's ethical stance, for example, may be affected by belief in a loving God and by reflection on what a person created by a loving God should do. The centrality of one's conception of God highlights the fact that religious ethics typically involve a triadic relationship between oneself, God, and fellow human beings.[10] In orthodox Christianity, Jesus is considered both divine and an example of an ideal human life; the accompanying outlook on ethical matters is often Christocentric,[11] the attributes of Christ figuring prominently in one's sense of what is right behavior. Conceptions may also be formulated about other spiritual exemplars. Someone approaching a hard choice might, for instance, ask how a faithful follower of St. Francis of Assisi or of Martin Luther King, Jr., would respond.

A person who believes strongly in direct inspiration may believe that, in prayer or meditation, God will vouchsafe to him how he should act. Though conceivably such inspiration might eventuate in the form of general propositions, such as "you should never lie," it might instead yield a distinct sense of how one should act in a particular situation unaccompanied by any generalizable standards for dealing with other situations.

The typical Christian will regard the diverse sources and kinds of religious insight as offering not mutually exclusive alternatives but possibilities of reinforcement and reciprocal correction.[12] Nonetheless, depending on the kind of guidance that is emphasized as central, the picture of what Christian ethics is really like differs dramatically.[13] One possibility is that the ethical life is largely a matter of conforming to fairly detailed propositions, laid down in scripture or in authoritative church statements, about what constitutes right action.[14] Another possibility is that the central message of Christianity is that one should act lovingly, that is, with agape or unselfish love toward others.[15] If this message is taken as a kind of flexible standard for behavior, it may be thought to require attention to the particular situation and to the relationships involved[16] in preference to more precise and general rules of conduct. If the injunction to act with love is thought mainly to concern one's character and attitudes,[17] one may believe that what is critical to right action is a good heart and openness to God's inspiration, that considered reflection about what one should do is relatively less important.[18] Yet another general outlook is that conscious reflection about desirable behavior is a critical aspect of the moral life, but that the fundamentals of Christian faith have relatively little specific to say about what one should do, leaving the believer to discover what is morally right in much the same manner as the nonbeliever.[19] It is over matters such as these that controversy swirls in Christian ethics.

Religious people not only differ widely in the kinds of guidance they think they receive from religious sources, they vary in the degrees of confidence they assign to their conclusions. A person who supposes that scripture is inerrant and contains clear moral prescriptions may believe with complete assurance that certain kinds of acts, such as adultery, are always wrong. Similarly, someone who is convinced God communicates directly and clearly to him during prayer may harbor no doubt what he should do after receiving God's inspiration. Other religious persons, more skeptical about clear ethical mandates in revelation and distrustful of claims of private communication with God, may strongly doubt their ability to ascertain ethical truth, or may think that general ethical guides, such as promoting human love, provide unsure resolution in many concrete contexts; but these persons may still believe that the religious perspective holds out an important means for highly fallible creatures to try to understand what is right.[20]

As I have said, the point of this book is not to try to resolve disputed questions in theology, and this disclaimer extends to theological ethics. I do comment occasionally on how well particular approaches fit with premises of liberal democracy, but for the most part when I speak of religiously influenced ethical choices, I group these quite diverse sources and kinds of guidance together. The preceding simplified and schematic presentation is largely designed to forestall any mistaken apprehension that the manner in which believers rely on religious faith to arrive at ethical choices can be placed in a single pigeonhole.

Not every religious conviction that concerns the moral life is, of course, directly relevant to particular moral choices. According to the Christian tradition, the ethical failures of men and women critically reveal their place in the world and their relationship to God; these failures are understood as sins against God, requiring forgiveness. Whether people need special divine grace and revelation to live morally[21] and whether their efforts to be moral contribute to their salvation are questions that have divided Christians through the ages and touched the heart of their respective faiths, but these questions do not immediately concern either correct personal behavior or just political outcomes. Nor do religious convictions that are understood to strengthen one's responsibility to do what is right, whatever that may be.[22]

Among religious convictions that do bear on correct ethical choices, many do not involve political decisions. When a person relies on religious grounds to decide how much of his income to give to help the starving, the decision has no direct import for public laws and policies. Even some choices touching responses to the law do not deal with its proper content. A person who has decided on nonreligious grounds that a law is grossly unjust might seek religious guidance about the moral propriety of disobedience. His religiously informed response to that issue might not involve religiously based evaluation of the merits of the law.

Yet when these various connections between religion and ethics and law are put aside, critical connections remain that are of the utmost importance for our purposes. The person who believes scripture enjoins him to donate a great deal to help starving people in other parts of the world may also conclude that his government should play an active role in that effort. Many people who seek religious guidance from prayer and consultation with fellow believers to help make personal ethical decisions will follow these avenues when they must make political choices. Perhaps most important, religious premises that pervade one's view of social reality and justifiable human actions will almost certainly affect what one thinks the government should do.

Succeeding chapters in this book illustrate how religious convictions can touch various political issues, but a moment's reflection shows their potential relevance to matters like military and foreign policy, capital punishment, welfare distribution, animal rights, and abortion. Max Stackhouse speaks of faith and theology as inevitably "public and political";[23] Jurgen Moltmann claims that a theology may be naive and politically unaware but cannot be apolitical;[24] Lynn Buzzard urges that "[p]olitics, art, science and philosophy are all part of the arena of activity by the believer community;"[25] and Basil Mitchell says it is scarcely possible for anyone who takes religion seriously to acquiesce in its being treated as a private matter.[26] Unless there are good reasons for religious believers to discount the evident relevance of religious convictions for political choice, those convictions will affect some political decisions they make. Short of demonstration that the convictions themselves are misguided, the good reasons must concern either the inaptness or superfluousness of reliance on religious conviction. The next chapter deals with the general possibility that liberal democratic premises render reliance on religious convictions inapt. Much of the remainder of this chapter is devoted to the possibility that such reliance is unnecessary.

What Constitutes Reliance on Religious Convictions

Before I turn to that subject, I pause to clarify what exactly I mean when I refer to reliance on religious convictions in political choice. The preceding discussion about the diverse ways religious premises and involvements can figure in ethical choices obviously applies to political decisions as well as to more personal matters.

Here, I want first to make the simple point that the tightness of connection between the religious source of guidance and the conclusion about a particular issue can vary considerably. When someone supports a law against homosexual acts because he believes inerrant scripture unambiguously condemns such acts or because he thinks a troubled prayer about the correct position to take has been decisively answered by God, the link between religious conviction and practical conclusion is strikingly direct. In other circumstances, say when competing welfare proposals are at stake, certain general religious premises, such as the inherent selfishness of people and the importance of caring for the needy, may figure in an extended weighing of pros and cons, indirectly affecting what one finally concludes is the best proposal. I shall from time to time consider the possible relevance of these differences in the proximity of the religious conviction to the final practical conclusion; but I start with the assumption that these differences are not in and of themselves critical for purposes of liberal democratic theory, and when I speak of a person relying on religious convictions, I mean to include convictions that are general and lie in the background of some chain of evaluation as well as those that figure more directly.

A related and troublesome conceptual problem concerns a person's consciousness about the connection between his religious convictions and his political decisions. The clearest instances of reliance on religious convictions occur when the person is certain that he would make a different choice if he disregarded those convictions. If a person knows he would oppose a law proscribing homosexual acts but for their scriptural condemnation, he is patently relying on religious conviction when he supports the law.

A person is clearly not relying on religious convictions when his choice rests firmly on independent grounds. It is important to recognize that in some instances of clear nonreliance the religious convictions of the person himself or of others will be *causally related* to the conclusion that the person reaches. Suppose that Mabel, who had grown up as a nonreligious humanist believing in the basic goodness of human beings, was converted to fundamentalist Protestantism and began to believe on scriptural authority that people are fundamentally and irrevocably selfish. Her conversion led to deep reflection on her own life experiences and to extensive reading of social science literature. She *now* thinks that an objective appraisal of human psychology and history establishes the truth of the view that people are irreducibly selfish, and she is confident she would continue to believe that even if she were to lose her fundamentalist religious faith. If her belief in human selfishness were critical to her reaction to some political program, she would not be relying on her religious convictions, though fully aware that causally she might not now have the belief that she does but for her conversion. In other situations, religious convictions may play a causal role that is not apparent to the person involved. Suppose that Mabel is firmly convinced that a moral premise, say the importance of caring for the needy, is self-evidently correct, something that any sensible person would accept regardless of religious belief. A psychologist might observe that the explanation why Mabel takes this view is that when she was younger she accepted the premise on religious grounds; or a sociologist might say that the premise has evolved to being widely accepted as self-evident in the culture because for many generations it was self-consciously held on religious grounds. In either event Mabel's present acceptance of the premise is not grounded in religious convictions; she thinks it is fully sustainable without reference to any such convictions.

The more difficult exercises in classification arise when unselfconsciousness or uncertainty infects the connection between religious conviction and practical choice. People often make moral and political choices without consciously tracing conclusions to basic premises; in a particular instance they may fail to be aware of the role of religious convictions. For these cases, I want to assume that what counts is how the person's present views should be systematically explicated, in the way they might be if a constant series of "why's" compelled him to explain the grounds of his position ("Well yes, I guess the reason I think people are irreducibly selfish is because that's what the Bible teaches"). If such questions, answered *without any change in belief*, revealed the centrality of premises that are religious, then the person is relying on religious premises though he may not actually realize it at the moment of choice. This notion of systematic reconstruction is somewhat tricky because, in the face of such persistent "why's," many people will actually alter their beliefs to a degree, usually in the direction of greater coherence. I do not want to claim that a person is relying on religious convictions if such reliance *would* be necessary to sustain the conclusion were his beliefs more coherent than they presently are. Such a claim would involve a creative reconstruction by the observer, employing his own notions of coherence and soundness, that I want to avoid, instead sticking more literally to the chooser's present beliefs.

A person can be relatively conscious of the place of religious convictions and still be highly uncertain about how critical they are to his final choice. This can happen because he is not sure of the weight a premise unmistakably derived from religious sources bears on a practical conclusion or because he is not sure how far an underlying premise depends on religious convictions. Suppose a person thinks that both scripture and some scientific evidence support a prohibition on incest. If he thinks that together they make the case for prohibition overwhelming, he may not have a judgment about what he would conclude were he to disregard the religious conviction. And if Mabel thinks that the basic premise that caring for the needy is more important than improving average welfare is supported both by scripture and some reasons of secular moral philosophy, she might be uncertain whether the latter reasons alone would be strong enough to sustain the premise against counter arguments. It is often the case that someone who is confident that arguments in combination are strong enough to yield a conclusion will not bother to decide whether the conclusion could survive elimination of one or more of the supporting arguments. This uncertainty is especially likely to arise for broad premises like inherent selfishness, as to which common experience supplements religious insight.

For our purpose, a person is relying on religious convictions if their abandonment would force him seriously to reconsider the position he takes. If he is now confident of the position he takes and is uncertain what he would think absent the force of the religious convictions, he is presently relying on those convictions to a degree, even though *it is possible* that he would eventually arrive at the same conclusion without them. It might be objected that this classificatory decision implicitly overstates the significance of reliance on religious convictions, because in some percentage of instances people disregarding their convictions would end up taking the same positions they now do. But this objection would misconceive the main point of my inquiry. The point is to ask whether it is reasonable to ask people in a liberal democracy not to rely on their religious convictions. If people should try to forgo reliance on religious convictions, then all those who are now uncertain about the practical significance of their religious convictions should reexamine their political choices to see what the import of nonreliance would be. A norm of nonreliance has implications for their process of choice as powerful as its implications for those who know their conclusions would be different absent their religious convictions.

How Reliance Relates to the Idea That Religious Sources Confirm What Is Discoverable by Reason

I turn now to the relationship between moral truths believed to be discoverable from religious sources of guidance and what can be known without reference to these sources. We can roughly distinguish three basic positions. The first position, that what is morally right is determinable without reference to religious truth, was reflected in the eighteenth century belief in natural religion[27] and is accepted by many modern "liberal" Protestants; it has long been a dominant theme of the Roman Catholic natural law tradition deriving from Aquinas.

Under this view, what specifically religious sources in their various forms tell us is true about ethics is confirmatory of what we can understand by reason and ethical intuition. A powerful contemporary illustration is found in John Finnis's *Natural Law and Natural Rights*,[28] an exposition of traditional natural law that proceeds to develop a comprehensive moral theory without reference to God, suggesting only in a final part of the book that the discovery of self-evident goods and moral truth points toward the existence of God. Some other Roman Catholic writers who are more skeptical about scriptural and hierachical authority than is Finnis assert that ethical thought should be autonomous, rooted in the human condition rather than special religious insights.[29]

Radically opposed to the idea that all or most moral truth can be discovered by the use of ordinary insight and natural reason is the view that one's religious perspective critically affects the resolution of every moral question. Thinkers who have regarded human reason as deeply infected by sin have often stressed the necessity of revelation. Jonathan Edwards, the dominant figure in the Great Awakening of the eighteenth century, put the point powerfully: "The least beam of light of knowledge of the glory of God in the face of Jesus Christ is worth more than all the human knowledge that is taught in all the most famous colleges and universities in the world."[30] Some modern evangelical Protestants also believe that on their own human beings are largely blind to moral truth, incapable not only of doing but also of understanding what is morally right. For them, salvation becomes the dominant event in the moral as well as the religious life of the believer. Among leading modern Protestant theologians, Karl Barth has most emphasized the distinctiveness of religious morality. Asserting that the reality of God is so different from the things of this world that one cannot arrive at truth from "rational" nonrevealed premises, Barth claims that "true man and his good action can be viewed only from the standpoint of the true and active God and his goodness."[31] If natural reason is considered radically incapable of reaching moral truth, philosophizing in these terms may be regarded not only as ineffective, but as "the invasion of a false and misleading element in the moral life of the believer."[32]

An intermediate position is that ordinary human sentiments and rational understanding can go a good distance toward settling what is morally right but that on some important moral questions, perhaps including some questions of justice and political morality, these sources of insight are unhelpful or fail to yield as precise a resolution as is needed; on those occasions the believer's final judgment may depend on reference to religious premises. The ways in which religious sources of insight might supplement rational understanding are various. One possibility is that certain discrete moral truths not establishable on the basis of reason are revealed; these truths presumably are not incompatible with what reason shows[33] but go beyond it. Some Catholic writers have suggested that the indissolubility of marriage,[34] the virtue of chastity, and the universal wrongfulness of fornication[35] may fall into this category. A more subtle and more interesting second possibility is that revelation can provide a depth or shading of understanding that is not attainable by unaided reason. Perhaps ordinary moral thought suggests duties of care for other people, but revelation may be needed to support the full dimensions of self-giving agape. Although love is likely to be counted as desirable in virtually any moral system, there may be a distinctively Christian conception of this virtue and of how it fits with other virtues, such as humility and forgiveness.[36] Though the basic moral principles may not require reference to the Christian faith, that faith may contain an account of human goods and ideal relations that suggests particular interpretations of those principles[37] and affects more "borderline" moral choices.[38] Under this conception of religious morality, it may be hard to say exactly where natural reason runs out and revelation begins, but specifically religious sources of insight will sometimes make a critical difference. A third possibility is that for the believer the threads of revelation and reason intertwine more fully still. His very use of reason will be enlightened by some premises that are derived from revelation, and distinguishing the products of unaided reason from those of revelation will be an elusive task.

We can quickly see that for people who think that religious sources of guidance are frequently a ground for politically relevant ethical truth that is unavailable elsewhere, any injunction to disregard these sources in political choice would be an instruction to make decisions on the basis of only part of what they regard as relevant data. For religious believers who adopt either the (extreme) position that reason is radically inadequate or the (intermediate) position that reason often receives critical supplementation from religious sources, any thesis that reliance on religious grounds is inappropriate has obviously disturbing implications.

At first glance, such a thesis may not seem to threaten the person who is confident that in all relevant respects, revelation merely confirms what reason can discover. If denied revelation as a source of judgment, can such a person not turn to reason and come up with the same conclusions? I want now to indicate why this "first glance" appraisal is woefully mistaken in light of commonly held views about how revelation actually confirms natural reason. I shall concentrate on the widely held, relatively optimistic, traditional natural law position whose dominant spokesman has been Aquinas and which finds recent expression in the work of Finnis[39] and others.

If reason uninformed by religious insight allowed everyone without strenuous intellectual efforts to reach correct conclusions about all political issues, religious sources would only confirm what was otherwise evident or help illuminate matters whose rational importance was obvious once attention was directed to them. In that event, whenever a person took an ethical position indicated by religious conviction he could unambiguously state that his position was fully supportable on nonreligious grounds he understands.

If, however, the confirmatory role of religious sources is less modest, if those sources are actually used to resolve uncertainties, then people influenced by them will sometimes be relying on religious convictions in a way that would be barred by any full-blooded principle that religious grounds are illegitimate.

One way in which religious sources may play this role concerns the limits of ordinary human capacities. Suppose that many ethical questions, while yielding to reasoned resolution, are quite complex. Perhaps most people are *incapable* of resolving these questions on rational grounds; as Finnis says, some derivations from first principles to moral norms require "wisdom, i.e., a reasonableness not found in everyone or even in most people."[40] Even some of those people who have the intellectual capacity to resolve issues on nonreligious grounds with sufficient effort will lack the time, inclination, or disposition[41] to do so. Among people who are incapable of reasoning fully about a complex question or who have not devoted the necessary effort, some will believe that scripture or authoritative church statements give them correct answers.[42] These persons may believe that religious sources confirm what uninstructed reason can discover, and thus may also believe that the positions they accept are demonstrably correct on nonreligious grounds, but they will not understand on nonreligious grounds why that is so, nor will they be able to defend their positions on nonreligious grounds against major competitors. They have in fact adopted the positions they now hold on religious grounds and cannot be sure what positions they would accept if they abandoned the religious grounds. We see therefore that religious convictions can make a critical difference in the formation of political views of many people if the nonreligious grounds for some positions cannot be grasped with comparative ease. We need look only to the traditional Roman Catholic perspective, which joins belief in natural law with a vitally important role for authoritative statments of the church hierarchy, to see how much religious premises may affect the ethical outlook of ordinary believers. Church leaders have often insisted that Catholics should give assent to authoritative teachings,[43] evidencing an attitude expressed in this quote from Germain Grisez: "Those who really believe that there exists on this earth a community whose leaders are appointed and continuously assisted by God to guide those who accept their authority safely through time to eternity would be foolish to direct their lives by some frail fabrication of reason instead of by conforming to a guidance system designed and maintained by divine wisdom."[44]

A more subtle role for religious sources concerns the inquiries and conclusions of those who are most competent to resolve issues on grounds of reason and who make the effort to do so.[45] Some problems may have rational solutions but solutions that are hard to grasp for anyone. It is a familiar process for legal scholars to shift from thinking one answer to a problem is right to thinking that the choice is a toss-up for which there is no right answer, to thinking that a contrary answer is correct. Even scholars committed to the view that every legal problem has a rationally correct answer will often be uncertain what it is. Now, if the same were true about ethical problems, a person who believed religious sources confirmatory of uninstructed reason might attain from those sources a much higher degree of certainty about an answer than he would otherwise have.[46] And sometimes a person might accept on the basis of religious authority a position that conflicted with his highly uncertain judgment reached on rational grounds. This would be especially likely if he assumed, in accordance with traditional Catholic teaching, that hierachical pronouncements are more reliable than one's use of unaided reason if the two conflict; but even if someone thought that church teaching was as liable to error or misconstruction as reason, still on occasion a strong teaching would be followed in preference to a weak conclusion of reason.[47] Of course, people rarely have the psychological objectivity and self-awareness to know that what they firmly believe is right on one basis is something they would uncertainly believe is wrong on another basis. But a principle of eschewing religious convictions would demand such an inquiry and would occasionally lead the uncertain person to reject the position arrived at through religious sources.

In some instances of decision about laws and policies the degree of certainty of moral judgment will itself be important. Someone who is highly uncertain about the correctness of his own position may be much less willing to impose it on others and much more willing to accept some sort of compromise. An unqualified principle foreclosing reliance on religious convictions would presumably also foreclose any increments in degree of certainty that these convictions provide.

I want to pause here to consider a possible response to my assumption that reliance on the church's teaching or on scripture is, in fact, a reliance on religious conviction. It might be said that these are instances of deference to authority and that such deference is often rational quite apart from religious premises. In matters of fact and even in some matters of evaluation, we all defer on occasion to the judgments of those who understand more than we do.[48] Perhaps deference to church teachings is just acceptance of the authority of the morally wise.

I began by acknowledging that any sensible view of political choice must include reliance on factual authorities as part of a citizen's exercise of his political responsibilities. On many issues, we must assume that experts know roughly what they are talking about. It is rational to accept the judgments of people who are established as experts by criteria of training, experience, and peer recognition, and to accept the judgments of those who have proven right in the past. It is less apparent that such acceptance is appropriate for fundamental evaluative judgments, but it cannot be ruled out. Suppose that on five previous occasions I have tentatively reached a judgment opposed to that of Socrates. On each occasion I have failed to be persuaded by his arguments at the time, but futher experience and long

reflection have persuaded me, and most other people, that Socrates definitely had the better of the arguments and that I was wrong. The sixth
occasion arises and the issue is whether capital punishment is morally
acceptable. My assessment of the arguments is that it is not, but Socrates
concludes that it is. I am asked whether I believe, overall, that capital
punishment is acceptable. On the basis of previous experience I might
rationally say: "Because at this point I have more confidence in Socrates's
judgment than my own, I think it is probably acceptable." On this basis, I
might rationally support capital punishment though not presently understanding why the arguments for it are stronger than the arguments against it.
No sensible model of how citizens and officials should make political
decisions can exclude such possible reliance on "moral authority."

Something like this account might be part of the explanation why
religious believers accord weight to the positions derivable from scripture
and church teachings; perhaps these sources have, for the individual,
established reliability in judgments about moral matters on other occasions.
But such an account is not most of the explanation for most religious
believers. The authority of the religious sources derives mainly from
separable beliefs about the way in which these sources reflect God's will. It
is, for example, often said that the Church's teachings are guided by the
Holy Spirit. Confidence derives not so much from successful prior resolution of moral issues as from religious convictions that establish authorita-
tiveness. If I am right about this, the reliance of Roman Catholics on the
teachings of the Church typically do involve a distinctive reliance on
religious convictions.[49]

Thus, we see that even on important versions of the view that religious
convictions and institutions merely confirm what is discoverable by uninstructed human reason, any barring of reliance on religious convictions
would preclude sources of insight with considerable practical significance
for vast numbers of religious persons. If a principle were accepted that
religious grounds of judgment are illegitimate for political choices within a
liberal democracy, a very high proportion of Christians and Jews, if they
wanted to perform as conscientious liberal citizens, would have to eschew
religious sources of insight that they would otherwise regard as relevant and
on some issues critically determinative.

A serious effort to live by a principle excluding reliance on religious
convictions would be particularly difficult for a reason that has so far been
only intimated and which helps to explain why the topic I address in this
book has not more often received focussed attention. The reality is that
many believers do not apprehend how the distinct threads of religious

morality fit in the development of their moral and political positions. Although sometimes a religious person may believe that ordinary arguments have little to say on the issue at hand, more often he will suppose that they are fairly powerful and that the ordinary arguments that fit with his religious convictions are correct. In part because they want to convince nonbelievers and in part because they have a vague sense that such arguments may be more acceptable in our political order, believers often cast public arguments for their positions in nonreligious language. Identifying the special role his religious convictions play would thus be particularly difficult for the believer himself and for others. And even when a person's degree of self-awareness and self-expression allows relatively clear identification of the place of his religious premises in a structured account of his position, neither he nor others may know whether initial religious conviction has led to moral judgment or initial moral intuition has led to adoption of religious convictions that support the intuition.

These complications conceal the degree to which religious convictions influence the political judgments and actions of citizens, and, they along with much else said in this chapter, begin to indicate how taxing it would be for an individual believer to try to dispel the influence of his own religious convictions in his political life. Although thought about the proper place of religious convictions in our polity is important enough to warrant the somewhat artificial separation of religious from other considerations for analytical purposes, the practical difficulty of real people making that separation is a subject to which I shall return.

Notes

1. See generally D. Little and S. Twiss, *Comparative Religious Ethics*, pp. 53–74 (San Francisco, Harper & Row 1978); N. Smart, *The Philosophy of Religion*, pp. 4–34 (N.Y., Oxford Univ. Pr. 1979); K. Greenawalt, "Religion As a Constitutional Concept," 72 *Calif. Law Review*, pp. 753–81 (1984)

2. Ninian Smart, supra note 1, points out that contemplative mystical experience may not be well captured by the idea of experience of the "Holy." Though both Christianity and Judaism embrace groups with mystical traditions, mystical experiences have figured less prominently in them than in Hinduism and Buddhism.

3. See D. Little and S. Twiss, supra note 1, at pp. 54–62; N. Smart, supra note 1, at pp. 4–34.

4. See R. Swinburne, *Faith and Reason,* p. 128 (Oxford, Clarendon Pr. 1981).

5. In K. Greenawalt, supra note 1, I discuss in some depth the "definition" of religion for constitutional purposes. I explain why it is mistaken even to expect an

adequate definition in the sense of a simple statement of necessary and sufficient conditions. The views I express there also apply to the broader purposes of this book.

6. The idea that "ultimate concern" is the proper standard for legal purposes is one that has enjoyed some currency; I suggest that it is fundamentally flawed in id. at pp. 806–11.

7. Of course, Marxist atheism is a (negative) religious belief concerning a transcendent God.

8. See K. Ward, *Ethics and Christianity*, p. 156 (London, George Allen & Unwin 1970).

9. See id. at pp. 93–94; V. MacNamara, *Faith & Ethics*, pp. 106–7, 116–17 (Wash., D.C., Georgetown Univ. Pr. 1985).

10. W. Beach and H.R. Niebuhr, *Christian Ethics: Sources of the Living Tradition*, p. 5 (N.Y., Ronald Pr. 1955).

11. See. E.L. Long, Jr., *A Survey of Christian Ethics*, pp. 110, 118 (N.Y., Oxford Univ. Pr. 1967).

12. The idea of reciprocal correction is tricky here. One does not believe that what God has actually inspired him to do by prayer would conflict with what God has actually instructed him to do by authoritative scripture; it is the fallibility of human receptivity that generates the need for reference to diverse sources.

13. Very helpful summaries of various points of view are contained in E.L. Long, Jr., supra note 11, and E.L. Long, Jr., *A Survey of Recent Christian Ethics* (N.Y., Oxford Univ. Pr., 1982). Divisions among modern Catholic theologians are illuminatingly explained in V. MacNamara, supra note 9.

14. See, e.g., id. at p. 90, suggesting that the Vatican I theology treated revelation as a set of truth propositions and that some modern Catholic thinkers believe that the Bible contains revealed moral truths.

15. See, e.g., J. Robinson, *Honest to God*, p. 115 (London, S.C.M. Press 1963). This notion in fact unites many who have highly divergent understandings about the implications of a "love ethic."

16. Among Protestant writers who have most strongly emphasized the importance of relationships and particular situations are Paul Lehmann, *Ethics in a Christian Context* (N.Y., Harper & Row 1963), and Joseph Fletcher, *Situation Ethics: The New Morality* (Philadelphia, Westminister, Pr. 1966). From within the Catholic tradition, Charles Curran has proposed "a relational model for understanding the Christian life" (*Transition and Tradition in Moral Theology*, p. 22 [Notre Dame, Ind., Univ. of Notre Dame Pr. 1979]). See also J. Fuchs, *Christian Ethics in a Secular Arena*, pp. 36–44 (Wash., D.C., Georgetown Univ. Pr. 1984) (emphasizing the discovery of concrete moral truths).

17. See, e.g., K. Ward, supra note 8, at p. 79.

18. Bishop Robinson, supra note 15, at p. 37, suggested that "Love alone, because as it were, it has a built-in moral compass, enabling it to 'home' intuitively upon the deepest need of the other, can allow itself to be directed completely by the situation." This point of view is criticized for placing too much emphasis on

motive and not enough on sources of illumination in J. Macquarrie, *Three Issues in Ethics*, p. 39 (N.Y., Harper & Row 1970).

19. See, e.g., G. Hughes, *Authority in Morals* (Wash., D.C., Georgetown Univ. Pr. 1978); B. Schuller, *Wholly Human* (Wash., D.C., Georgetown Univ. Pr. 1986), Catholic writers who stress the autonomy of ethics. Hughes mounts a sustained attack on the idea that scripture or authoritative church statements can give clear answers to modern moral problems. Id. at pp. 8–23.

20. J. Philip Wogaman has written of the tentativeness of moral judgments and has proposed that certain general guides, such as human sinfulness and the value of individual life, be treated as "methodological presumptions." See *A Christian Method of Judgment*, pp. 36–114 (London, S.C.M. Press 1976). Joseph Fuchs, supra note 16, at p. 83, acknowledges that rigid deontological rules can produce greater security in concrete moral judgments than more flexible approaches, but claims that the price in terms of moral error is too high. Gerald Hughes, supra note 19, at p. 29, disputes the assumption that people will inevitably be tormented by doubt and insecurity if unsure that they have correct answers to moral questions.

21. By special grace, I mean a grace that is not extended to and received by everyone. Compare G. Hughes, supra note 19, at p. 7, who suggests that grace is needed for humans to live morally but that a kind of grace is offered to humans generally, even those lacking an opportunity for explicit Christian belief.

22. John Macquarrie, for example, supra note 18, at p. 146, says that the placing of morality in the context of faith "should lend depth to moral obligation, seen as unconditional demand, and it should encourage moral effort by relating it to an objective ground of hope." For a sensitive account of why actions that are responsive to God's love and performed to please God do not fall neatly into either the selfish or altruistic category, see S.L. Ross, "Another Look at God and Morality," 94 *Ethics*, pp. 87–98 (1983).

23. M. Stackhouse, "An Ecumenical Perspective on Neoevangelical Politics," 1 *Journal of Law and Religion*, pp. 204–14 (1983).

24. J. Moltmann, "The Cross and Civil Religion," in J. Moltmann, H.W. Richardson, J.B. Metz, W. Oelmuller, M.D. Bryant, *Religion and Political Society*, p. 19 (New York, Harper & Row 1974).

25. L. Buzzard, "The Evangelical Rediscovery of Law and Politics," 1 *Journal of Law and Religion*, pp. 187, 199 (1983).

26. B. Mitchell, *Law, Morality, and Religion in a Secular Society*, pp. 124–25 (London, Oxford Univ. Pr. 1967). See also V. MacNamara, supra note 9, at p. 132; R.J. Neuhaus, *The Naked Public Square*, pp. 60, 235 (Grand Rapids, Mich., William B. Eerdmans Pub. Co. 1984).

27. See, e.g., W.W. Sweet, "Natural Religion and Religious Liberty in America," 25 *Journal of Religion*, p. 45 (1945); H.F. May, *The Enlightenment in America*, p. 12 (N.Y., Oxford Univ. Pr. 1976).

28. J. Finnis, *Natural Law and Natural Rights* (Oxford, Clarendon Pr. 1980). See also C. Curran, supra note 16, at pp. 65, 87.

29. In *Toward a Christian Ethic*, pp. 19–20 (N.Y., Newman Pr. 1967), W.H.M.

Van Der Marck says that because scripture "does not give us an ethic," it is "strictly necessary" to set up moral theology in an "autonomous, human way." See also G. Hughes, supra note 19, and B. Schuller, supra note 19.

30. H.F. May, supra note 27, at pp. 54–55 (1976).

31. K. Barth, *Church Dogmatics*, vol. III, pt. 4, G. Bromiley and T. Torrance, trans., p. 3 (Edinburgh, T. & T. Clark 1961), quoted in E. L. Long, supra note 11, at p. 29.

32. E.L. Long, supra note 11, at p. 53.

33. See id. at p. 46.

34. See, e.g., V. MacNamara, supra note 9, at p. 74.

35. See, e.g., J.G. Milhaven, "Moral Absolutes and Thomas Aquinas," in C. Curran, ed., *Absolutes in Moral Theology*, p. 177 (Wash., D.C., Corpus Books 1968).

36. Keith Ward, supra note 8, at pp. 93–94, talks of a "distinctively Christian doctrine of the nature of those values which men ought to realize," and describes how the Confucian idea of benevolence differs from the Christian idea of love. See also V. MacNamara, supra note 9, at pp. 80–83, 100.

37. See B. Mitchell, supra note 26, at p. 107.

38. See S.L. Ross, supra note 22, at p. 93. By a "borderline moral choice" I have in mind a choice in which strong arguments support at least two possible courses of action and that the manner in which one conceives of a principle, like showing love for others, may be determinative.

39. J. Finnis, supra note 28; J. Finnis, *The Fundamentals of Ethics*, especially at p. 110 (Wash., D.C., Georgetown Univ. Pr. 1983).

40. See J. Finnis, supra note 39, at p. 69 (Wash., D.C., Georgetown Univ. Pr. 1983). Charles Curran, supra note 16, at p. 188, says that "given human weakness and sinfulness, human beings need the help of divine revelation and of the teaching office of the church in order to have a clear and adequate knowledge of natural law." See also McNamara, supra note 9, at p. 43; Mitchell, supra note 26, at p. 105. Though recognizing a basic moral law written on the hearts of all men, Augustine thought that ignorance and misguided will had almost effaced that law, that we are "so readily subject to vanity that we judge the false for true, reject the true for false, and hold as uncertain what is actually certain" (H. Deane, *The Political and Social Ideas of St. Augustine*, p. 61, compare pp. 85–95 [N.Y., Columbia Univ. Pr. 1963]).

41. St. Augustine's emphasis on sin as a barrier to understanding lies close to traditional Protestant views.

42. I put the point in the text as if the religious sources give an easy and clear answer. That indeed is the viewpoint of some religious people on some issues. That viewpoint is challenged in G. Hughes, supra note 19, at pp. 11–23. Even if the religious sources do not yield a clear answer, the believer's conclusion may be affected by them. See id. at pp. 92–93.

43. According to Basil Mitchell, supra note 26, at pp. 124–25, "the Roman Catholic Church has regarded supernatural revelation as a moral or practical

necessity, although not a theoretical one, for knowing the Natural Law without an admixture of error; so that neither in theory or in practice does the doctrine of Natural Law, whatever its merits, provide a means of determining moral questions without reference to controversial religious claims." Joseph Fuchs, supra note 16, at p. 137, speaks of the tradition since the Council of Trent that the teachings of the magisterium "demand assent" and that the task of moral theologians is mainly reflection on and confirmation of those teachings. See also C. Curran, supra note 16, at pp. 17, 43. In his *Syllabus of Errors* (1864), Pope Pius IX condemned the view that philosophical and moral insights can be obtained by reason alone. See G. Grisez, *Abortion: The Myths, the Realities, and the Arguments*, pp. 345–46 (N.Y., Corpus Books 1970).

45. Of course, it is possible that some moral questions are beyond the intellectual capacity of any human being or that sin seriously undercuts all attempts at objective evaluation. Bernard Haring speaks of revelation as "an undeserved, gracious, divine intervention bringing men to an awareness or understanding of realities that are simply beyond the horizon of man's intelligence or at least transcend the level which he could reach at that moment without such an intervention" ("Dynamism and Continuity in a Personalistic Approach to Natural Law," in G. Outka and P. Ramsey, eds., *Norm and Context in Christian Ethics*, p. 204 [N.Y., Charles Scribners' Sons 1968]).

46. See V. MacNamara, supra note 9, at p. 108.

47. Gerald Hughes, who strongly challenges the idea that scripture or church· teachings can, apart from reason, provide certain answers to contemporary moral questions, nevertheless indicates circumstances in which appeal to authority is proper and speaks of a dialectical relationship between the authority of tradition and one's own moral conclusion. Hughes, supra note 19, at pp. 92–93, 96–97.

48. See generally R.T. DeGeorge, *The Nature and Limits of Authority*, pp. 22, 201, 203 (Lawrence, Kans., Univ. Pr. of Kansas 1985), distinguishing "epistemic" authority from "executive" authority and speaking of epistemic moral authority.

49. James T. Burtchaell, in "The Sources of Conscience," *Santa Clara Magazine* (Summer 1985), at pp. 25–29, criticizes Archbishop John O'Conner and Governor Mario Cuomo, in their debate respecting a proper political position regarding abortion, for their common assumption that a good Catholic's resolution of the moral question is mainly a matter of loyalty to church teaching. William J. Rewak responds to Father Burtchaell's criticism and defends reliance on the authority of church teaching. "Abortion: Three Comments," in id. at pp. 30–31.

4

Publicly Accessible Grounds
of Decision and
Religious Convictions

In this chapter, I explore more closely claims that religious convictions are not appropriate bases of political judgment in a liberal democracy. Though such claims often derive in part from specific concern about religious grounds of political decision, and *may* limit any proposed exclusion to those grounds, some prominent modern theorists relegate certain other possible grounds of decision to the same disfavored status as religious grounds. I concentrate in this chapter on their position, an understanding of which requires a broader categorization of grounds of decision and the place of religious grounds in that broader categorization. After presenting some accounts of the position, I explain why religiously derived convictions that affect moral judgment fall within the broader category of premises that are to be excluded. I also examine in a preliminary and general way the plausibility of the contention that grounds of political decision should be restrained in the way this position envisions.

The discussion in this chapter largely underlies the consideration of particular political problems in most of the following chapters. These chapters explore whether citizens can reasonably be expected to restrict themselves to nonreligious grounds of decision. In them I develop a twofold argument. I claim that theories that exclude many nonreligious premises as well as religious convictions do not leave ample grounds for citizens to resolve many political issues; I also claim that no adequate reason exists for preferring all nonreligious premises to religious convictions as bases for political judgments.

The Position That Citizens Should Rely on Nonreligious Judgments

The idea that citizens and officials in a liberal democracy should rely on nonreligious bases for judgment is one that finds fairly frequent expression and occasional systematic defense.

In an admirable recent introduction to ethics and law, David Lyons suggests that political morality should be governed by principles and arguments "accessible to all persons." He says that to reject the idea of "a naturalistic and public conception of political morality . . . is to deny the essential spirit of democracy."[1] Two decades earlier, in a well-known article on obscenity as sin, Louis Henkin wrote: "The domain of government, it is suggested, is that in which social problems are resolved by rational social processes, in which men can reason together, can examine problems and propose solutions capable of objective proof or persuasion, subject to objective scrutiny by courts and electors."[2] In an earlier discussion of the role of the criminal law in respect to subjects like suicide, euthanasia, and abortion, Glanville Williams said: "For the legislator, it seems sufficient to say that theological speculations and controversies should have no place in the formation of rules of law, least of all rules of the criminal law which are imposed upon believers and non-believers alike."[3] In a book defending reliance on religious convictions, Basil Mitchell groups Henkin and Williams with other thinkers as representing a new liberalism that presumes that religion is a private matter that "belongs to the realm of ideals, not to that of interests. It follows that religious considerations, as they affect morality, should have no place in law making."[4]

What are the dimensions of this "liberal" view? Since Lyons, Henkin, and Williams have not written systematically on the subject, any attempt to draw out the implications of their positions risks omitting nuances they themselves would introduce. The point of the exercise is not to pinpoint their precise intentions but to capture a range of possibilities for evaluation. Most obviously, the notion of a naturalistic and public conception of political morality affects official behavior. In a religiously pluralist society, officials act improperly if they ground their decisions on religious bases. Though a claim about restricted bases of decision might be limited to officials, the idea of a naturalistic conception of political morality is broader. Since ordinary citizens are also political actors, the idea concerns their actions as well. Citizens violate the spirit of liberal democracy if they make political arguments or press political objectives on religious grounds. But the thesis seems to go deeper yet, touching not only the way people defend their positions but the way they arrive at those positions. Canons of morality typically concern personal bases for decision as well as public justifications. If political morality is naturalistic and public, then good liberal citizens should not rely on other than naturalistic and public arguments in deciding how to vote or what political alternatives to support.

I do not mean to suggest that no line exists between personal grounds of decision and public justifications; indeed I shall argue later in the book that public justifications should often be more circumscribed than the entire range of considerations appropriate for decision. But since the line between grounds of decision and stated justifications is not explored by the theorists who propose the exclusion of religious grounds from political morality, and since the full logic of their positions extends to excluding religious convictions as self-conscious bases for personal political decisions, I usually treat the liberal argument for exclusion as embracing these decisions.

As Chapter 3 partially indicates, even this exclusion would not totally eliminate the *effect* of religious convictions for one's personal political life or for public policy. A person initially led by religious insight to understand some fact or moral position that he now believes is fully sustainable on nonreligious grounds could act on the basis of that position. Further, religious convictions might affect the allocation of one's energies in the political sphere. So long as one's position on an issue was grounded on other bases, one's commitment of time and effort might be influenced by a religious sense of the issue's importance. Nothing said by Lyons, Henkin, or Williams would render such choices illegitimate.

There is also at least one respect in which the thesis about exclusion would permit religious conviction to figure indirectly in political decisions. If a legislature must decide which day of the week is to be a day off, and the majority of the population wish strongly, for religious reasons, not to work on Sunday, satisfying general desires about which day of the week to make a holiday is a rational secular ground for choosing Sunday.[5] Similarly, *if* there are good secular reasons why polygamy is harmful in a country in which the vast majority of the population is committed to monogamy, a generally held religious belief that monogamy is called for by God might lead indirectly to a decision to not authorize polygamy.[6] Though direct reliance on religious convictions for what the law should be may be barred, neither citizens nor legislators would need wholly to disregard the effect of practices that are embedded in the culture because of religious beliefs.

The sort of liberal view sketched by Lyons, Henkin, and Williams receives systematic explication and defense, if only incomplete application, in John Rawls's *A Theory of Justice*.[7] Rawls's theory is noted both for its ''original position'' approach for developing principles of justice and for the substantive principles of justice he endorses, including the "difference principle." Though what is particularly critical for our purposes is the manner in which real people are to resolve debated political issues in a society, what Rawls says about that needs briefly to be put in the context of the rest of his theory.

Rawls imagines people in an original position who have general knowledge but do not know their own personal characteristics, social position, or particular conceptions of the good. Behind this "veil of ignorance" they choose principles of justice that will best serve their own interests.[8] The device of choice behind a veil of ignorance is designed to produce principles that are fair, because everyone chooses without knowing what principles would favor him in his actual place in society with his actual beliefs and abilities. The principles chosen, according to Rawls, will consist of equal liberty, which has priority over other social objectives; fair equality of opportunity; and a "difference principle," which permits inequalities of income and wealth only insofar as these benefit a representative person in the worst off group.[9]

At first glance Rawls's original position approach may appear to exclude all reference to religion in establishing principles of justice and to do so by fiat. Plainly, the theory of justice that results from his analysis could hardly be expected to persuade those who think revealed truth calls for very different approaches. If, for example, all the members of a society actually were committed to a singular religious vision, such as Islamic fundamentalism, that assigns roles and opportunities on a basis varying from the equality of opportunity that would be chosen in the original position, we should expect members of that society to be guided by their revealed understanding of right ordering rather than principles that would have been chosen in an original position under conditions of ignorance about "ultimate truth." If Moslem women, as well as Moslem men, freely adopt the roles assigned to them by Islamic fundamentalism, even an outsider should concede that the society is not *unfair* in failing to afford women every opportunity available to men.[10] What might otherwise be unfair is rendered not so by the free choice of those who are disadvantaged socially to remain in their positions.

Robert Paul Wolff suggests that it is "obvious that the parties in the original position are rational, secular, scientific men and women";[11] and a good many readers of *A Theory of Justice* believed that Rawls assumed that a single set of principles of justice would result from rational self-interested choice under conditions of ignorance.[12] In subsequent writings, Rawls has disclaimed an ambition to establish a single, rationally best, set of principles of justice, aiming instead to develop the principles that best elaborate the "basic intuitive ideas that are embedded in the political institutions of a

constitutional democratic regime and the public conditions of their interpretation,"[13] most importantly the idea of "fair social cooperation between
free and equal persons."[14] These basic intuitive ideas are ones that are
accepted by an "overlapping consensus" that includes the opposing philosophical and religious doctrines likely to persist in a more or less just
democratic society.[15] Thus, what Rawls implicitly says about a strict Islamic
republic is that it is unjust by liberal conceptions, not that it is absolutely
unjust.[16]

Because Rawls asserts that his theory is based on shared ideas of liberal
democracy, he is not directly concerned with what might lead any individual to accept these ideas. We can imagine someone concluding that he
accepts the substance of Rawls's theory because God created human beings
to exercise their moral autonomy, and a Rawlsian society would best
promote that exercise. Rawls's theory, devoted to developing the implications of basic premises, does not suggest that religious grounds for accepting these premises are necessarily irrelevant or inappropriate.[17]

What is inappropriate is reliance on religious grounds to decide political
issues within a society that accepts Rawls's conception of justice.[18] Rawls
makes clear that citizens should be guided by this conception in their political decisions. Since the conception does not rely in any respect on any
particular religious perspective or standard of good, citizens deciding what is
just would not rely on religious perspectives or standards of good. Discussing
restrictions on exercises of religious conscience, Rawls says in *A Theory of
Justice* that the state "does not concern itself with philosophical and religious
doctrine but regulates individuals' pursuit of their moral and spiritual interest
in accordance with principles to which they themselves would agree in an
initial situation of equality."[19] Any reasonable expectation of danger, which
might underlie a restriction of liberty, must "be based on evidence and ways
of reasoning acceptable to all. . . . [A] departure from generally recognized
ways of reasoning would involve a privileged place for the views of some over
others, and a principle which permitted this would not be agreed to in the
original position."[20] More recently Rawls has written: "In public questions,
ways of reasoning and rules of evidence for reaching true general beliefs that
help settle whether institutions are just should be of a kind everyone can
recognize."[21] The relevant standards for political decision are the shared
principles of justice "and practices of common sense and science."[22]

Although Rawls does not explicitly discuss the point, I understand his
theory to embrace the ways in which a citizen justifies to himself the
political positions that he takes, as well as the reasons he communicates to
others. If this is correct, Rawls supposes that citizens in a liberal democracy
should resolve both value and factual questions that are relevant to justice
without relying on particular religious convictions.

One possible qualification to the conclusion that religious convictions should not determine political choice concerns topics that are outside the reach of his theory of justice. Treating only relations between human beings within an existing political community, Rawls does not address relations of human beings to animals or relations of one human society to another, though he recognizes that important political choices include these matters.[23] Perhaps reciprocal relations among members of different societies could be dealt with by some sort of extension of the original position;[24] but since reciprocity does not govern relations between human beings and other animals, it is less clear how sound principles for these might be derived. Rawls gives no hint, however, that a shift to a transcendental perspective might be appropriate here. Because political choices about treatment of animals will affect other human beings, and because Rawls's subsequent statements about reliance on shared standards and methods for ascertaining truth are not qualified, we may probably suppose that he thinks fairness to the other people involved requires that political choices about animals be made on grounds accessible to all.[25]

In summary, although Rawls does not explicitly and systematically defend the position that *all* political decisions should be made without reliance on religious convictions, he does indicate that about the large domain of questions of justice within a single political community and the tenor of many of his comments is still broader.

The inappropriateness of reliance on religious conviction in politics is stated more clearly and absolutely in Bruce Ackerman's *Social Justice in the Liberal State*.[26] Regarding constrained dialogue about power as the centerpiece of liberal political theory, Ackerman says:

> [n]obody has the right to vindicate political authority by asserting a privileged insight into the moral universe which is denied to the rest of us. A power structure is illegitimate if it can be justified only through a conversation in which some person (or group) must assert that he is (or they are) the privileged moral authority:
>
> *Neutrality*. No reason is a good reason if it requires the power holder to assert:
>
> a. that his conception of the good is better than that asserted by any of his fellow citizens, or
>
> b. that, regardless of his conception of the good, he is intrinsically superior to one or more of his fellows.[27]

As we shall see in subsequent chapters, not every political reliance on religious conviction amounts to asserting one's own "conception of good," though Ackerman's notion of what that covers is very broad. But Ackerman makes plain that the grounds for liberal political decisions should be nonreligious and rational. He talks for example, about the liberal state, "deprived of divine revelation," in developing a policy toward nature[28] and, in language that reflects less than enthusiastic sympathy with religious perspectives, he precludes restricting abortions "on the basis of some conversation with the spirit world."[29] Richard Flathman speaks of Ackerman's notion of "neutral dialogue" as tolerably familiar as an aspect of liberal theory, one designed to avoid destructive conflict.[30] The idea that "in politics each of us must cease to claim the superiority of our conception of the good and order our interactions by principles neutral among such conceptions" is a "self-denying ordinance" which was "historically first or at least most emphatically adopted in respect to religious beliefs . . . ."[31]

As suggested and developed by Lyons, Henkin, Williams, Rawls, and Ackerman, the thesis that political decisions should be made on naturalistic, nonreligious, publicly accessible grounds is a claim about the ethical import of liberal democracy. Short of arguments or ass mptions that directly challenge religious premises themselves, such a thesis, as I indicated briefly in Chapter 1, cannot claim to say what a member of a liberal democracy should, overall, do. This point is shown by the following example.

> Jody believes that God considers the drinking of alcohol to be sinful; that God wishes people to refrain from drinking alcohol and further wishes that organized societies stamp out this practice; that individuals who drink alcohol will be visited with heavy penalties after death; and that individuals within societies that permit the drinking of alcohol will be visited with similar penalties.

Jody would understandably seek to have her society enact laws against the drinking of alcohol, even while recognizing that many people in society do not share her religious convictions and believe they have a moral right to use alcohol. Persuading her that neutral dialogue or decision under the hypothetical conditions of an original position would lead to allowing adults to choose whether or not to drink alcohol would hardly change her mind given her present insight into transcendent truth. What she wants to accomplish makes perfect sense if she has correctly conceived religious truth. It is silly for her opponents to tell Jody that she should not impose her religious views on others, as if there were some common base of rational understanding that would allow Jody to acknowledge the correctness of that claim without abandoning an aspect of her religious faith.

What a sensitive understanding of Jody's position does not require is that others acknowledge that her aims are consonant with the premises of liberal democracy. A liberal democracy tolerates people like Jody, just as it tolerates people who wish to establish a dictatorship of the proletariat,[32] but Jody's political program is definitely not liberal democratic. Jody's opponents can say to her, "We understand why you are doing what you are doing, but we want to make it clear that your aims fall outside the boundaries of our traditions, and that were similar aims shared by many others, maintaining an open, pluralist society would be extremely difficult. In that important sense, you are not acting like a good liberal democrat." The thesis that excludes religious grounds makes a claim of this sort about good citizenship in a liberal democracy.

Naturalistic, Accessible Reasons and Religious Morality

Neither the systematic accounts of Rawls and Ackerman nor the proposals offered by Lyons and Henkin single out religious grounds specially for disqualification. The reasons for excluding them from political decisions also apply to certain other possible grounds of decision. The common theme of the writers is that the grounds of decision should have an interpersonal validity that extends to all, or almost all, members of society; decisions should be based either on commonly shared premises or on modes of reasoning that are accessible to everyone.

If such bases exist, those who defend political decisions will be able to claim that the results are justified by reasons that have general intersubjective validity, that the law and its restrictions on liberty are based on shared understandings, not on the happenstance that the people with a particular point of view are the more numerous or powerful. This aspiration is appealing; whether it is realistic is one of my major subjects.

In the remainder of this chapter I undertake a preliminary and general exploration of what constitutes commonly shared kinds of reasons, and then indicate the important sense in which I treat religious grounds for political decisions as falling outside that category. This abstract discussion may at times seem to wander rather far from my main concerns, but it is crucial that we avoid an overly simplistic view about what are shared premises and publicly accessible reasons. The ensuing comments underlie both my assumption in the rest of the book that reliance on religious grounds is not consonant with reliance on shared reasons and my claims about the inability of shared reasons to resolve many political issues.

Publicly Accessible Reasons and Shared Premises

It is tempting to summarize the thesis about shared bases of decision as a thesis that political decisions should be made on secular rational grounds: secular not in the sense of being antireligious but in the sense of not relying on religious assumptions,[33] rational in the sense of resting on reasoned arguments whose force is generally understood. If the thesis were so understood, the search to separate excluded grounds from permitted grounds would become an endeavor to provide elaboration of the concept of secular rational grounds relevant for this purpose.

The idea of distinguishing among rational, irrational, and nonrational grounds of decision has considerable appeal, lying partly in the familiarity of the terminology; I have employed that terminology in some initial attempts to address this subject.[34] How far standards of rationality are *genuinely* trans-cultural is a matter of dispute,[35] but it is clear that an argument that a particular society treats as rational at least reflects very widely shared canons of reason within the society. At a minimum, if most people in a society regard a judgment as irrational, it offends accepted ideas of reason. Thus, what are publicly accessible reasons in a society will overlap very greatly with what are widely regarded as canons of rationality in that society.

Criticisms of my previous efforts have persuaded me that the dangers of conceptualization in terms of rationality override whatever virtues inhere in the familiarity and apparent simplicity of the terminology. One danger is the misapprehension that I take Rawls, Ackerman and the others to claim more for rationality than they do, particularly that they must suppose that their premises of justice rest on grounds that can be rationally established. Another danger is that I may seem to rest my own analysis on a controversial theory of rationality that I do not even defend.[36] A third danger is the appearance that I relegate religious belief wholly to the spheres of the nonrational or irrational. To avoid these dangers, I speak here of shared premises and publicly accessible reasons. Roughly, we can distinguish among grounds for decisions that conform to these standards, grounds that are somehow in opposition to the standards, and grounds that deal with matters that these standards leave unresolved. Though these three critical categories are not entirely reducible to the language of rationality, nonetheless the overlap is considerable; and so in my exposition, I do not entirely dispense with the terms "rational," "irrational," and "nonrational."

LOGICAL, SCIENTIFIC, AND ORDINARY KNOWLEDGE

The clearest instances of judgments based on publicly accessible reasons are ones based on reasons whose force, rather than being a product of the particular persons making the judgments, would be acknowledged by any competent and levelheaded observer. That logical deduction and scientific or ordinary empirical inquiry may involve judgments of this kind is fairly straightforward.

Some time ago my eight-year-old son had to determine what the dollar value was of 5,000 ordinary pennies. Though two adults initially informed him that the correct answer was $500, the rationally demonstrable answer, derivable from the meaning of dollars and cents and the axioms of arithmetic, was $50. Whatever may be the ultimate theoretical status of analytical truths like this one—whether they like empirical conclusions are potentially open to revision[37]—an ordinary person who presently denies them has failed to respond to conclusive, publicly demonstrable proof.

If someone asked an empirical question, such as "Did it rain here yesterday?" or "At what temperature will water boil at 15,000 feet?", evidence would be forthcoming that would yield a rational answer. Roughly, very roughly perhaps, we can distinguish scientific empirical knowledge, based on predictive confirmation and experimental reproducibility, from ordinary empirical knowledge, based on observation and common sense reasoning. Scientific theories typically yield generalizations that help to predict what will happen.[38] A theory based either on past tests of water boiling at 15,000 feet or on an understanding of how air pressure at any given height acts upon heated water will yield a conclusion about the temperature at which water will boil, a conclusion confirmable by experiment. Among standards of a good scientific theory are predictive reliability, coherence with other established theories, and in the instance of competing theories that rank about equally by these standards, convenience or simplicity.[39] Though it is questionable whether a single distinctive scientific method exists and how far scientific knowledge and inquiry itself depends on ordinary knowledge and prior notions of rationality,[40] nonetheless the shared standards of scientists represent for our society the epitome of at least one form of rationality. If scientific inquiry can establish the certainty or the probability of something, then that something has been established according to publicly accessible reasons.[41]

The relation between ordinary knowledge and publicly accessible reasons is somewhat more complex. By ordinary knowledge, I mean to include information, other than analytical truths, that we acquire because of our own direct perceptions or because of reports of the direct perceptions of others, and also "common techniques of speculation and casual verification."[42] If I remember that it rained here yesterday or people tell me that it rained, I have good reason to suppose that it did rain. Much of what we believe is on the evidence of our personal experience and memories,[43] and other important evidence is grounded in what Richard Swinburne calls "the testimony principle: that other things being equal, if someone tells you that p, then probably p."[44] As he says, "most of what we believe we believe on authority."[45] If we arrive at a location and the people there say it rained yesterday, we believe that it did. Sometimes we lack anyone's direct perceptions to answer a question. Suppose that I want to know if it rained yesterday at an uninhabited spot to which I have traveled. If the ground is now wet and if I know from my own memories and the testimony of others that it rained long and hard yesterday at a place 200 miles to the west where the wind was blowing steadily eastward, I may conclude that it probably also rained at the uninhabited spot yesterday. People commonly make such judgments without consciously employing scientific theories or undertaking genuinely scientific inquiry. In principle, all these sorts of grounds for concluding that it rained here yesterday fall within the domain of publicly accessible reasons. If I can explain my reasons for reaching that conclusion and they are reasons that are commonly accepted as valid, then I have met the criteria of public accessibility.

INTUITIVE FACTUAL JUDGMENTS

The complexities arise when the basis for a perception or factual inference is neither obvious, as it is the case of a perception that rain falls, nor immediately explicable to others, as would be the connections between wet ground, rain 200 miles away, and eastward wind and the probability of rain having fallen. We sometimes intuitively reach conclusions whose bases we cannot immediately explain. Do our intuitive judgments themselves lie within the domain of publicly accessible reasons for believing the truth that our intuition supports?

Assuming that a judgment that is made intuitively concerns existing or future facts, the issue is whether reliance on the intuitive judgment can conform with a principle that reliance should be based on publicly accessible reasons? The answer depends on the nature of the intuitive judgment and how strictly the requirement of publicly accessible reasons is taken. We shall want to understand the requirement in terms of the idea that political decisions should be made only on such grounds and in light of Rawls's sensible inclusion of "practices of common sense" as lying within publicly accessible reasons. What then emerges as mainly critical is the extent to which judgments of the sort involved have proven out in the past.

We may roughly distinguish four kinds of circumstances in which intuitive judgments are made. A person may believe that an intuitive judgment is a kind of surrogate for a judgment based on a rational explanation that he could provide if given more time. A lawyer may be asked whether the state supreme court would hold that a certain transaction is legally permissible.[46] Based on distant study of analogous cases, she may have an initial sense about legality before she is capable of actually formulating any relevant legal principles. When she gives her initial response, she assumes, though without complete certainty, that she could back up her response with convincing interpersonal reasons. A second kind of situation arises when someone makes an intuitive judgment that he knows he cannot really *explain*, but he believes that people of variant personalities and general backgrounds would all make the same judgment given the same exposure to relevant circumstances. I may identify a person's voice over the telephone without being able to say what the voice qualities are that allow the recognition.[47] I assume that others familiar with the person speaking would also be able to recognize the voice. More controversially, experienced police officers may assert an ability to know intuitively what movements are suspicious;[48] the implication is that others who are similarly trained and have had similar police experience would have similar intuitions.[49] In other situations, a person making an intuitive judgment may doubt whether people generally or people with similar training and exposure to situations would have the judgment he does but he believes that their failure to reach the same judgment is the result of some identifiable inadequacy or defect on their part. Finally, a person, say a clairvoyant, may acknowledge that his intuitive judgment is simply not generalizable in an ordinary way, that it rests on some peculiar insight or perspective that he cannot fully explain and that he does not expect to be replicated by others.

The first kind of situation is perhaps easiest. If in the past the lawyer has proven to herself and others that her initial intuitive reactions are almost invariably followed by convincing interpersonal legal analysis that yields a highly certain prediction of what the supreme court will do, then she can reasonably assume that only a further expenditure of time and effort lies between her initial reaction and her provision of the publicly accessible reasons that support it. The client may or may not be able to understand the convincing legal reasons if they are provided; he is relying mainly on the lawyer as an authority who possesses an expertness he lacks. From his point of view the reliability of the lawyer's judgment may be only slightly diminished if the lawyer has not worked out the problem thoroughly; if the transaction in question is only marginally advantageous, the client *may* prefer to rely on the intuitive judgment rather than undertake added expense. In short, common sense sometimes leads people to rely on the intuitive judgments of experts because the exercise of developing a fuller reasoned explanation is not worthwhile. How this may occur for important political decisions is much more subtle. Rarely, then, will no explanation be provided; it will be worthwhile for an expert to develop and explicate the grounds of his judgment. But even then, as to marginal considerations or the balance of competing arguments, the expert may rely on intuitions that he believes he could support if he engaged in an even fuller explication. For minor political decisions, such as whom to hire for some low-level government position or which project to support with a grant of $3000, the role of expert intuitions about likely facts may be more prominent.

In the second kind of situation, providing an explanation in terms of publicly accessible reasons is not practically possible.[50] Most people simply are not capable of going very far in explaining how they recognize another person's voice over the telephone. But each of us has a degree of confirmation in past experience; we know how often we have been able to identify a particular voice or other voices. Absent some reason to the contrary, we may assume that our ability is roughly similar to that of other people; we also have experienced others identifying our voice and we know that others say they have successfully identified other voices. Thus, if a friend says, "I am sure that was John's voice," we have a substantial reason to think it was John's voice. If, in fact, arrest practice establishes that experienced police officers really can identify movements as suspicious,[51] though they are unable to say why they can do so, then reliance on such judgments also fits with common sense. In this context, the publicly accessible reason is not the basis for the judgment but the repeated success of similar judgments by similar people in similar situations.

So long as the defect in capacity is really readily identifiable, the third kind of situation is not fundamentally dissimilar from the second. Not all similarly situated people would make the same judgment, but we can explain why some people are unable to do so. If the defect can be identified separately from the failure to make correct intuitive judgments *and* those without the defect evidence a high degree of accuracy, we have reason to trust a judgment that someone without the defect makes. If instead, it is simply assumed that someone who makes incorrect judgments must have a defect, but that person evidences no independent defect that we can identify, then the third kind of situation is really like the fourth; some people make correct judgments and others do not for reasons no one can really explain.

We may consider the predictions of a clairvoyant as an extreme example of the fourth kind of situation. Reliance on what a clairvoyant says seems most in opposition to the notion of publicly accessible reasons. We must, however, carefully distinguish what one believes clairvoyants can actually accomplish from what the implications are of a principle that people should rely on publicly accessible reasons.

Margaret Popkin, the police chief of a large city, receives the following report from her deputy. Each day in the past month, in the presence of the deputy and a prominent scientist, Malcolm Morse has placed pins on a city map where he thinks attempted murders will take place on the following day. Every known murder and attempted murder has been accurately predicted by Morse and for each other pin placed by Morse, the possibility of attempted murder could not be confidently foreclosed. Morse has placed ten pins for the following day. Popkin must decide whether to assign police officers to the locations indicated by Morse.

Chief Popkin might simply assume that a great farce is being played upon her or that some fantastic coincidence has occurred; but it would certainly be rational for her to allocate her officers according to Morse's reported intuitions, though no one can *explain* his past success. That past success itself provides the publicly accessible reason for her to rely on Morse's intuitions. And if the past success involved Popkin's own intuitions about locations of crimes rather than someone else's, it would be rational for her to rely on them as well. If a person says that a police chief should never rely on a clairvoyant's intuitions, the basic reason must be skepticism about clairvoyance, not rigid insistence that on no conceivable facts could such reliance conform with publicly accessible reasons.

When intuitive judgments have not been vindicated in the past, a person's confidence in a present intuitive judgment is ordinarily not the source of a publicly accessible reason to believe the judgment is correct. Suppose that occasionally an impulsive gambler has had extremely strong intuitions that a coin toss will come up heads. Her intuitions have been wrong exactly as often as they have been right. She now has an extremely strong intuition that the next coin toss will be heads. Her present intuition is not a good reason for anyone else to believe that the next toss is more likely to be heads than tails, nor is it even a good reason for her if she is sufficiently reflective about her past experience.

The coin toss is an extreme example of an intuition about a result that seems rationally to depend on a random outcome, but that example provides a helpful introduction to cases in which present probabilities and past confirmations are less apparent, that is, most of life's circumstances. Suppose, first, that confirmation is unavailing but the great majority of people have the same intuition, and we can think of no external reason why they would have that intuition. I can make the point most easily in terms of a direct perception. If it is reported to me that 999 people say they perceived one panel as green and one panel as red, but that one person saw both panels as red, I believe that probably one panel is green and the other red. If the 999 people say they perceived no difference and only one person thought the panels were of different color, I shall suppose that the panels are the same color and that the defect is in the lone dissenter's perceptive capacities. But my opinion will change if I learn that the viewers were attending a convention for the color-blind. For otherwise unexplained intuitions,[52] the argument that the intuition that most people share is more likely to be correct may lie within the realm of publicly accessible reasons.

In respect to many subtle variations of fact, nonconfirmable intuitions will diverge substantially, and it is as to these that the question of publicly accessible reasons is most pressing. All but the most self-doubting persons[53] are inclined to place more confidence in their own intuitions then in the reported intuitions of others. If Josephine says she feels people are generally untrustworthy, I cannot be sure she is telling the truth and I do not know exactly what she means by "generally untrustworthy." These barriers of communication do not exist[54] if I reflect on my own perceptions. Further, my feelings are somehow connected, though in ways I may not fully understand, to other views about reality that I find the most persuasive.[55] I am aware that some of these views may be seriously in error, but if I could identify the errors I would not hold those views, so the combination of views is the closest I think I can come to error-free views. Since Josephine's intuitions may be connected to views I presently regard as erroneous, that possibility renders her intuitions less trustworthy from my perspective.

Beyond these reasons to credit their own intuitions, people have a normal psychological tendency to place confidence in their own strong feelings. In part, the point is that we just think that our feelings are more likely to be right than an objective appraisal might warrant; we tend to discount past disappointments of expectations or to suppose that somehow our present intuition is really different from the similar intuitions that have proved wrong in the past. In part, the point is that we feel more comfortable if we act in accord with our strong feelings. Suppose we are persuaded that people are really more trustworthy than we have always felt, but intellectual persuasion is not accompanied by emotional confidence in others. Giving people just that degree of confidence that our present rational appraisal would warrant[56] may make us uneasy and insecure, and we might prefer to act more as our original feelings would indicate. Of course, the psychological comfort of action that accords with strong feelings not only leads people to deviate from the course of action suggested by a detached evaluation; that comfort also constitutes an initial powerful barrier to the critical appraisal needed for a detached evaluation.

In any event, a principle that everyone should rely on publicly accessible reasons in making factual judgments for political decisions would presumably entail that people should give no more weight to their particular intuitions than could be defended in terms of persuasive interpersonal grounds for the present intuitions and the accuracy of similar past intuitions.

PRACTICAL DECISIONS

Political decisions are a branch of practical decisions about what *should* be done. As a number of my examples have indicated, these judgments typically involve factual components. When people determine which among possible means is actually capable of achieving an end, or which of various efficacious means will be least costly, they make empirical judgments. If accuracy mattered above all, ideally such judgments would be made in light of a thorough canvassing of all aspects of alternatives; but in ordinary life shortcuts are usually required. Given the need to make decisions in reasonable time and with reasonable effort, it is rational, usually necessary, to proceed with something less than a full review of relevant considerations.[57] In that effort, reliance on informed intuition is consistent with a principle of reliance on publicly accessible reasons to the degree I have just suggested.

Most practical judgments involve more than simple calculation and are not reducible to purely factual issues.[58] In some circumstances, all that is involved is the application of an authoritative rule to a particular situation. In simple cases of this sort only an exercise in logical derivation is needed, as when a judge imposes a mandatory sentence on an offender. More often, a person facing a practical judgment must make a direct choice among ends or a choice between means that considers the harms and benefits of subsidiary effects as well as capacity to achieve the immediate end.

At least when rough agreement exists about the importance of various ends, publicly accessible reasons can determine the outcome, though the correctness of such a judgment will usually not be demonstrable beyond question. One reason for the absence of demonstrability is that the alternatives and all their implications will rarely be laid out in a systematic way. A second reason why the judgments will not be demonstrably correct involves a deeper understanding of reasoning about conflicting values. Much discourse in law and morality assumes our ability to identify in context which arguments are stronger than others, though nothing that amounts to proof of their various strengths may be possible.[59] As Rawls has said, when proof is not possible, one can still hope, in the phrase of John Stuart Mill, to "present considerations capable of determining the intellect."[60]

When value judgments must be made, certain standards of reasoning are deemed appropriate, including standards of generality, coherence, and regularity.[61] An apt resolution for one problem should have implications for other problems; it should be based on value assignments that are consonant with value assignments made in other areas, and it should be consistent with resolutions made before and after it. Relevant considerations should be presented and assessed in a suitably detached manner so they may be given their fair weight,[62] and in assessing ends, people should order the satisfaction of present and future preferences in some defensible way.[63] When people's judgments about particular resolutions do not initially fit the general principles they accept, they should reconsider resolutions and principles in light of each other in an effort to reach "reflective equilibrium."[64] These rather vague notions can be viewed as standards of rationality concerning value judgments, and one who follows them employs publicly accessible forms of reasoning.

It is unlikely, however, that even rigorous and detached employment of these standards will produce answers to all questions concerning the assessment of values. There is a strong, though always controversial, tradition in liberal philosophy that treats ultimate values as subjective.[65] What matters for our purposes is not whether ultimate values have some objective grounding, say in God's relation to human life, but whether human beings have the capacity to arrive at objective judgments about ultimate values. Any view that they do not have this capacity may seem to pose a substantial obstacle to any recommendation of exclusive reliance on publicly accessible reasons for political decisions, since ultimate value judgments may be assumed to figure in such decisions.

We need to be clear about what is at stake here and what constitutes a relevant threat to the thesis about publicly accessible reasons. We can put aside the troubling question in moral philosophy whether it is irrational, or otherwise wrong,[66] for an individual to pursue his long-term interest at the expense of others. In the political context, an analogous question is whether an individual acts immorally in pursuing his own self-interest within the political process at the expense of the public interest.[67] I indicated in Chapter 1 that at least as to some issues, the good citizen is constrained to promote the public interest, not his or her own selfish interest, but I did not undertake to defend that position or indicate how far that constraint applies. The main reason why that issue is not central for our purposes is that someone who relies on a religious conviction to make a political judgment will almost always think that the position one supports is best overall, not just best for oneself or best for people who happen to believe similarly.[68] A subsidiary reason for not focusing more carefully on constraints on the pursuit of selfish interests is that almost all the issues I discuss are ones in which the idea that people should not proceed on the basis of pure self-interest is widely accepted. Insofar as a claim about the subjectivity of values raises problems about whether we should be moral at all or about whether we should act on behalf of the general interest in the political process, these are problems I can disregard.

Thus narrowed, the troublesome question is whether determinations about what is ultimately right or good are inevitably subjective. An answer that they are poses a serious threat to the thesis that political decisions should be made on the basis of shared premises and publicly accessible reasons. How might this possible threat be met?

There are at least three general ways in which a challenge based on the subjectivity of values might be answered. One is to meet the challenge head on: to assert that, contrary to what that challenge supposes, moral truths can be established objectively, either by publicly accessible reasons or by means which for these purposes are just as good as publicly accessible reasons. The second way is to assert that the relevant moral questions are settled by shared premises in a society. If value premises are universally shared, or nearly so, within a society, perhaps they legitimately underlie political decisions, even if the premises themselves cannot be *established* by the forms of reasoning that are publicly accessible. The third response acknowledges that subjectivity may infect some areas of morality, but contends that these do not include the appropriate range of political decisions. In a liberal democracy, it may be claimed, political decisions appropriately take a neutral stance about whatever debatable questions of value are unsettled by liberal democratic premises themselves.

The first, most obvious, response to the worry about the subjectivity of value determinations asserts that the domain of objective value judgments is considerable. Some of what appear initially to be irreducible conflicts between claims of value may on examination prove to be complicated factual questions.[69] Other apparent conflicts may be reined in by canons of consistency as they apply to practical choice. If a person or society has desires or ends whose satisfaction will defeat other desires or ends that are regarded as more important, we can say that attempts to satisfy the first desires or ends are irrational, that they do not fit within the pattern of what overall will best serve the person's or society's objectives.

Beyond these possibilities lie more controversial claims about objectivity. It may be thought that fundamental goods are discoverable from an understanding of human nature[70] or are self-evident to rational beings,[71] that our understanding of what it is to be a person among persons commits us to certain conclusions about values,[72] or that the nature of moral language implies a way to resolve value conflicts.[73] A view that was influential at the time of our country's founding and that finds modern expression in intuitionism is the idea that people have a separate moral sense that tells them what is good and right.[74] Exactly how to characterize any such shared sense among human beings may be debatable,[75] but its conclusions would certainly be an appropriate starting point for deliberations on political issues.

This cursory canvas is barely a beginning for thinking about objectivity regarding values, but we can see how a proponent of decisions based on publicly accessible reasons might argue that judgments about good and ought are much more susceptible to reasoned judgment than any extreme subjectivist view admits.

The possibility of such objectivity however is hardly sufficient to dispel the worry about the status of ultimate values. Most modern secular philosophers who have wished to stress the supracultural objectivity of many values and moral judgments have not supposed that *all* judgments about values and right action have correct, rationally determinable answers.[76] Even if various ways of establishing values objectively can reduce what would otherwise be the domain of subjectivity, it does not follow that separately, or jointly, they eliminate that domain. If they do not do so, the dimensions of the problem for reasoned grounds of decision are lessened, but the problem remains.

A philosophically more modest response to the subjectivist worry is to claim that one's particular culture settles what is valuable and what sorts of actions are right, and that these understandings appropriately underlie political decisions. In that event the relevant ultimate values would constitute shared premises of the society, rather than being grounded on independent publicly accessible reasons. To lawyers especially, this approach may be appealing. The law may be viewed as embodying an immense number of judgments about values and resolutions of conflicts between them, and legal decision in novel and difficult cases understood as an attempt to resolve a particular problem in light of the rich materials of the law. This view of legal decision, notably exemplified in the work of Ronald Dworkin,[77] might be extended more broadly to decisions about what the law should be. Citizens and officials would then be drawing from the rich materials of their culture to resolve novel problems; the value judgments they would appropriately deploy would be drawn from the culture. Even if in some sense the culture's "choices" were ultimately subjective, the fact of the culture's adoption of them would be reasonably determinable and their explication and application could be a part of reasoned discourse within the culture.

In respect to culturally determined values, it is highly doubtful any comprehensive ordering of values exists that totally eliminates the domain of subjectivity. There are incoherencies, crosscurrents, and debated questions. A common theme among modern thinkers is that the interpretation of complex phenomena requires normative judgments by interpreters that are not dictated by the underlying materials being interpreted. In any event, whatever may be true *for officials*, citizens of a liberal democracy are free to urge and vote for measures that would represent a shift in many widely prevailing values. No doubt they must communicate in terms that people understand; to that extent their discourse must connect to what people presently understand about values, but people are free to argue that their society has badly misconceived what really matters. A private citizen is not doing anything at odds with the spirit of liberal democracy, for example, if he urges that the society is too materialistic and that people should care much less than they presently do about physical well-being. A private citizen acts within the spirit of liberal democracy if his voting and other political actions are determined by objectives that are not widely shared at present. Liberal democracy does not preclude citizens from self-conscious rejection of many accepted values and from efforts to have laws made that would reflect other values.[78]

The third possible response to the concern over the subjectivity of values is to concede its possible truth as far as ultimate values are concerned but to claim the irrelevance of that conclusion to political decisions. One conceivable possibility is that other-regarding morality is not affected by the doubtful status of ultimate values. Since political decisions involve the relation between the representatives of organized society and others, they make up a special branch of interpersonal morality. If it were the case that the subjective aspects of morality concerned only self-regarding pursuit of the good life, and that all elements of other-regarding morality could be rooted in publicly accessible reasons, then the concern about subjectivity would not touch political decisions. That possibility is illusory, however. One reason is that a significant part of other-regarding morality is encouraging others to live a life that is good for them. Most obviously in the case of parents toward children, but also between friends and acquaintances, a person's own notion of the good life will affect how he treats others.[79] Moreover, one person's attempts to live in ways he thinks good often impinge on other persons in ways that some regard as harmful or destructive, so disapproval and outright prohibition to protect the other persons loom as possibilities. If no ideas about the good for individuals can be established objectively, it will be impossible to establish all of other-regarding morality objectively.[80]

Perhaps a more promising line is that at least political decisions need not be infected by the subjectivity of determinations of ultimate value. This is essentially the approach that both Rawls and Ackerman take. Rawls asserts that people with very different life plans, and ideas of the good, will all want liberties, opportunities, and wealth. The theory of what is just, the theory relevant to political decision, can be developed from this "thin theory of the good."[81] Ackerman's whole theory is built on the inappropriateness of political decisions that rest on any controversial assumptions about what is valuable. Though Ackerman makes arguments why people who believe in absolute values should still be liberals, his own position is made clear by his comment that "[t]here is no moral meaning hidden in the bowels of the universe."[82] His postulate of dialogue constrained by a principle of neutrality is precisely designed to take many questions of ultimate value, all these that are involved in a person's conception of the good, out of the political arena. Like Rawls, Ackerman supposes that almost everybody wants the means to accomplish their ideas of the good in their own lives, and these desires for wealth and power are a sufficient basis for reaching political decisions. Thus, political decisions can be made employing publicly accessible ways of reasoning even if many value assumptions are not established by shared premises or techniques of reason. The theories of Rawls and Ackerman do, without doubt, rest on at least *some* ultimate value assumptions, such as that people in a society are owed equal respect and concern;[83] but granting this point does not undermine the possibility that their theories will permit reasoned political decisions. Conceivably the necessary premise of equality might be drawn out of the nature of persons or moral concepts and thus itself be given an objective status, but even if it cannot, *this premise* may be a shared one that underlies liberal democracy, a premise that a good liberal democrat cannot deny. That avenue would be sufficient to establish the equalitarian premise as a starting point for liberal democratic theory.

If all political decisions could be made with a combination of this premise, and perhaps other shared premises of liberal democracy,[84] plus generally accessible forms of reasoning, then the aspirations of Rawls's and Ackerman's approaches would be vindicated. Much of my burden in Chapters 6 to 10 is to show that more is required in many areas of political importance.

Religious Morality as Outside Shared Premises and Publicly Accessible Reasons

It remains to explain why I treat religious morality and religiously grounded moral judgments as beyond shared premises and publicly accessible reasons. The basic idea is that some of the crucial premises that underlie such judgments are not the subject of general acceptance or of persuasive demonstration by publicly accessible reasons, but this basic idea obscures and oversimplifies in ways that warrant explication.

INFLUENCES OF PUBLICLY ACCESSIBLE REASONS ON
RELIGIOUSLY BASED MORAL JUDGMENTS

I want first to make clear three important connections between publicly accessible reasons and religiously grounded moral judgments that I by no means wish to challenge. The first connection concerns the substantive content of moral perspectives. Any religious morality is likely to include many elements that are found in secular moralities and that can most plausibly lay claim to being self-evidently true, universally accepted, or demonstrable on the basis of accessible reasons. Judaism and Christianity strongly condemn the unjustified taking of life or infliction of pain. In these elements, revelation may most straightforwardly be seen as confirming what is apparent to natural reason. Thus, some *elements* of any religious morality may be establishable by reason, but these elements are precisely those for which the religious ingredient is inessential. When I speak of religious morality as going beyond shared premises and publicly accessible reasons, I refer to elements that owe their apparent force to the religious perspective, elements that might have no force or less force if one limited oneself to reasoning in the absence of the religious insight. It is for these elements that the status of the religious claim matters.

The second connection between publicly accessible reasons and religious morality concerns the elaboration and application of central religious premises. Suppose that a religious belief about the inerrancy of scripture or the overarching importance of self-sacrificing love is not establishable by reason. Nevertheless, ordinary processes of reason may be employed to interpret the meaning of a scriptural passage written in an ancient language or to develop the practical significance of being guided by love. A claim about the import of the biblical passage or the ethic of love might then depend both on a reasoned account of its significance and on a belief in its prescriptive force that reaches beyond reason. When I say that religious morality is not founded on publicly accessible reasons, I do not mean that such reasons are wholly absent from the development of positions, only that some critical underlying component is not *based* on those reasons.

The third connection between publicly accessible reasons and religious morality partly exposes the oversimplification even in the position that the underlying religious premises are not based on such reasons. At a minimum those reasons operate as sorts of negative criteria of believability. Basic religious beliefs are, for most people at least, subject to tests of internal coherence and compatibility with experience. What reasoned scrutiny of religious claims amounts to is complex, but Ninian Smart has suggested a number of bases for assessing historical religions like Judaism and Christianity:[85] (1) Are its historical claims roughly in accord with actual historical events? (2) Were the leaders of the faith flagrantly unethical?[86] (3) Do the elements of its faith involve self-contradiction or an intolerable tension? (4) Does acceptance of the faith produce the fruits that the faith values? (5) Does the faith produce a deep and meaningful account of the problems of life that are hardest to explain? (6) Do the founder and prophets have force and style? (7) Is there a solidity and aesthetic coherence to the narratives of the faith? All, or most, of these inquiries involve elements that are subject to thought and discussion in reasoned terms. What seems ethically compelling on other than religious grounds is one basis for assessing religious beliefs with clear ethical implications. It is also a standard for construing the implications of general positions whose precise ethical import is not clear. A person's ethical sense, thus, affects both what general religious views he may adopt and also the manner in which he understands the ethical significance of these views. If, as I assume, reasoned analysis plays a part in the development of nonreligious ethical positions, morality developed by publicly accessible reasons and shared premises is for many people a kind of straining device and check on religiously grounded morality.

ACCESSIBLE REASONS AND RELIGIOUS TRUTH

All these preliminaries about undeniable connections bring us to the central question: Can publicly accessible reasons and shared premises actually establish the truth of some particular religious position? If we assume that a substantial number of religious perspectives, including here atheism and agnosticism, can meet minimal requisites of rational scrutiny and ethical acceptability, how is an individual to choose one rather than another of these perspectives and how can he defend his choice? If he cannot make a defense on grounds of publicly accessible reasons and shared premises, then any ethical position that critically derives from the religious perspective cannot be so defended.

Referring to liberal democratic premises and to the obvious fact that natural reflection alone cannot yield the sets of truths claimed by historical religious like Judaism and Christianity, one is tempted to dispose of the problem simply by saying that religious premises go beyond shared premises and publicly accessible reasons; but the problem warrants somewhat deeper exploration. That exploration can yield a richer understanding of the bases for religious belief and also provides an important standard for comparison with the bases for certain nonreligious beliefs.

I turn first to the premises of our liberal democracy, among which I have included both religious liberty and government nonsponsorship of religious truth. Does acceptance of these premises logically compel, or point more weakly toward, acceptance of the skeptical conclusion that religious truth cannot be settled on publicly accessible grounds? One *might* believe that publicly accessible grounds are capable of showing the validity of a particular religious faith, but also believe that, given the present diversity of religious beliefs, the intensity of feeling about religion, and the inappropriateness of government involvement, religious liberty and nonsponsorship are warranted. But if these two premises of liberal democracy are not strictly incompatible with a belief that publicly accessible reasons can settle religious truth, the premises do fit more comfortably with an attitude that for political purposes one religious view is as valid as another, at least as long as neither view itself conflicts with liberal premises. As I shall suggest in more depth in Chapter 12, the present paucity of public political arguments cast in narrowly religious terms reflects the present dominance of an attitude that accessible reasons cannot establish the soundness of any particular religious perspective.

Are there more decisive grounds than present attitudes and weak emanations from basic liberal democratic premises to suggest that religious truth reaches beyond publicly accessible reasons and shared premises? I want initially to draw a distinction between a relatively rationalist approach to religious belief and one that emphasizes personal inspiration. A person who accepts the first approach may acknowledge that naturalist reasoning cannot *directly* establish many religious truths but believe that it can discover these truths in steps. He may think, as have many people throughout the ages, that rational argument can show that a powerful and morally beneficent God exists, or probably exists,[87] and that further rational argument, based on miraculous occurrences,[88] accurate scriptural prophecies of future events,[89] and the moral persuasiveness of its basic teaching, can establish the content of God's revelation to human beings. It would then conform with practical common sense to do some actions that revelation indicates are desirable,[90] even though one's independent reason would not reach the conclusion that those actions were called for. Even if a person with this sort of approach to religious truth supposed that full participation in the religious life requires a commitment of will that in some sense goes beyond reason, he might think his beliefs themselves and their practical implications were wholly defensible in term of publicly accessible reasons.[91]

This sketchy picture of a rationalist approach to religion provides a sobering corrective to an easy assumption indulged in by a great many highly sophisticated people[92] that religion is necessarily a matter of the heart and not the mind. In fact, upon sufficient reflection, almost everyone would acknowledge that some publicly accessible evidences in our world do, or could, count for or against particular religious beliefs.[93] But a great many people, perhaps including most religious people, think existing evidences of the sort discussed so far are radically inconclusive, that they alone cannot anchor particular religious perspectives of the kind familiar in our society.

What if someone takes the view, which has dominated modern Protestant thought, that some kind of personal inspiration or even "leap of faith" is necessary for religious truth to be confirmed?[94] It is initially attractive to suppose that on such a view, publicly accessible reasons are rendered wholly irrelevant, but our previous examination of the place of intuitive judgments reveals the fallacy of this supposition. That examination has shown that in certain circumstances even intuitions that are not explainable may have interpersonal force, and we need to ask whether intuitions about religious truth may be of this variety.

Unless a person accepts a religion unthinkingly on grounds of tradition, he will have a deep sense that the religious perspective conforms with his own personal experience and his understanding of social experience. If one has not grown up within a tradition, the religion must have an initial appeal that "speaks to his condition." If he accepts the religion, there must be continuing sense that it illuminates life's possibilities and meaning. To take a Christian perspective, an account of life that emphasizes love and redemption and puts Jesus in a position of central importance is seen as giving a more persuasive interpretation of the significance of human existence than any alternative.

Though needs and responses of this sort are highly personal, they are not totally idiosyncratic. Most people seek answers to deep questions of existence and want their lives to have meaning. A person's explanation of how a particular set of religious beliefs has met his own particular perplexities and anxieties may well have some persuasive force for others with similar concerns.

We can imagine at least three other ways in which personal religious insights might be confirmed for others. One way, a variation on the clairvoyant example, is similar to the idea of accurate scriptural prophecies. Suppose that a person believes that God has communicated to him directly that an event will occur or believes that God will answer petitions made during prayer and has offered prayers for future occurrences. If events occur just as he believes they will, and if the occurrence of these events would otherwise have been impossible for anyone to foretell,[95] their occurrence constitutes some evidence in favor of the truth of his set of beliefs.

A second possibility of confirmation lies in the number of people who have a particular religious intuition. If almost everyone believed in a single

God, the sheer fact of such belief might constitute some evidence for its truth. However, were some alternative explanation available, such as that belief in God is the product of social conditioning or compensates for some widespread psychological inadequacy, the potential force of such evidence would be countered.[96]

The third kind of confirmation concerns the fruits of belief. Suppose that people who accept a particular religious faith are widely understood to lead lives that are, even judged by outsiders, particularly harmonious and satisfying.[97] It is, of course, logically possible that some set of false beliefs will make human life most satisfying, but perhaps most people would judge that such clear fruits of faith constitute some evidence of truth, particularly, again, if no alternative explanation that assumes falsity can account for why a faith so richly affects the lives of its adherents.

I have enumerated a number of ways, touching both external arguments for particular religious beliefs and arguments that turn on the experiences of adherents, in which publicly accessible reasons may bear on assertions of religious truth. Perhaps one point obliquely illustrated in the discussion is that the edges of publicly accessible reasons are themselves rather uncertain. Is the fact that most people have a particular intuition *any* evidence, in and of itself, for the truth of the intuition? We may not be sure whether or not widespread intuitions are standing alone a publicly accessible reason for belief.

The discussion of accessible reasons for religious belief leads us to two other points that are important for our purposes. People have radically different ideas about the force of various publicly accessible reasons that bear on the truth or falsity of particular religious claims. And in the area of religious belief, where confirmation is certainly not easy, people are especially likely to give great weight to their own intuitions and the fruits of their own experience.[98]

If we consider the reasons for Christian belief, we must quickly realize that many highly intelligent people aware of all the arguments in favor of such belief find those arguments wholly unconvincing. It is not just that they accede to powerful contrary arguments, they see virtually no force in the arguments in favor of Christianity. This is a pretty strong basis for doubting that the truth of Christianity can be established by publicly accessible reasons. Of course, it might be responded that these who do not see the force of these reasons suffer some defect, but there is no evident defect that can be identified in a noncircular way. If the defect is a lack of special grace from God and the truth of Christianity is not accessible to those who lack this grace, then nonbelief itself becomes the only practical way for humans to identify who suffers the defect. If instead, the supposed defect is some ordinary human failing, such as inordinate self-love, then in theory the defect could be separately identified, but in reality there seems no strong observable correlation between those with the defect and those who are not believing Christians. In sum, acceptance of Christianity, or another religion, includes elements of belief whose tenability is not subject to fully interpersonal examination.

When people must decide about claims that gravely affect their lives and are not subject to easy external confirmation, they understandably give great weight to their own personal experiences, to what feels right for them. A person who regards the existence of God as self-evident and who strongly feels that his own experience confirms the truth of a particular Christian perspective is not likely to alter his faith upon being told that others have arrived at different conclusions. Part of the point, as I indicated in connection with nonreligious intuitions, is that their own experience appears to people as the most reliable basis for assessing the truth of competing perspectives. But beyond that lies the more subtle psychological reality that people are drawn to beliefs that fit with their own sense of themselves and their place among others. To some extent, they can trim their feelings to conform with convincing arguments about truth; but when ordinary rational grounds for assessing the truth are highly inconclusive, people are likely to believe what conforms with their deepest feelings.

In succeeding chapters, I shall assume that claims about religious truth are outside the domain of publicly accessible reasons. I believe that for purposes of this book that assumption is roughly accurate, but the reader should remember that this assumption reflects the more complex reality to which the last few pages have been devoted.

I turn now briefly to a different possible objection to my position that religiously grounded morality is, in a critical sense, outside shared premises and publicly accessible reasons. Perhaps certain religious views, whatever their grounding in reason, are so widely shared they can provide the basis for political conclusions. I want to concede the theoretical possibility that in an otherwise liberal society, religious convictions might be so uniformly held they could provide a shared basis for political reasoning, though I am doubtful that could occur in any modern prosperous society with substantial nondiscriminatory immigration. In any event, in present American society, significant numbers of people dissent from even the most widely held religious beliefs, such as belief in the existence of God; and a much higher percentage dissent from any belief specific enough to yield significant ethical conclusions that are not obvious on nonreligious grounds.[99] Further, any notion that particular religious premises whose force cannot be established by accessible reasons should nevertheless be a general starting point for consideration of political issues is in some tension with principles of religious liberty and government nonsponsorship. Thus, both the size of the dissenting group and ideas of liberal democracy provide strong reasons against a view that a consensus about religious premises allows them to be used as shared principles for political decision.

In the following chapters, I endeavor to circumscribe the appropriate range of reliance on religious premises, using specific illustrations to draw out conclusions that are then formulated in more abstract form. My aim in treating a number of important social issues is not to contribute to their practical resolution but to show when religious convictions appropriately come into play and when they do not.

Notes

1. D. Lyons, *Ethics and the Rule of Law*, pp. 191–92 (Cambridge, Cambridge Univ. Pr. 1984).

2. L. Henkin, "Morals and the Constitution: The Sin of Obscenity," 63 *Columbia Law Review*, p. 441 (1963).

3. G. Williams, *The Sanctity of Life and the Criminal Law*, p. 229 (N.Y., Alfred A. Knopf, Inc. 1966).

4. B. Mitchell, *Law, Morality, and Religion in a Secular Society*, p. 100 (London, Oxford Univ. Pr. 1967).

5. Whether to grant special days off to people of different religions is another question.

6. Whether such good secular reasons exist is debatable. Even if they do, nonauthorization of polygamy need not entail a criminal prohibition against entering relationships deemed by some religious persons to constitute plural marriages.

7. J. Rawls, *A Theory of Justice* (Cambridge, Mass., Harvard Univ. Pr. 1971).

8. Id. at pp. 17–22, 118–50.

9. Id. at pp. 150–61, 175–83, 60–90.

10. There is a tricky point here. A Rawlsian might say that it is unfair not to afford all women equal liberty and opportunity, even if all women, or the vast majority of women, choose to restrict themselves. I assume that if all women of one generation and their growing daughters freely choose not to have certain opportunities, it would not be unjust to educate women in a way that would impair access to those opportunities, even were it thought that the daughters had not yet reached a fully mature judgment about the opportunities. That assumption is debatable, as, of course, is the notion that any group could ever *freely* choose to be as subservient as Moslem women, in the fundamentalist vision, are supposed to be.

Perhaps an even clearer example of a practice not being unjust that would be barred by the original position analysis would be keeping the least advantaged group at a very low level of income and wealth if all members of that group freely believed their religious salvation depended on their having only a subsistence income.

11. R.P. Wolff, *Understanding Rawls*, p. 127 (Princeton, N.J., Princeton Univ. Pr. 1977).

12. Some readers of Rawls doubted that any single set of principles could be so derived, worrying that the conditions of the original position are not specific enough to yield one set of principles, or that the conditions are manipulated to reach the results Rawls happens to favor, or that both problems are present in various aspects of the conditions. See, e.g., B. Ackerman, *Social Justice in the Liberal State*, pp. 225, 328–29, 339 (New Haven, Conn., Yale Univ. Pr. 1980); J. Fishkin, *Tyranny and Legitimacy* (Baltimore, Johns Hopkins Univ. Pr. 1979); J.P. Sterba, *The Demands of Justice*, pp. 34, 55 (Notre Dame, Ind., Univ. of Notre Dame Pr. 1980); R.P. Wolff, supra note 11, at pp. 131–41; B. Barber, "Justifying Justice: Problems of Psychology, Politics and Measurement in Rawls," in N. Daniels, ed., *Reading Rawls*, pp. 292, 294–301 (Oxford, Basil Blackwell 1975).

13. J. Rawls, "Justice as Fairness: Political not Metaphysical," 14 *Philosophy and Public Affairs*, p. 225 (1985). For a sympathetic explanation and defense of Rawls's position, see R. Rorty, "The Priority of Democracy Over Philosophy," in M. Peterson and R. Vaughn, eds., *The Virginia Statute for Religious Freedom* (N.Y., Cambridge Univ. Pr. 1987).

14. J. Rawls, supra note 13, at p. 229; see J. Rawls, "Kantian Constructivism in Moral Theory: The Dewey Lectures," 77 *Journal of Philosophy*, p. 527 (1980), indicating that aspects of his theory of justice may depend on a particular "conception of the person" in the original position.

15. J. Rawls, supra note 13, at pp. 225–26.

16. See J. Rawls, supra note 14, at p. 518.

17. See J. Rawls, supra note 13, at p. 250.

18. The point that reasons for adopting a theory of justice might differ from the reasons permitted to actors making practical choices in a society in which the principles of the theory were accepted is made clearly in B. Ackerman, "What Is Neutral About Neutrality?" 93 *Ethics*, p. 387 (1983).

19. J. Rawls, supra note 4, at p. 212.

20. Id. at p. 213.

21. Rawls, supra note 14, at p. 539.

22. Id. See also pp. 540–41.

23. J. Rawls, supra note 4, at pp. 17, 504, 512.

24. See C. Beitz, *Political Theory and International Relations*, pp. 126–83 (Princeton, N.J., Princeton Univ. Pr. 1979).

25. If there are any political decisions about treatment of people within a single society that do not concern justice in any obvious sense, say the design of a state capital or the numbers of lifeguards at a public beach, the same rationale would point to their being made on grounds accessible to all.

26. B. Ackerman, supro note 12.

27. Id. at pp. 10–11. See also A. MacIntyre, *After Virtue*, p. 112 (Notre Dame, Ind., Univ. of Notre Dame Pr. 1981), summarizing Ronald Dworkin's position as being "that the central doctrine of modern liberalism is the thesis that questions about the good life for man or the ends of human life are to be regarded from the public standpoint as systematically unsettlable."

28. B. Ackerman, supra note 12, at p. 103.

29. Id. at p. 127.

30. R. Flathman, "Egalitarian Blood and Skeptical Turnips," 93 *Ethics*, p. 357 (1983).

31. Id.

32. As Ackerman, supra note 23, at p. 302, says, "No liberal government can expect all its citizens to behave like liberal statesmen all of the time."

33. See R.J. Neuhaus, *The Naked Public Square*, pp. 21–22 (Grand Rapids, Mich., William B. Eerdmans Pub. Co. 1984).

34. See K. Greenawalt, Religious Convictions and Lawmaking, 84 *Michigan Law Review*, pp. 352–404 (1985); "Religiously Based Premises and Laws Restrictive of Liberty," 1986 *Brigham Young Law Review*, pp. 245–97 (1986); "The Limits of Rationality and the Place of Religious Convictions: Protecting Animals and the Environment," 27 *William and Mary Law Review*, pp. 1101–65 (1986).

35. When we speak of an argument as rationally compelling we tend to believe that it has a persuasiveness that is transcultural, that reaches all human beings, or at least all human beings of adequate training, intelligence, and openmindedness. If we are informed that some people just do not see the force of the argument at all, we are inclined to ascribe the failure to some personal or cultural inadequacy, not to some equally valid but quite different concept of rationality.

36. The power and boundaries of rational thought are, of course, a deep and unending problem in philosophy and culture. As Hilary Putnam has said, "there is no neutral conception of rationality to which to appeal." *Reason, Truth and History*, p. 136 (Cambridge, Cambridge Univ. Pr. 1981). See also J. Rawls, supra note 14, at p. 529, suggesting there is no one best interpretation of "rationality"; B. Barry and R. Hardin, eds., "Epilogue," *Rational Man and Irrational Society?*," pp. 367, 368 (Beverly Hills, Calif., Sage Pubs. 1982), suggesting that too much weight is now placed on the concept of rationality. For a useful discussion and taxonomy of notions of rationality, see J. Elster, *Sour Grapes: Studies in the Subversion of Rationality*, pp. 1–42 (Cambridge, Cambridge Univ. Pr. 1983). My aim is not to make a fresh contribution to these topics.

37. See H. Putnam, supra note 36, at pp. 82–83, speaking of the steady erosion of confidence in a priori truths since the publication of Quine's "Two Dogmas of Empiricism" in 1951.

38. Even when an investigator's interests lie exclusively in past events, a theory may be of a sort that permits prediction that a conjunction of similar circumstances in the future would produce similar results.

39. See S. Toulmin, *The Place of Reason in Ethics*, p. 95 (Cambridge, Cambridge Univ. Pr. 1950); R. Swinburne, *Faith and Reason*, p. 38 (Oxford, Clarendon Pr. 1981). See generally E. Nagel, *The Structure of Science* (N.Y., Harcourt Brace and World 1971).

40. See H. Putnam, supra note 36, at pp. 189–98. Science may, for example, rest on assumptions about causality and continued regularities that it cannot itself establish, and the choices of what problems to investigate is obviously not determined by science. For the view that ordinary knowledge looms much larger in much social science work than is usually acknowledged, see C.E. Lindblom and D.K. Cohen, *Usable Knowledge*, pp. 13, 17, 37–38 (New Haven, Conn., Yale Univ. Pr. 1979).

41. See J. Rawls, supra note 14, at pp. 537: "Keep in mind that we aim to find a conception of justice for a democratic society under modern conditions; so we may properly assume that in its public culture the methods and conclusions of science play an influential role."

42. See C.E. Lindblom and D.K. Cohen, supra note 40, at p. 15.

43. Richard Swinburne, supra note 39, at p. 20, talks of "basic propositions" that include propositions reporting perceptions and memories and which a person believes "not solely because he believes something else, but because he is inclined to believe that they are forced upon him by his experience of the world."

44. Id. at p. 40.

45. Id. at p. 40. Reliance on authority in this sense includes reliance on what we read in a history book or the daily newspaper or hear from television reporters.

46. I carefully put the question this way so that the lawyer is being asked to make a hypothetical prediction. It is decidedly not my view that an open question about what "the law provides" is always reducible to a question about what courts will, or would, decide.

47. See H. Putnam, supra note 36, at p. 184, denying that a capability of being publicly checked is an aspect of rational belief. See also B. Williams, *Ethics and the Limits of Philosophy*, p. 18 (Cambridge, Mass., Harvard Univ. Pr. 1985), criticizing the drive toward a rationalist conception of rationality that requires that decisions be based on grounds that can be discursively explained.

48. The idea of suspicious movements is itself complex. We might say that genuinely suspicious movements are movements that are associated with attempted criminal behavior in a much higher percentage of instances than are nonsuspicious movements. Suspicious movements need not be associated with attempted crime in every one of their instances or even in more than half of their instances. The claim I am suggesting is that police officers sense a difference between suspicious and ordinary movements that they cannot fully explain. If they have this capacity, then forms of investigation may be warranted when suspicious movements are involved that would not be appropriate or worth undertaking if no such movements had occurred.

49. In a sharp attack on rationalism, Michael Oakeshott emphasizes the impor-

tance of "practical knowledge," knowledge incapable of being formulated in doctrinal terms, in training for all concrete human activities. *Rationalism in Politics*, pp. 8–11 (London, Methuen & Co. 1967).

50. See R. Swinburne, supra note 39, at p. 22. Extensive education designed to increase conscious awareness of relevant factors might produce an ability to explain that was previously lacking, but on many matters such education is unwarranted.

51. Success here would mean a relatively high correlation between movements perceived as suspicion and independently provable criminal efforts. See supra note 48. If, for example, in 80% of the cases in which people were stopped because they were acting suspiciously, illegally concealed weapons were discovered, that would constitute very considerable success.

52. By an explanation here, I mean some account that indicates why people might have the intuition even if it is not accurate.

53. Richard Swinburne, supra note 39, at p. 35, points out that people have different degrees of confidence in their initial propositions.

54. At least they do not exist in anything like the same degree. To some extent, we are prisoners of our own labels and have some difficulty cutting through the general conceptual terms in which we often frame our perceptions to recapture the perceptions as accurately as possible.

55. The connection exists not only with our other factual appraisals but also with our judgments of value.

56. Depending on one's objectives, it is, of course, often prudent to treat people as more or less trustworthy than one thinks they really are. If the consequences of untrustworthiness are slight and monitoring is expensive, it makes sense to "trust" people one doubts; if the consequences of untrustworthiness are catastrophic, one may monitor persons one is quite sure are honest. It is also not uncommon to treat people as more trustworthy than rational prudence would dictate in the hope that the showing of trust will itself have beneficial effects.

57. See generally J. Elster, supra note 36, at p. 18; C. Lindblom, "Some Limitations on Rationality: A Comment," in C.J. Friedrich, ed., *Nomos VII: Rational Decision*, p. 227 (N.Y., Atherton Pr. 1964); D. Braybrooke and C. Lindblom, *A Strategy for Decision: Policy Evaluation as a Social Process* (N.Y., Free Press of Glencoe 1970); C. Lindblom, "The Science of 'Muddling Through'," 19 *Public Administration Review*, pp. 79–88 (1959); C. Lindblom, "Still Muddling, Not Yet Through," 39 *Public Administration Review*, pp. 517–26 (1979).

58. Using the entertaining example of the design of bloomers for ladies to wear riding bicycles in the late nineteenth century, Michael Oakeshott expresses skepticism than any decisions are ever purely ones of means to ends. M. Oakeshott, supra note 49, at pp. 80–110.

59. See B. Williams, supra note 47, at pp. 96–98, discussing how critical similarities and differences are identified absent any statable rule; S. Hampshire, *Two Theories of Morality*, p. 51 (Oxford, Oxford Univ. Pr. 1977), discussing legal interpretation.

60. J. Rawls, supra note 7, at p. 125.

61. See generally K. Ward, *Ethics and Christianity*, at p. 130 (London, George Allen & Unwin 1970).

62. See generally R. Brandt, "The Concept of Rational Action," 9 *Social Theory and Practice*, p. 153 (1983), which in its careful exploration of the requisites of rational action includes an interesting excerpt from Benjamin Franklin describing his strategy for decision making.

63. It has been suggested that a pure time preference is inappropriate. See J. Rawls, supra note 7, at p. 297; T. Nagel, *The Possibility of Altruism*, pp. 58–60 (Princeton, N.J., Princeton Univ. Pr. 1970).

64. See Rawls, supra note 7, at p. 48; S. Hampshire, supra note 59, at pp. 5, 25.

65. See, e.g., A. MacIntyre, *After Virtue*, pp. 11–12, 20 (Notre Dame, Ind., Univ. of Notre Dame Pr. 1981); J.L. Mackie, *Hume's Moral Theory*, p. 45 (London, Routledge & Kegan Paul 1980), explaining Hume's view that reason is the slave of the passions; S. Toulmin, supra note 39, at p. 2; F. Oppenheim, "Rational Decisions and Intrinsic Valuations," in C.J. Friedrich, ed., supra note 57, at p. 217.

66. To pursue one's own interest regardless of the cost to others may be morally wrong by definition. The issue is whether an individual who chooses not to be guided by moral considerations is wrong in some sense that is not dependent on the meaning of morality.

67. One could, of course, think that people generally are constrained by moral duties, but may appropriately pursue their self-interest in the political process, just as, according to capitalist ways of thinking at least, they may appropriately pursue their own self-interest in their choices about work and what products to purchase.

68. I pass over the possibility that a decision that is best overall from the transcendent point of view may actually be worse from the point of most members of the society. A decision to help bring about Armageddon might be thought to conform with God's plan but to be disastrous for the majority of citizens, who lack the requisite beliefs to be saved. I am assuming, as I think is almost always the case for major religious groups in American society, that the policy indicated by religious conviction is thought to be best for all or most members of the society.

69. See C.E. Lindbloom and D.K. Cohen, supra note 40, at p. 46.

70. See H. Veatch, *Aristotle: A Contemporary Appreciation* (Bloomington, Ind., Indiana Univ. Pr. 1974).

71. J. Finnis, *Fundamentals of Ethics*, pp. 20–21 (Wash., D.C., Georgetown Univ. Pr. 1983). This notion of self-evidence places greater emphasis on appraisal by one's intelligence than does a typical view that moral truths are intuitively perceived.

72. See T. Nagel, *The Possibility of Altruism*, pp. 83–88 (Princeton, N.J., Princeton Univ. Pr. 1970); T. Nagel, "The Limits of Objectivity," in S.M. McMurrin, ed., *The Tanner Lectures on Human Values 1980*, Vol. I. pp. 108–12 (Salt Lake City, Univ. of Utah Pr. 1980). See also T. Nagel, *The View from Nowhere*, pp. 138–207 (N.Y., Oxford Univ. Pr. 1986).

73. R.M. Hare, Freedom and Reason (Oxford, Oxford Univ. Pr. 1963).

74. See G. Wills, *Inventing America*, pp. 181–213 (Garden City, N.Y., Double-

day & Co. 1978). The basic idea is captured by Thomas Jefferson's opinion that if you state "a moral case to a plowman and a professor," the plowman "will decide it as well and often better than the [professor] because he has not been led astray by artificial rules." Quoted in H.F. May, *The Enlightenment in America*, p. 296 (N.Y., Oxford Univ. Pr. 1976).

75. Some value judgments, however one may derive then, may simply be associated with rational persons. As Isaiah Berlin has suggested, if someone derives pleasure from sticking pins in people and displays complete indifference to the pain his actions cause, we conclude that the person is irrational. I. Berlin, "Rationality of Value Judgments," in C.J. Friedrich, eds., supra note 57, at p. 221.

76. See, e.g., J. Rawls, supra note 7, at p. 88; A. MacIntyre, supra note 65, at pp. 8, 20 (1981); H. Putnam, supra note 36, at p. 148 (1981); T. Nagel, "The Limits of Objectivity," supra note 72, at pp. 135–36 (1979); G.S. Warnock, *The Object of Morality* 29, pp. 144–66 (London, Methuen & Co. 1971).

77. R. Dworkin, *Taking Rights Seriously* (Cambridge, Mass., Harvard Univ. Pr. 1978). In Dworkin's subsequent work, the independent judgments of the interpreter of legal materials have loomed larger and larger. See especially R. Dworkin, *Law's Empire* (Cambridge, Mass., Harvard Univ. Pr. 1986).

78. This comment is subject, of course, to whatever preclusion may exist upon promoting values of a particular sort because the values conflict with liberal democratic premises or because, given those premises, the values are not subject to promotion within the political process.

79. That is not to say that an individual will necessarily suppose that what is a good life for himself is a good life for others or that he will communicate every opinion he has about what is probably a good life for others.

80. It might be possible to have a complete other-regarding morality that left open some questions about the good for individuals.

81. This theme is developed throughout *A Theory of Justice* and is further explained in later writings, including "Justice as Fairness: Political not Metaphysical," supra note 13, at pp. 229, 248.

82. B. Ackerman, supra note 26, at p. 368.

83. Ronald Dworkin discerns this as the fundamental concept of Rawls's deep theory. "The Original Position," in N. Daniels, ed., supra note 12, at pp. 16, 50–51.

84. One might or might not think that all other premises of liberal democracy can themselves be drawn out of the notion of equal respect and concern or some variation of that. I am skeptical that they can.

85. N. Smart, *The Philosophy of Religion*, pp. 114–23 (N.Y., Oxford Univ. Pr. 1979).

86. This inquiry is not circular if we assume some basic moral premises against which to judge leaders' lives.

87. For the existence of God and other matters of religious truth, as with matters of nonreligious truth, one may believe with less than certainty. Though disagreeing with the idea he takes as implicit in Pascal's famous "bet" about God

that one can actually believe what one thinks is improbable, Richard Swinburne argues persuasively that it may be rational to live as if some fact is true even if one thinks it probably is not true. R. Swinburne, supra note 39, at pp. 161–63. If, for example, one strongly believes that eternal life, if it exists, will only be available to those who seek on earth to do the will of God, if God exists, it would be rational to try to perform what one thinks may be God's will, even if one believes that it is more probable than not that neither eternal life nor God actually exists. Despite the clear rationality of such a choice, I think the division of believed probability from life commitments is one few religious persons make for extended periods and that that division is very hard for anyone to maintain psychologically over time. I shall omit in this book discussion of intriguing questions about what is a fair political posture for one whose personal choices are governed by premises he thinks are probably not true.

There is a related complexity about probability I also do not address. One may think something more probable than any relevant alternative but less probable than not. When one says of a complex historical reconstruction, "This is probably how it happened," one means only that this is the most probable reconstruction, not that its accuracy in all details together is more probable than not. For some practical decisions, one must act on this lower kind of probability. If among ten job candidates, it appears 35% likely that J will perform best and the probability for each other candidate is lower, J will ordinarily be hired. If, however, J is quite different from the other nine who have similar strengths and weaknesses, it may be that some of them would be more promising than J in an individual pair-off. In that event, one of the other nine would be hired. I shall not try to work through how similar complexities about the probabilities of premises behind moral positions should affect political choice.

88. Id. at pp. 177–79; N. Smart, supra note 85, at p. 113.

89. R. Swinburne, supra note 39, at p. 183. The importance of miracles and prophecies in establishing revelation for eighteenth-century believers in natural religion is briefly described in H.F. May, supra note 74, at p. 12.

90. I here pass over the arguments for why we morally should do what God wants us to do, once it is granted that God's wishes are perceived. See S.L. Ross, "Another Look at God and Morality," 94 *Ethics*, pp. 87–98 (1983). Even if one supposed, as I do not, that God's wanting us to perform certain actions would not bear on their morality, we might well have prudential reasons to perform them.

91. See R. Swinburne, supra note 39, at pp. 27–28, 199.

92. See, e.g., S. Toulmin, supra note 39, at p. 217.

93. One can fantasize about a self-proclaimed religious prophet in a rigorously atheist society who predicts her execution on a certain Monday and her bodily resurrection two days later. The regime executes her on the predicted day and loyal atheist troops put her ashes in a tomb which they constantly watch. To show the foolishness of religious beliefs, the regime has live television cameras, open to viewing by citizens, trained on the tomb on Wednesday, the predicted day of resurrection. All those connected with the television transmission have, like the

patrolling troops, been carefully screened for political loyalty and atheism. At noon on Wednesday, the cameras show the prophet emerging through the stone wall of the tomb. Her bodily features are clearly recognizable and she speaks in her distinctive and familiar voice. Virtually everyone who was then watching the TV channel, most of whom were previously atheists, as well as those on the scene, agree in their account of what has occurred. No doubt, even these events would not create belief in everyone, some sort of mass hallucination or secret conspiracy is always a possibility, but it is hard to say that what has occurred would not be *some evidence* for the existence of a supernatural force and for the authenticity of this prophet.

94. In contrast with the simpler idea that intuitive religious conviction, given by God's grace, precedes commitment and rational understanding, the "leap of faith" idea, arrestingly presented by Sören Kierkegaard, supposes an initial commitment to live by faith, with the making of the commitment or the living by it bringing conviction. As Ninian Smart has suggested, supra note 85, at p. 125, it may not be possible even to understand a religion unless one enters into its life with sympathetic imagination. See also id. at 139.

95. I am not assuming here any event that appears miraculous by itself but a degree of accuracy about predicting particular events that seems inexplicable on any natural bases.

96. In theory at least, a social conditioning explanation could be tested by conditioning children not to believe in God. If they, nonetheless, developed belief in God, the social conditioning hypothesis would be undercut. In reality, the widespread difference in religious beliefs among different cultures is rather convincing evidence that social conditioning is of great importance in the incidence of particular religious beliefs.

The significance of some deep-seated psychological need to believe is more complex. The presence of such a need, though not positive evidence of falsity, could indicate why people would believe, even if belief were false. The religious believer may respond, however, that if such a need is virtually universal, it tends to suggest something in external reality capable of satisfying the need.

97. See, e.g., K. Ward, supra note 61, at p. 202.

98. As Richard Swinburne, supra note 39, at p. 23, one may believe in God while admitting that the public evidence is against that belief.

99. I assume, as I indicate in somewhat more detail in Chapter 12, that the principles of America's "civil religion" are not specific enough to yield significant ethical conclusions.

II

POLITICAL CHOICES
AND
RELIGIOUS CONVICTIONS

5

Inappropriate Grounds of Restriction:
Consenting Sexual Acts as Sins

Because the point of this chapter differs from the message of the following ones and represents a sort of diversion from the primary themes of the book, I need to explain how this chapter fits with the rest. The next five chapters deal with various political issues. I briefly examine possible grounds for their resolutions and conclude that many citizens will have to reach beyond shared premises and publicly accessible reasons to determine their positions. I contend that it would be mistaken to regard religious grounds of decision as less appropriate than other grounds that are not rooted in shared premises and publicly accessible reasons. I do suggest in Chapter 11 that perhaps liberal citizens are committed to follow publicly accessible reasons when they yield clear answers to problems, but the main drift of the following chapters is that religious convictions cannot fairly be excluded as bases for decision in the manner that the liberal theorists I have mentioned suppose or imply.

In this chapter I focus on a different sort of relationship, that between the moral conviction that is derived from a religious belief and the particular reasons given for restraining someone's liberty. I argue that some *reasons* for restraint are barred by liberal premises. This argument indicates what I mean when I say that in a liberal society legislation must rest on a proper secular objective.

In Chapter 1, I indicated my support for one major assumption that all the theorists who argue against reliance on religious convictions make about a citizen's responsibility: namely, that not only some outcomes but some grounds for outcomes are foreclosed by premises of liberal democracy. That assumption involves rejection of what we might call the interest accommodation view that liberal democracy is just a set of procedures for people to satisfy whatever wishes they have, with some limits on what the majority can do. For any restriction on liberty as serious as a prohibition on consenting sexual acts, the grounds on which people may properly rely poses a serious question for liberal democratic theory.

The extent to which sexual expression reflects people's deepest feelings and affects the quality of their lives makes the legitimacy of prohibitions of sexual acts highly important, but my central purpose here is neither to argue that the domain of sexual choice should be especially protected in a liberal society nor to substantiate overall conclusions about appropriate regulation. I am focusing on a particular sort of argument that I claim is not by itself an appropriate basis for restriction, whether of sexual acts or any other activity. I do set that problem in the context of other relevant arguments, but my comments about those should not divert the reader from what the chapter is mainly about.

Consenting Sexual Acts and Reasons Consonant with Liberal Democratic Premises

Three simple arguments exist against criminalizing acts that directly affect and substantially affect only those adults who freely choose to engage in them, a class of acts into which many consenting sexual acts fall. The first argument is that such matters of individual choice are none of the state's business. The basic idea, going back at least as far as Locke,[1] is that government should protect the rights of individuals against infringements by others. Since consenting acts by two people that do not directly or significantly affect others do not infringe the rights of others, and since people do not need the protection of government against their own inclinations to perform such acts, no occasion for criminal penalties arises.

The second argument against restrictions, found most familiarly in John Stuart Mill's *On Liberty*[2] is ostensibly utilitarian. It urges that people should have the power to live their own lives as they wish, so long as they do not harm others. A denial of this power by a regime of penalties that inhibits desires will inevitably cause suffering and frustration and will stunt capacities for human development that could have benefited the individuals involved and contributed indirectly to broader enlightenment about fulfilling forms of life.

The third argument against prohibition pays attention to actual and likely patterns of enforcement. This argument claims that the unavoidable ineffectiveness of efforts to enforce and the injustice of having occasional rare convictions fall on a few unfortunate persons are strong reasons to eschew criminal measures.

What arguments in terms of secular objectives can be mounted to the contrary? There is first a paternalistic claim that prohibition *is* necessary to help protect people resist their own temptations to engage in acts that are psychologically self-destructive or likely to cause harm to them in their social relations. This claim has some plausibility for adultery, but it rings hollow in respect to most people who want to engage in homosexual acts. They apparently are firmly committed in their sexual preferences and suffer serious frustration if they refrain from homosexual encounters. Whether in some sense, heterosexual acts are healthier or more natural than homosexual ones seems largely beside the point for people whose powerful inclinations are homosexual. Even if one supposes that "homosexual actions are biologically deficient,"[3] they may be psychologically healthy for the irreversible homosexual[4] and, at least in "the context of a loving relationship striving for permanency," morally good.[5]

A second ground for prohibition is protection of family life. Understood as a concern about deleterious effects on family relations, the argument applies most strongly to incestuous relations between close relatives. Sexual involvements among parents and children or brothers and sisters may gravely impair family relations even when the persons involved are adults. The prospect of such relations in the future could adversely affect interactions before children reach maturity. The argument about protecting family life hardly is relevant for homosexual acts committed by persons who are not married, except insofar as any sexual relations outside of marriage compromise an ideal that all sex occur within marriages.[6] The argument has some application to acts of heterosexual intercourse that may lead to conception and birth of children outside of ordinary family situations.[7] The argument reaches with greater force to extramarital sexual acts. The main worry about these is not that they may reduce the number of children born into families, but that they undermine marriages and that failing marriages are bad for children. Extramarital acts can also be seen as impairing family life in a way that does not depend on harmful consequences. They may be viewed as infringing the rights of spouses, at least when married couples have no understanding that permits them. The idea of forbidding adultery to protect spousal rights and stable family environments for children founders, however, on the frequency with which adultery is committed and the impossibility of effective enforcement.

Another ground for penalizing consenting sexual acts rests on protection of children from sexual advances by adults, but bars on sex between adults do not bear much plausible relation to the avoidance of sexual impositions on children.

A fourth argument, now applicable most strongly in the United States to male homosexual acts, concerns physical dangers of unrestrained sexual relations. In addition to the traditional worries about venereal disease, there is now the grave danger of Aquired Immune Deficiency Syndrome (AIDS), a killing disease so far, in the United States, passed mainly during homosexual intercourse.

Finally, a claim may be made that the general moral tone of the community will deteriorate if acts most people regard as morally obnoxious are not treated as illegal. In its most plausible version, this claim rests on a connection between sexual morality and parts of morality that are undoubtedly the state's business. The assumption is that people will be so dismayed or alienated by the state's failure to enforce powerful sexual mores, they will be less inclined to respect the liberty and property of their fellows and to contribute to the common purposes of all society.[8] Since the posited connection is virtually impossible to prove or disprove,[9] estimating the strength of this argument in any particular society is very difficult. The consonancy of such an argument with liberal premises is itself a somewhat troubling question, which I briefly address below.

With the exception of the criminal prohibition of incest, which I believe supportable on rational secular grounds,[10] and putting aside the threat of AIDS, which one hopes will pass, my own judgment is that when one considers the arguments that rest on commonly accessible reasons, the arguments against prohibiting private sexual acts among adults are far stronger than the arguments in favor of prohibition. This judgment is made despite my acceptance of a conservative premise that existing practices and laws may often have a degree of social value that is not immediately apparent.[11]

As I have indicated, for our purposes what matters is not the correctness of my judgment about the balance of arguments but its implications. I want to assume that Sam is persuaded that this judgment of the balance of commonly accessible reasons is right but *also* believes that homosexual acts are sins that God wants stopped. He supposes that public coercion and the law's symbolic condemnation are proper devices to curtail these acts.

The aim to forbid homosexual acts *on this ground* is at odds with the basic premises of liberal democracy. A liberal society, as Chapter 2 indicates, has no business dictating matters of religious belief and worship to its citizens. It cannot forbid or require forms of belief, it cannot preclude acts of worship that cause no secular harm, it cannot restrict expression about what constitutes religious truth. One needs only a modest extension of these uncontroversial principles to conclude that a liberal society should not rely on religious grounds to prohibit activities that either cause no secular harm or do not cause enough secular harm to warrant their prohibition. As John Plamenatz said about Locke's argument for toleration of belief, "logically, it follows from this that no man ought to be punished for any action which is merely immoral and not injurious."[12] Freedom of worship and expression may enjoy a special place in a liberal democracy but, as liberals have recognized at least since Mill's *On Liberty*,[13] freedom to choose one's pattern of life is also very important. Though the claim for liberty to determine one's sexual activities might itself be strongest if it rested on some religious or conscientious ground, the curbing of these activities simply because they conflict with the religiously based convictions of others is unwarranted in any event. The inappropriateness of the state's pursuing religious objectives or promoting particular religious views implies the inappropriateness of its relying on particular religious views to foreclose actions whose impact would not warrant restraint on secular bases.

Though I suppose that the balance of secular arguments is substantially against prohibition, that supposition is not critical. My view is that the possible sinfulness of sexual activities is not *by itself* a legitimate consideration. Even if a person believes that the secular arguments tip only weakly against prohibition, he should either refrain from seeking the prohibition or should acknowledge that his aim to prohibit is at odds with the model of liberal democracy presented in Chapter 2.

A religious advocate of prohibition might try to meet the thrust of my argument with a more expansive version of the paternalist argument or by an extended claim about the freedom and welfare of himself, his family, and others.

The paternalist concern about the welfare of the actors might be extended to reach their spiritual welfare, what will happen to their souls or personalities after death and what their relationship to God will be in this life. That such an argument trespasses the boundaries of what is left to individuals in a liberal democracy is evident enough not to require lengthy explication: the fate of someone's soul or personality after death and the healthiness of his relationship to God in this life are not matters for the state, given the separation of religion and government and other liberal democratic premises.

A more complex reliance on religious grounds to justify paternalist prohibition is possible. Sam might claim that those who commit immoral sexual acts will be less happy and will suffer psychological maladjustments, understood in ordinary secular terms, that could be avoided by a successful prohibition.[14] So put, the argument seems a straightforward paternalistic one, subject to ordinary factual evidence. But suppose when challenged as to the factual basis of his claims, Sam responds:

> I realize the ordinary factual evidence is now inconclusive about whether prohibition will more greatly relieve or cause unhappiness and maladjustment; but I am confident that no one living in a continual state of sin can be happy or well adjusted, so I am sure that the prohibition will improve matters.

In this form, an ordinary paternalistic argument is based on factual claims that are grounded in religious convictions about the nature of sin and its consequences. In Chapters 9 and 11, I tackle the problem of religiously informed factual judgments; it is enough here to say that this version of the paternalistic argument is not subject to the simple objection concerning wholly inappropriate grounds for state interference with individual lives.

Sam might make another response: that his own freedom is involved, that the toleration of sinful sexual activities impinges on the lives of himself and his family. Is he not justified in trying to prevent offense to his own religious sensibilities and to foreclose the presence of what he regards as examples dangerous to the religious life of those dear to him? No doubt, toleration of sinful acts may be so viewed by some people, but so also may toleration of sinful beliefs and expressions. Of course, if liberty is understood to include the freedom to do anything one wants, the frustration of Sam's wish not to have homosexual acts committed is a restraint on his liberty; but this is an oddly expansive notion of liberty. In a liberal society the knowledge that others are performing acts that one regards as sinful cannot count as a violation of the liberty of oneself and one's family. Nor can any indirect danger to the religious life of loved ones created by the known existence of sinful acts constitute a basis for prohibition.

What of the unhappiness that the knowledge of sin causes? Can the prevention of such unhappiness be a permissible secular ground for prohibition? So long as the religious basis for the unhappiness is treated as essentially irrelevant, the prevention of unhappiness is a secular reason, but that does not necessarily mean it will count very heavily; perhaps it should not count at all. The aim to prevent unhappiness over the performance of sexual acts by others will typically be a reason of much less power than the religiously based concern to which it is related. Someone's damnation is a terrible consequence; Sam's actual unhappiness over the acts that cause another's damnation is likely to be less momentous, since Sam has his own life to live. Further, liberal democracy may well be understood to make illegitimate, or highly suspect, any argument for prohibition that rests simply on the unhappiness that some people feel about knowing that others are committing certain kinds of acts.[15] Permitting prohibition on this basis could undermine principles of respect for individual liberty and minority rights;[16] thus, reliance on unhappiness over knowledge that acts are taking place may be viewed as improper whatever the reason for the unhappiness.[17]

A somewhat related basis for prohibition is the notion that social cohesion will suffer if people's strong moral feelings are not supported by criminal sanctions. Analysis of this possibility is slightly more complex. Perhaps if all members of society fully accepted the implications of liberal democratic premises, adequate cohesion would not depend on suppressing acts that do not cause harm. But if adequate cohesion is necessary to sustain a healthy respect for the rights and interests of fellow citizens, and if so many persons will feel alienated in a society that does not prohibit acts they regard as seriously wrong that adequate cohesion is threatened, the model liberal citizen must choose between defending liberty and preserving adequate cohesion. Were careful appraisal of the facts to indicate that such a choice was necessary, something I strongly doubt, then a choice in favor of adequate cohesion, which every society needs, would not be ruled out by the premises of liberal democracy. However, it should be recognized that a compromise of principle would be involved, that liberal citizens would be finding it necessary to respond to illiberal feelings of many of their fellows.

Yet another conceivable justification for prohibiting acts simply regarded as wrong is that those acts are unnatural and represent some kind of a harm to the natural order. If the idea of harm is stretched so far, one is left with no principled limit on reasons for prohibitions. I reject that extension, but I consider at the end of the next chapter the consistency of this conclusion with what I say about preservation of the natural environment.

The observations about the liberty and happiness of those who wish wrongful acts to be curtailed highlight a profound theoretical difference between nonprohibition and more positive aspects of a program seeking nondiscrimination against those who perform "deviant" sexual acts. If a private employer is told that in hiring he may not discriminate against someone he believes is engaging in sinful practices, his religious liberty is implicated, at least if the employer will have continuing personal contact with the employee.[18] Religious liberty is also implicated if religious institutions are told they cannot discriminate on grounds they regard as religiously appropriate. Since protection of religious freedom and autonomy *and* the promotion of equal opportunity against socially unwarranted discriminations are both legitimate governmental objectives in a liberal society, the model of liberal democracy yields no easy resolution to *this* legislative dilemma.

Nondiscrimination on grounds of sexual activities or sexual preferences in employment of public school teachers is also troublesome, even if the basic objection to particular sexual activities is religious. Parents who must send their children to school may have a legitimate interest in not having their children taught in the only free schools by role models that they regard as abhorrent. Though I favor a rule of nondiscrimination in public employment, including school teaching, that position follows much less easily from the premises of liberal democracy than the principle that religious notions of wrong are not an appropriate basis for prohibition.

The continued and fairly widespread existence in the United States of laws prohibiting consenting homosexual acts does not disprove a thesis that such laws may be at odds with the proper conception of liberal democracy.[19] Societies, like individuals, often are not wholly faithful to their own premises and ideals; inertia leaves intact many laws that would not be freshly adopted; and other currents run against the implications of liberal premises. All these are reasons why one may find illiberal legal constraints in liberal democratic societies. Further, there are genuine secular arguments for prohibitions and some people are honestly convinced that these outweigh the secular arguments against prohibition. *Their* support of criminal laws is not at odds with the liberal premise that religious views and their moral consequences should not be forced on people.

If my analysis in this chapter is sound, we can identify one kind of religious reason that should not count for good liberal citizens in a liberal democracy. The aim to prevent a wrong judged purely from a religious perspective is not a proper ground to legislate a prohibition. Though I have illustrated my thesis with consenting sexual acts, the important conclusion is not about whether prohibitions of those acts can be justified. For all I have said, other reasons, including some reasons tied to religious premises, may properly support such prohibitions. My point is about a certain kind of religious reason that is not consonant with liberal democracy. *If that kind of reason is not properly relied on with respect to consenting sexual acts, it is not properly relied upon with respect to any other social issues either.*

Conceptually, the claimed bar on this sort of reason is not one that relates peculiarly to religious reasons. The analysis can be generalized to conclude that a simple belief that acts are morally wrong, whether religiously based or not, is never an appropriate ground of prohibition. To support prohibition in a liberal society, one must be able to point to some genuine damage to individuals or society (or other entities). So understood, the bar on this basis for legislation extends to some possible nonreligious as well as religious views of wrong.

However, because a nonreligious moral view is much less likely than a religious one to have notions of wrong that can be detached from notions of ordinary harm, the bar I have discussed does mainly concern religious reasons for prohibition. Further, given the special concern over imposition of religious positions, historically grounded and reflected in the religion clauses of the constitution, the bar is of particular practical importance as it applies to religious notions of wrong.

Notes

1. J. Locke, *A Letter Concerning Toleration*, (1689), J. Tully, ed. (Indianapolis, Hackett Pub. 1983); J. Locke, "Second Treatise of Civil Government," in P. Laslett, ed., *Two Treatises of Government*, P. Laslett, ed. (Cambridge, Cambridge Univ. Pr. 1960).

2. J.S. Mill, *On Liberty* (1859), E. Rapaport, ed. (Indianapolis, Hackett Pub. 1978).

3. See M. Novak, *Confession of a Catholic*, p. 168 (San Francisco, Harper & Row 1983), quoting an article by Edward Vacek, S. J.

4. Id.

5. C.E. Curran, *Transition and Tradition in Moral Theology*, p. 71 (Notre Dame, Ind., Univ. of Notre Dame Pr. 1979).

6. See generally B. Mitchell, *Law, Morality, and Religion in a Secular Society*, pp. 25–30 (London, Oxford Univ. Pr. 1967).

7. If pregnancies outside marriage more often lead to abortions, the wish to curb abortions could be a subsidary reason for curbing sexual relations that lead to a particularly high incidence of them.

8. In my view, this is the interpretation of Lord Patrick Devlin's argument in *The Enforcement of Morals* (Oxford, Oxford Univ. Pr. 1965) that gives it the most persuasive power. See also B. Mitchell, supra note 6, at p. 22.

9. H.L.A. Hart is thoroughly skeptical about it in *Law, Liberty and Morality*, pp. 50–51 (Stanford, Calif., Stanford Univ. Pr. 1963).

10. Both the universal taboo against incest and the intuitive sense that family life is disturbed if one's parents, children, and siblings are regarded as potential objects of sexual attachment are sufficient to sustain the prohibition in respect to close relatives unless clear evidence is forthcoming of the harmlessness of incest or the futility of criminalization. Not only are the arguments for prohibition of incest especially powerful, the impairment of liberty is highly circumscribed. Whether in a modern society the prohibition should reach cousins may be debatable.

11. The hesitancy to abandon established practices and laws is most eloquently defended in Edmund Burke's writings. See especially E. Burke, *Reflections on the French Revolution*, T. Mahoney, ed. (N.Y., Bobbs-Merrill Co. 1955). As H.L.A. Hart has put it, "There is a presumption that common and long established institutions

are likely to have merits not apparent to the rationalist philosopher." See Hart, supra note 9, at p. 29. A simple preference for what exists is not in itself a rational argument, but belief that changes are disruptive and that people are often unaware of all the ways in which institutions serve shared social ends may well be rationally based. See M. Oakeshott, *Rationalism in Politics*, pp. 1–36, 59–79 (London, Methuen & Co. 1977).

12. J. Plamenatz, Man and Society, vol. I, p. 84 (London, Longmans, Green & Co. 1963).

13. J.S. Mill, supra note 2; see also D.A.J. Richards, "Conscience, Human Rights, and the Anarchist Challenge to the Obligation to Obey the Law," 18 *Georgia Law Review*, pp. 771, 778 (1984).

14. Lying somewhere between spiritual paternalism and psychological paternalism is moral paternalism, the aim to protect people from having "corrupted or degraded" characters. See B. Mitchell, supra note 6, at p. 71. If the reason for preventing corrupted character is that such character makes life unsatisfying or inflicts pain on others, the argument for prevention is one of secular paternalism or protection of others. If the reason for prevention is that God does not want corrupted character, the argument is a form of spiritual paternalism. If the reason is that corrupted character is a bad thing per se, I am inclined to think, for reasons indicated in the last three paragraphs of the chapter, that the argument for prevention is close enough to spiritual paternalism to be subject to the same basic objection.

15. Joel Feinberg, suggesting that in a liberal society criminal punishment is warranted only if someone harms or offends another, *Harm to Others*, pp. 14–15 (N.Y., Oxford Univ. Pr. 1984), argues that causing an unpleasant state of mind in another by one's own private sexual behavior is not a wrongful offense because it is not a wrong to the offended party (J. Feinberg, *Offense to Others*, p. 68 [N.Y., Oxford Univ. Pr. 1985]). See also R. Dworkin, *Taking Rights Seriously*, pp. 233–37, (Cambridge, Mass., Harvard Univ. Pr. 1978), arguing that "external preferences" about the behavior of other people should not count for legislative decisions.

16. See H.L.A. Hart, supra note 9, at pp. 46–47, who makes this point in a passage that is eloquent but may be interpreted to support the mistaken proposition that perfect application of a thoroughly utilitarian approach, one that counted all the unhappiness caused by sins, would obviously produce a high degree of suppression. The degree of suppression would depend not only on the numbers of people on each side but the intensity of their feelings, and perfect application of the utilitarian standard might actually yield considerable freedom for deviant minorities. The passage is discussed in J. Feinberg, supra note 15, at pp. 63–64.

17. A good deal remains to be said as to exactly which grounds are improper. If the acts of others create real insecurity about how one might be treated, as consensual euthanasia might engender fear that others will fabricate one's own consent when one is old, such insecurity would be a proper ground for prohibition.

18. More precisely, the matter may be one of degree. The religious liberty of an owner of a large firm may be slightly affected if the firm must hire persons who

offend the owner's religious sensibilities, but the owner's religious claim is much graver if he is in continuing association with his employees.

19. As I indicated in Chapter 2, one might draw from our tradition a somewhat different model of liberal democracy, one that permits limited support of some broad religious positions, though not a preference for any particular denomination. I believe that prohibition of homosexual acts is in tension even with that alternative model, though the tension is less evident than with the model I have supposed is best.

6

Borderlines of Status I:
Animal Rights and Environmental Policy

This chapter commences analysis of the ways in which people formulate judgments about what secular objectives to pursue and how to resolve conflicts among those objectives. In this and the next five chapters, I discuss three different sorts of judgments: judgments about status, judgments about facts, and judgments involving clashes of value. Chapters 9 and 10 deal mainly with the latter two inquiries, Chapter 9 exploring three broad social issues (welfare assistance, military policy and punishment, and one narrower question of legal choice), and Chapter 10 focusing on three typical church-state issues. In Chapter 11, I tackle the different topic of judgments and reasons that are in opposition to what reasons accessible to all strongly indicate. Chapters 6, 7, and 8 deal with borderlines of status. I devote so much space to these borderlines because they present the starkest political questions about reliance on religious grounds and because they expose most clearly the difficulties of a thesis that citizens should rely exclusively on shared nonreligious premises and forms of reasoning accessible to all.

Some basic disagreements about policy reduce to how much protection, if any, particular entities are thought to warrant. One's initial determination of how much living human beings owe to fetuses, nonhuman animals, plants, and ecosystems can have a crucial bearing on whether one favors legislation protecting individual beings of various kinds or the natural environment in some larger sense. Chapter 7 addresses the highly sensitive topic of abortion. This chapter treats "animal rights" and environmental policy. So far, these subjects are much less controversial than abortion because only a small minority presently favors a radical shift in existing legal approaches and because no policy now being seriously considered will impinge on human liberty to nearly the same extent as would restrictive abortion laws. Nonetheless, for my purposes, many of the critical questions are similar, and discussing these questions first in connection with nonhuman interests may allow a degree of detachment when we reach the emotionally freighted subject of abortion. Chapter 8 draws together the common themes of the two chapters and pursues some of the abstract questions they jointly raise.

It is important to stress initially what Chapter 9 makes clear, that the conclusions I draw about religious convictions and borderline questions of status are by no means restricted to such questions. The conclusions have much wider scope, covering many different kinds of political and moral issues. I start with the examples I do because of their present importance and because of the clarity with which the limits of publicly accessible reasons are shown, *not* because borderline questions of status are subject to unique consideration.

Human Morality and Moral Consideration for Nonhuman Entities

What do human beings owe to other animals and to the rest of the natural environment? This question can be subdivided into what we owe to other individual entities in their individual capacities and what we should do about preserving nature in some broader sense. The drowning of cats terminates the lives of particular sentient creatures but does not threaten the environment; constructing a ski resort above timberline alters a natural setting but may only incidentally affect nonhuman creatures.

Someone who is concerned about the interests of individual animals may be relatively indifferent to whether particular species or features of the physical world survive over time, and someone who cares deeply about preservation of species and natural settings may be indifferent to the survival of individual members of plentiful species. Indeed, for some ethical choices, such as the propriety of sport hunting,[1] an environmental ethic may point in an entirely different direction from an animal rights ethic. Nonetheless, both sorts of ethics and the subjects they address take us beyond a morality that concentrates exclusively on relations *among* human beings. In doing so, the two sorts of ethics share common themes and raise common questions.

An ethic that claims a morally protected status for entities other than human beings must face a possible threshold difficulty, one that is immediately terminological but that has underlying substantive implications. Morality is often viewed as a means by which human beings achieve a tolerable social existence together. The subjects of moral duties must undoubtedly have moral capabilities, and among creatures on this earth, those capabilities *may* exclude all but human beings.[2] If rights and justice are understood as involving reciprocal moral relations among members of the same social community, then, barring the possibility of significant enough interaction between animals with moral capacity and human beings, only human beings, perhaps only human beings with enough mental capacity to be moral agents, may qualify as bearers of rights who are owed justice. Both Rawls and Ackerman, for example, assume that justice concerns relations among people.[3]

That a morality may include duties owed to creatures without moral capacity is perfectly clear.[4] Most people think they have moral duties towards members of the human species who lack moral capacity, and they also think they have duties towards at least higher animals not to subject them to gratuitous cruelty. Among systematic moral views utilitarianism has traditionally counted the pains and pleasures of all sentient creatures. Rawls explicitly recognizes that "how we are to conduct ourselves toward animals and the rest of nature" are moral questions "of the first importance," which his contract theory does not cover.[5] Ackerman goes beyond Rawls in saying something about how these problems might be resolved, but what he says is notably inconclusive: that people may divide over whether animals and the rest of nature are simply to be regarded as means to human goods or should be preserved, and that the liberal state must recognize the tentativeness of any policy established toward nature.[6]

If moral duties can be owed to nonhuman creatures, as they undoubtedly can be, the purely terminological question whether such creatures are potential subjects of rights or justice is not particularly important.[7] What is important is whether duties of the type and stringency associated with rights and justice are owed to nonhuman entities. Were a moral bar to exist against killing innocent animals that was as absolute as the bar against killing innocent human beings, we could speak of the duty as having the stringency of the duty associated with the right to life. No doubt some kinds of duties, such as truth telling, do not apply to relations with nonhuman animals, and other duties, such as the duty of fair play, may depend on reciprocal interactions;[8] but duties not to cause harm and duties of benevolence are potentially applicable to animals and cannot be foreclosed by some conceptual bar. For this reason, I shall not attempt to restrict the terms "rights" and "justice" to relations among creatures with moral capacity, rather assuming that entities incapabable of being moral subjects may have rights and claims of justice, even though others must make the claims of their behalf.[9]

The second common subject of animal rights and environmental protection concerns the place of human beings in the world. The relative predominance of human beings is critical for what they owe to other entities. At one extreme we can put the view that nature, including animals, is for human dominion. At the other extreme is the idea that nature is sacred, an aspect of God or the gods. An intermediate conception is one of stewardship, that human beings have a responsibility for preserving the welfare and integrity of the natural world.

A third common problem concerns the standard for judging a proper moral conception: is the question of whether something is owed to nonhuman entities to be viewed in terms of the intrinsic worth of those entities or in terms of the manner of thinking that will be best for human beings in the long run?[10] I need to explain this distinction briefly. If the proper moral standard for protecting animals and natural objects were explicitly the welfare of present and future human generations, then the standard would still concern morality among human beings, including intergenerational duties. Duties to other human beings might include not harming some animals, just as these duties might include not harming some automobiles, but no duties would be owed to the animals themselves. If, instead, duties were owed to animals and other natural objects because of their inherent worth, then a proper moral conception would transcend the interests, even broadly conceived, of human beings. What of the following kind of intermediate possibility?

> It is critically important for human beings to respect animals and nature itself. If they are insensitive and cruel to animals, they will become hardened in their relations to other people.[11] If they do not respect nature, they will recklessly squander the earth in a way that will deprive future human beings whose interests they are not now competent to assess. A respectful attitude toward nature teaches people to accept the severe restrictions on human endeavors and helps lower their level of frustration. An attitude that animals and nature are not to be dominated contributes to less domineering and aggressive attitudes among people and thus enhances our social existence.

The attitude being favored is one in which ordinary people would attach intrinsic value to animals and nature; but the ultimate philosophic justification for the attitude is that it will be good for people.[12] A supporter of a practical ethic favoring protection of animals or nature might, of course, claim both that it is required by the inherent worth of nonhuman entities and that it is best for humans in the long run.

For the rest of this chapter, I shall assume that the crucial questions are whether entities other than human beings intrinsically deserve protection and, if so, how much. Given fundamental uncertainty about the import of attitudes toward animals and nature on the behavior of human beings toward each other, much of my basic points would remain if the questions were reformulated in terms of the attitudes that are ultimately best for human beings, but I shall not pursue the extra step of complexity at each stage.

Once one outlines the major alternatives about the place of humanity in the universe, alternatives whose relevance to animal rights and environmental protection are immediately evident, the potential relevance of religious convictions is also apparent. A major theme of religions is to interpret the place of human beings in nature. Indeed, in some attacks on present environmental attitudes, the Judeo-Christian view that nature was created for man's domination has been portrayed as the major villain.[13] In response it has been argued that the major strands of Judaism and Christianity place stewardship responsibilities upon human beings, and that the modern secular notion of progress is rather the main threat to protection of nature.[14] One author has suggested that the break between human beings and nature is much sharper in Judaism than in Christianity, which, in his view, resanctifies nature with its doctrine of the Incarnation.[15] Without question, some eastern religions accord greater respect to nature and animals, and conceive a much less sharp break between human beings and the rest of nature, than do the major western religions.[16]

The central question for us is whether citizens should eschew religious perspectives in resolving what protection to accord animals and nature. The plausibility of the position that they should disregard those perspectives depends considerably on the promise of commonly accessible reasoning to resolve matters.

Animal Rights

I first turn to the moral consideration owed to individual entities as such, loosely the subject of animal rights. The label is loose because, as I have noted, use of the term "rights" in this context is disputable, however stringent the duties of human beings. The label is also loose because I mean to include here a position that animals are owed significant moral consideration, even if the manner in which their interests should be taken into account by human beings is by some sort of utilitarian calculus, rather than in terms of stringent duties. Further, the category of entities warranting protection might be narrower, or conceivably broader, than all animals.

The Borderlines of Consideration

What I mean by consideration owed to the entities as such is that the consideration does not depend either on the interests of some other kinds of entities, such as human beings, or on the number of similar entities in existence, protection being owed for some reason other than an entity's being one of the last remaining members of a species or other set of natural objects.

The three major questions for public policy are: which entities are owed moral consideration in their own right; how does that consideration relate to the consideration owed to human beings; and how far should judgments of this sort be embodied in law and other governmental decisions? The idea that some moral consideration is owed would not necessarily dictate that legal protection is appropriate; one might simply leave choices to the private sector. But the existence in many countries of laws forbidding cruelty to animals shows that at least at the edges legal protection is often regarded as warranted. I shall take it for granted that on many views of the moral consideration owed animals, some protection by law is appropriate.

An extreme version of the human dominion view would be that other entities exist solely for the benefit of human beings. That basic view could be given a nonreligious cast along one of two lines. The first would be that because the critical capacities of ordinary human beings[17] are unique or so far superior to other existing creatures, any action that contributes to human welfare or satisfaction is warranted, no matter how small the contribution and no matter how great the impairment for other creatures. A traditional version of this position is the notion found in Aristotle and Kant that the ability to reason abstractly is the basis for moarl respect and that only human beings have that capacity.[18] On a view such as this, human beings need accord no inherent value to any other animals.[19] This view claims to be objective, in the sense that it presents reasons that highly intelligent creatures from another planet should find persuasive and that should lead them to accord moral consideration to human beings and to deny it to other animals.

The second version of unqualified dominion would be a kind of "law-of-the-jungle" approach. According to it, the interests of human beings and other animals come into conflict; since (we assume) human actions are incapable of eliciting moral restraint from other animals,[20] human beings have nothing to gain by extending moral consideration to them. Thus, in human morality, which is designed to make social life tolerable for human beings, no consideration need be given to other animals. This perspective is the substantive analogue of the terminological claim that animals cannot be subjects of rights and justice because they are not participants in moral practices. The force of this perspective is limited to the domain of human morality; it does not provide any reason why the highly intelligent creatures from another planet should similarly accord preference to human beings, unless they are capable of moral interactions with human beings and not animals.

Neither defense of the absolute dominion view is very compelling. The uniqueness of some human capacities and the superiority of others hardly seems adequate reason to accord no moral significance at all to the interests of any other animals. The law-of-the-jungle view either is circular, restating an undefended assumption that morality must be entirely reciprocal, or it is confused. The propositions that many moral norms embody notions of reciprocity and that enrichment of human social life is a crucial aspect of morality do not entail the conclusion that the proper boundaries of morality are so set.[21] Perhaps human beings should consider the welfare of other beings whom they can injure or benefit, though their own lives will not be enriched by doing so. It is commonly assumed that we owe something to distant generations who cannot enrich our own social life; if the propriety of those duties is acknowledged, no reason appears why duties are limited to present and future human beings to the exclusion of other occupants of the planet. Most people's strong intuitive sense is that we do owe something to at least some other animals.

If consideration is owed to some animals, how is the outer line of those covered to be drawn? We seem confident that we do not owe anything to a stone or a dead twig. If an individual has a fancy to crush a small stone or break a twig, he commits no moral wrong in doing so, at least as far as the stone or twig is concerned.[22] The other side of the border of consideration requires an entity to have some capacity or characteristic that stones and dead twigs do not have. Among the possibilities for what is essential are moral capacity, capacity for language, self-consciousness (e.g., conceiving oneself as a distinct being), fear of death, fear of other consequences and anxiety, consciousness, ability to experience pleasure and pain, ability to have interests, having a good of their own, being alive.[23]

Deciding what animals deserve protection is, of course, complicated by the difficulty of our understanding what their experience is like; but we can be virtually certain that many of them are conscious and do experience pleasure and pain,[24] and we can be pretty confident that many mammals are also self-conscious in the minimal sense of being aware of their distinctness and of certain of their future interests.[25] Since avoidance of pain is a dominant aspect of human morality, the idea that we should not cause unnecessary pain to animals is an appealing beginning point, and that idea is reflected both in the traditional utilitarian view and in statutes forbidding cruelty to animals (which, however, might be defended as preventing human brutalization). As Bentham put it, "The question is not, Can they Reason? nor Can they talk? but, Can they suffer?"[26]

Whether painless death for animals is a moral consequence is more complicated. If a healthy animal is killed and its death does not cause pain to other animals, say its offspring, death still cuts off the possibility of future pleasurable experiences, and viewed by itself death is a harm to the animal, even if it has no consciousness or fear of death. What is more troublesome is whether that harm can be effectively cancelled by the life of another similar animal. Often the infliction of death on some animals is part of a practice that permits life for a larger number of animals than would otherwise exist.[27] The relevance of "replacement" is a critical question for the killing of animals in order to eat meat. Were every human being a vegetarian, much smaller numbers of animals of some species, including cattle, would be alive. On one view, meat-eating practices can be viewed as good for these species, and the painless death of some members of the species might be thought fully justified by the prospects of life of other members. People would in effect owe no moral consideration to preserve the life of an animal to be killed when death is part of practice in which another similar life will be substituted. In that event, slaughter for food would be acceptable quite independent of any human interests served by the practice.

The problem of replaceability exposes a critical distinction between a consequence-oriented approach to the treatment of animals and a genuine rights, or stringent duty, approach. If good treatment is based on utilitarian grounds, then killing that is painless, and not productive of fear and anxiety in other animals, is cancelled morally by substitution. If an individual animal has a *right* not to be killed because the intentional killing of an innocent creature is morally wrong, then its death is a moral wrong even if the result of "nonkillings" will be a marked decrease in the population of that part of the animal kingdom. Of course, the "replacement" argument need not be adopted all or nothing. Peter Singer has suggested that it can justify the killing of animals who are not self-conscious, but not those who are self-conscious, a category he thinks may include apes, chimpanzees, whales, and dolphins, and perhaps monkeys, dogs, seals, cats, pigs, and bears.[28] As Tom Regan suggests, the utilitarian premises that Singer embraces are not conducive to this sharp distinction;[29] but under some other approach to basic moral questions, self-consciousness more plausibly might be thought to form an appropriate dividing line between those animals who should be recognized as having rights and those who should not.

If ability to experience pleasure and pain creates a basis for minimal moral concern, not all animals qualify on that ground. Some apparently do not have such experiences. Many people have no moral compunctions about how they treat things like insects and worms, believing that these animals suffer little, if at all.

The basic standard of moral consideration could be broadened in various ways. Were it broadened to reach all living entities or all entities capable of having "a good of their own," it might reach all animals, and plants as well.[30] Although a defender of this position has acknowledged that the moral significance of plants can be "almost infinitesimal,"[31] on this view a tree's good can be frustrated, and not only chopping it down but tearing a leaf off it involves some moral harm.[32]

Since I am concerned with the interests of entities for their own sakes insofar as these might bear on public policy and legal protection, we can perhaps disregard plants and lower forms of animals. Even if individual flies and oak trees are entitled to some moral consideration, they are not on that basis likely candidates for protection by law.[33] Perhaps the threshold of moral consideration necessary to influence the government's activities as owner may be lower than the threshold necessary to justify government restriction of private choice. If individual trees warrant moral consideration, that might affect what the government should do in national forests, even if it does not properly affect what the government demands of private owners of forests. But we may pass this subtlety and concentrate on legal protection.

For that, judgments must be made about which animals warrant enough moral consideration to make them fit subjects for legal protection and about which of their interests qualify in this respect. Is painless killing, for example, a harm against which legal protection is possibly appropriate; and if so, is it possibly appropriate even if the factual conditions for replacement are met?

Comparison with Human Interests

Decisions about the appropriate use of the law also require moral assessments of animal interests against human interests, and here the difficulties become even greater. The spectrum of general approaches extends from equality, in some sense, to an extreme priority for human interests. The latter position can be said to be the import of present law. No protection based on the capacities and characteristics of individual animals is given to animal life per se. Wanton, unnecessary cruelty is forbidden. Rules regulating the use of laboratory animals do provide safeguards regarding their care and the conditions in which these animals are kept; the rules also constrain the infliction of pain in the absence of demonstrable research needs. Still, virtually any tenable human interest carries the day, justifying severe imposition on the lives of animals. Extensive loss of animal life is permitted, though the products being tested are luxuries; indeed a common test of toxicity is to see how intensive a dosage is needed to kill half of the experimental animals.[34] No rules exist against factory farming, which allows animals to grow in terribly confined conditions, so that their development will be quicker and less expensive, and their bodies plumper, than if they roamed free. The restrictions on how owners can treat pets are very limited.

Some of those favoring animal rights argue that we should move to a form of equality. The form of equality most favorable to the interests of animals would be that each life of each relevant animal would be counted as much as each human life. On this view, enhancing the life prospects of ten human beings would count no more than enhancing the life prospects of ten chimpanzees. No investigation would be made whether human beings or chimps have greater capacities for fulfillment and happiness. Now, many people do adopt something like this standard for human beings, that is, improvement of life prospects is thought to count regardless of an individual's capacity for realizing the goods of life.[35] But few, if any, would extend this egalitarianism to animals.[36]

We may assume that a relevant principle of equality will take different capacities into account. The simple pain of a cat would count as much as the simple pain of a human being, but it would be recognized that for some beings the interest in avoiding pain "involves an interest in forgoing the fear and confusion which would accompany the pain; and for some humans it further involves an interest in being able to have unsullied memories and to form and implement future plans with confidence, and in being spared a sense of humiliation and rejection."[37] On this view, because of all these correlative elements, pain of the same amount would be treated as a worse if it occurs in a human being. Of course, any attempt to apply an egalitarian position runs into the problem of assessing the "pure" pain an animal feels in comparison with what a human being feels and then weighing the significance of the correlative elements. Although these "factual" questions[38] may seem insurmountable, the equality approach at least provides an answer to the basic issue of valuation when the harm done to people and animals is similar. The equality approach is less helpful when the harm is one only people can suffer, say destruction of the capacity to understand abstract concepts and complex facts. If maintenance of that capacity is rated much more important than pleasure or physical well-being, an equality approach will sometimes yield great priority for human interests. When the deaths of animals and human beings are to be compared under the equality approach, one would have to decide how far human death is worse because of foresight, fear, and the sense of loss of those who survive, and how far it is worse because greater potentialities are foreclosed.

The extent to which these troublesome questions of comparability would compromise an attempt to apply an equality approach could depend very much on the assumptions made about what moral consideration entitles one to. The comparability questions are most acute if one accepts some sort of consequentialist balancing of harms and benefits. They are largely avoided if one adopts the view that animals have rights in a fairly strong sense. Tom Regan provides a lucid explication of one such view.[39] As innocent beings with a right to life, animals, he says, may not be used as means for the greater good. Thus, even if it could be shown that the death of 1000 animals in experimentation would save 1000 human lives that would otherwise be lost,[40] the experiments would not be morally justified. On the other hand, when a direct choice must be made between human and animal lives, for example, when humans or animals must be thrown from a lifeboat, the human lives should be preferred because a human death is a worse harm than an animal's death.[41] Indeed, Regan says, since imposing a lesser harm on many creatures is better than imposing a greater harm on one, even when the *total* of the lesser harms exceeds the greater harm, it is better to save one human life than to save any number of animals lives when a direct choice must be made.[42]

Though managing to sidestep many of the dilemmas of comparability, Regan has done so at the cost of resolutions that are strongly counterintuitive. Regan recognizes this, but claims that only a genuine rights approach can avoid inconsistency or indefensible differentiation, the inconsistency of treating animals worse than members of the human species whose capacities are no greater than those of the animals, or the indefensible differentiation of moral agents from those lacking moral capacity in terms of moral consideration.

Even Regan, however, does not press the argument from consistency to its full logic. Human beings lacking moral capacity are not only protected from being caused harm by other people, they are actively nurtured and protected from outside dangers. Were human beings appropriately to take an equivalent attitude to mammals, we should aim to protect weaker species from predators. Of course, such actions might upset the "natural balance," but under Regan's theory, that would not be a sufficient reason to refrain from protecting rights of individual animals we are capable of protecting. The idea that people should undertake to protect all mammals from predators and natural disasters is close to absurd, but a rejection of the idea substantially undermines the consistency argument that moral consideration for animals must be understood as conferring strong rights.[43]

Between near absolute human priority and some version of equality lies an intermediate view that the higher capacities of people give their interests some greater weight per se. From this standpoint, the pain of a person is worse than the pain of the cat just because the person has greater capacities, quite apart from the ways in which these capacities actually enhance the pain and its effects.

The Limits of Publicly Accessible Reasons

I shall not develop the arguments for and against these various positions in a systematic way. There is a growing literature on the subject, but what I have said thus far is enough to suggest the tenor of the competing assertions. Without reviewing each claim carefully, one cannot confidently reach a conclusion about the limits of publicly accessible reasons to resolve the issues, but I shall report my own sense that while common grounds of argument can answer some questions here, and can raise new, often disturbing, avenues of inquiry that challenge complacent assumptions, nevertheless much is left unsettled.

Rational argument may be able to establish that conscious animals capable of experiencing pain and pleasure should receive *some* moral consideration and that the pain or death of any such animal is, viewed by itself, a harm to be avoided. But these premises alone do not get one very far in respect to the proper bounds of legal protection. Critical questions remain, including: Is the replacement argument sufficient to justify painless killing as part of a practice in which more animals live than would otherwise do so? In the sense in which equality is plausible, should animal interests be counted equal to human interests and, if so, how much should interests derived from unique human capacities count? If animal interests should not be counted as equal, how much priority should be given human interests? In dealing with conflicts of human and animal interests, is some kind of consequentialist weighing or some notion of strong rights appropriate for animal interests? For these problems, analogies drawn to future generations or to treatment of defective human beings are so far afield and themselves of such uncertain resolution that they provide no sure footing. I am left with the sense that the place of convincing interpersonal argument is decidedly limited, that on the critical questions one must resort to one's own personal sense of life and a reflective view that makes one comfortable.

If I am right, people must inevitably go beyond the boundaries of persuasive publicly accessible reasons in assessing the proper legal protections of animals. That does not mean that argument in terms of such reasons has no place. Most people in this society unthinkingly relegate the interests of animals, except for domestic pets, to a very low plane, largely disregarding their consciousness and capacity to suffer pain or frustration. Rational argument, as well as emotional appeal, can shake people loose from any complacent and unthinking acceptance of near absolute human priority. But once people begin to think seriously about the problem of animals, analysis in terms of common forms of reasoning is incapable alone of resolving a number of the questions that are critical to appropriate legal protection.

Environmental Ethics

Resolution of the question whether the environment is intrinsically owed protection seems as intractable for publicly accessible reasons as animal rights. Though one might include within environmental ethics the possibility of protection of individual plants and individual natural objects, like stones, the line drawn in this chapter is between protecting individual entities as such and safeguarding some more inclusive category of thing, such as species, the land, the natural setting, ecosystems, or the biosphere.[44] For my purposes, an environmental ethic concerns itself with protections of one or more of these larger categories of beings over time. The worry is not the death, or destruction or pain of individual entities, but human destruction of, or failure to preserve, the environment. The fundamental ethical issue is whether humans owe any moral duty to protect the environment that goes beyond what they owe to other individual humans,[45] including future members of the human race, and beyond what they may owe to individual animals. Because there are inevitably possible future human interests that may be served by protective attitudes toward the environment, it is less clear than with animal rights that a decision to protect nonhuman interests will have critical implications for law and policy, but the underlying question of an independent duty is still important.

Although a judgment that some duty to the environment is owed will probably have implications for private individual action, the extensive coordination needed to prevent despoilation or alteration of the environment makes this a problem that largely matters for public policy and legal rule.

A dam that will cause substantial human benefit risks extinction of an obscure species of fish, a species that has made no apparent contribution to human welfare in the past and is highly unlikely to make such a contribution in the future. Should the dam be built?

The answer may depend on one's attitude toward the environment. Someone who focuses on the welfare of human beings exclusively will weigh the benefits of the dam against the scientific and aesthetic interests in preserving species and the remote chance that this fish will contribute to human life in some unforeseen way in the distant future. Someone who instead starts with a fundamental notion of respect for the environment, believing that humans have a responsibility not to work an irremediable change in the nature of the world they inhabit, might think that the dam should not be built, even if the weighing of human interests was favorable to the dam.

Even getting a rational secular handle on this borderline question of valuation is difficult, unless the focus is on the attitudes that are psychologically healthy for human beings to have. If crushing one stone raises no moral question, why does destroying the Grand Canyon raise a question except in terms of aesthetic and other losses to people[46] and to other creatures warranting moral consideration. Why should the life of one nearly extinct snail darter count for more than the life of one salmon, if the salmon's capacities are at least as great? At least with the subject of animal rights, the inquiry could proceed by asking what capacities that are thought deserving of moral protection in people also exist in animals; here even this exercise in analogy to ordinary moral problems is unavailable.

That socialized human life will alter the environment in some ways is inevitable; species of animals affect the settings they inhabit.[47] Yet many people feel concern about the extermination of other species.[48] John Rawls, for example, talks in passing of "destruction of a whole species as a great evil."[49] Others, devoting themselves more intensely to the problem of environmental ethics, have talked about diversity as a good in itself,[50] of the well-being of species, wildernesses, and ecosystems,[51] or of the importance of "preserving the integrity, stability and beauty of the biotic community."[52]

One argument in favor of this view is that humans should recognize themselves as members of a community with interdependent parts. Such recognition will, of course, necessarily affect our actions toward the environment, but why should it preclude a human-oriented perspective, one that allows manipulation of the environment so long as long-term human interests are not undermined? The idea that we are simply an insignificant part of a vast chain of being is itself as consonant with a law-of-the-jungle view, that we should get all we can for ourselves, as it is with the view that we must respect the other parts of being. Stuart Hampshire has written with some eloquence that "nature can sustain those emotions associated with the superhuman," that it "is principally for this reason that the careless destruction of a species seems disgraceful," since such destruction "expresses an ignorant attitude, and a false philosophy, of dominance, as if men were situated in the world as in their own garden."[53] Granting Hampshire's point that the world is not our garden, the question remains why we should not take all we can out of it. If the main point is that nature deserves respect because of the emotions that respect for it can sustain, then either we revert to a complex plea about psychological health or to some judgment reaching beyond publicly accessible reasons that such an attitude is one human beings *should* have.

Unless it is justified in terms of psychological health or as a needed corrective to present human ignorance of future possibilities, or serves as a shorthand for a more complex assertion about the interaction of human knowledge and pleasure with natural objects,[54] the claim that people should respect nature in its own right and try to preserve species because of their inherent value is not one that can be successfully grounded in publicly accessible reasons. People have radically different reactions to what nature in some larger sense is owed by human beings, and neither analogies to ordinary moral constraints nor other forms of reasoned analysis provide much assistance in settling who is right. Chief Seattle spoke of the rivers as "our brothers" to whom we owe "kindness."[55] This manner of looking at the natural world is so contrary to our own that is seems odd, but, unless it is based on some plain mistake about the location of spirits, Chief Seattle's view is not irrational. Attaching value to the preservation of species, and even to maintenance of the physical environment, is not contrary to publicly accessible reasons, but such views do require some judgment of value that extends beyond those reasons.[56]

The Place of Religious Convictions

If people must rely on evaluations that are not based on commonly accessible reasons to arrive at positions regarding animal rights and environmental protection, and these positions have important implications for what the law should be, the religious believer has an argument that he should be able to rely on his religiously informed view of humankind's place in the world as he struggles with the relevant moral questions and their political and legal implications. As I have mentioned, different religious traditions take radically different perspectives on how human beings fit with the natural environment; if commonly shared moral perspectives and forms of reason provide no evidently correct perspective, it is hard to understand why a liberal democrat should eschew his deeply held religious premises in favor of some alternative assumptions that also lie beyond public reasons and can yield a starting point. In this context, the religious premises help inform the citizen's view about what entities warrant the ordinary secular protection of their lives or physical existence.

In the example of the dam, only a government choice, not the rights of other people, is directly involved; but many rules protecting the environment do constrain the choices of those who own, occupy, or use parts of that environment. Some of those people whose choices are constrained will take the human dominion view of nature, believing that they have a moral right to exploit nature for human advantage. From their point of view, an environment-protecting regulation may infringe on their moral rights. Nevertheless, as I shall argue at the end of Chapter 8, reliance on religious convictions remains appropriate, since protection of the physical integrity of entities deserving moral consideration is a kind of protection that is called for in terms of secular objectives, and the religious convictions are used to reach judgment about which entities deserve protection.

In Chapter 8, I shall defend in greater depth the twofold claim summarily made here: namely, that everyone must reach beyond commonly accessible reasons to decide many social issues and that religious bases for such decisions should not be disfavored in comparison with other possible bases. It remains in this chapter to respond to a perplexing objection to the relation between my treatment of environmental protection and my treatment of prohibitions directed at sexual acts because they are regarded as sinful.

The attack on my position denies the difference between these two kinds of issues.

> You (Greenawalt) say that actions that don't harm anyone cannot be prohibited just because they are viewed as wrong. I can understand how an animal can be harmed but we really can't think of the Grand Canyon as an entity that is harmed. Thus, the only wrong done in destroying the Grand Canyon (if all human interests are put aside) is that the natural order is disturbed; but if that is a legitimate bases for prohibition, then why can't someone say that consenting homosexual acts should be prohibited because each one of them is a violation of the natural order?

This objection does not threaten what I have said about animal rights, or will say about abortion, but if it is sound, I must revise either my view that prohibiting wrongs per se is barred by premises of liberal democracy or my view that protecting the environment for its own sake is consistent with premises of liberal democracy. Forced to such a choice, I should wish to surrender my position about the environment, because the view that society could appropriately prohibit any disturbance of the metaphysical order would be so sweeping in its implications. On that view, masturbation and cursing to oneself would potentially involve matters of public concern. The domain of unreachable personal liberty in a liberal society should be substantially broader than it would be if laws against such disturbances of the metaphysical order were deemed appropriate.

This thought helps to explain why protecting the environment is different. We have an intuitive sense that causing a substantial and irrevocable change in the physical order is distinguishable from a fleeting action that does not cause any ascertainable permanent change in the external world. If I perform the fleeting action I do not seem to be acting for humankind in the way that I do if I destroy something no person can rebuild. The fleeting action is much more within my domain and much less a matter of legitimate concern for others. These differences help to support the essential position that the domain of liberty in a liberal society must include acts that produce no observable harm to anyone *or* anything and whose only shortcoming is that they may breach a view of the requisites of a natural order.

In what follows I shall assume that environmental issues are essentially similar for our purposes to those involving protection of animals; readers who find the objection just sketched more compelling than I have conceded may view any notion of environmental protection "for its own sake" as much more vulnerable given liberal democratic premises.

Notes

1. See, e.g., Loftin, "The Morality of Hunting," 6 *Environmental Ethics*, p. 241 (1984).

2. For the position that some animals ought to be viewed as moral agents, see J. Rachels, "Do Animals Have a Right to Liberty?" in T. Regan and P. Singer, eds., *Animal Rights and Human Obligations*, pp. 205, 214–19 (Englewood Cliffs, N.J.: Prentice-Hall 1976); R. Watson, "Self-Consciousness and the Rights of Nonhuman Animals," 1 *Environmental Ethics*, pp. 101, 128 (1979); P. Miller, "Do Animals Have Interests Worthy of Our Moral Interest," 5 *Environmental Ethics*, pp. 319, 331–32

(1983). Exactly what are the minimal conditions of being a moral agent is itself a complex question I shall not pursue.

3. See, e.g., J. Rawls, *A Theory of Justice*, p. 17 (Cambridge, Mass., Harvard Univ. Pr. 1971): B. Ackerman, *Social Justice in the Liberal State*, pp. 79–80 (New Haven, Conn., Yale Univ. Pr. 1980) (recognizing that a nonhuman animal could qualify for citizenship if it could engage in dialogue with human beings).

4. See, e.g., G.J. Warnock, *The Object of Morality*, pp. 149–51 (London, Methuen & Co. 1971).

5. J. Rawls, supra note 3, at p. 17; see id. at pp. 504, 512. Tom Regan interprets the cryptic passages in Rawls's book somewhat differently, seeking to provide a coherent account of how what Rawls says about duties to nonhuman animals can be fitted within his contract theory. T. Regan, *The Case for Animal Rights*, pp. 163–74 (Berkeley, Calif., Univ. of California Pr., 1983). Regan amply shows that what Rawls says about duties to animals cannot comfortably be accommodated within his contractarian approach; the impossibility of such an accommodation is one reason I conclude that Rawls did not intend such a fit.

6. B. Ackerman, supra note 3, at pp. 102, 111–13.

7. It may be true, as Donald Regan suggests, in "Duties of Preservation," in B. Norton, ed., *The Preservation of Species,* p. 197 (Princeton, N.J., Princeton Univ. Pr. 1986), that talk of rights serves no useful purpose, and invites confusion, when the central assertions are about duties. I agree with him that in respect to human relations toward nonhuman entities, the critical analysis is about duties.

8. That morality is not solely a matter of reciprocal interaction is shown by duties owed to future generations of humans. I assume, though I do not try to demonstrate, that such duties exist.

9. Readers who think the terminology of rights and justice is inapt in this context can translate passages of mine that use these terms into a terminology that refers to stringent human duties.

10. This dichotomy involves some oversimplification. See, e.g., the position of Donald Regan, supra note 7, discussed infra, at note 45.

11. See I. Kant, "Duties to Animals and Spirits," in *Lectures on Ethics*, trans. L. Infield (N.Y., Harper and Row, 1963); reprinted in T. Regan and P. Singer, eds., supra note 2.

12. See, e.g., M. Fox, *Returning to Eden: Animal Rights and Human Responsibility* (N.Y., Viking Pr. 1980); C. Stone, *Should Trees Have Standing?* pp. 48–54 (Los Altos, William Kaufmann 1974); B. Norton, "Environmental Ethics and Weak Anthropocentrism," 6 *Environmental Ethics*, pp. 131, 136 (1984) (asserting that Hindus and Jains proscribe the killing of insects out of concern for their own spiritual development rather than the lives of the insects). The relation sketched here between ultimate justification and actual attitude is closely similar to that posited by the claim that nonconsequential attitudes towards moral choices will produce the best consequences over the long run.

13. See, e.g., L. White, Jr., "The Historical Roots of our Ecological Crisis," in J. Barr, ed., *The Environmental Handbook*, (London, Pan Books, Ltd. 1971), pp. 3–16.

14. See R. Attfield, *The Ethics of Environmental Concern*, pp. 20–87 (Oxford, Basil Blackwell 1983). For one eloquent account of how a theological perspective can affect one's view of nature, see M. Ball, *Lying Down Together*, especially at pp. 119–38 (Madison, Wisc., Univ. of Wisconsin Pr. 1985).

15. S. Schwarzchild, "The Unnatural Jew," 6 *Environmental Ethics*, pp. 347–362 (1984).

16. Ninian Smart, *Philosophy of Religion*, p. 162 (N.Y., Oxford Univ. Pr. 1979), talks of the great divide in the Western tradition between people and animals. Lynn White, supra note 13, recommends the adoption of a new religion like Zen Buddhism or a modification of Christianity that would emphasise the pan-psychism of St. Francis.

17. I speak of ordinary human beings. Related to the issue of animal rights is the issue of how much consideration to give to members of the human species incapable of development to even the level of the higher animals. Proponents of animal rights often criticize "specism" and claim that severely retarded and handicapped humans are owed no more consideration than animals of equivalent capacity. See generally T. Regan, supra note 5, at pp. 232–65; P. Singer, *Practical Ethics*, pp. 52–53 (Cambridge, Cambridge Univ. Pr. 1979).

18. See P. Miller, supra note 2, at p. 321.

19. One might say that human beings should at least weight the interests of other animals when a matter is indifferent to them; but even having to think in these terms is something of an inconvenience, so disregard of animal interests might be warranted by the human interest in avoiding that inconvenience.

20. The assumption is that if other animals are capable of exercising moral restraint at all, human actions are incapable of generating that restraint in favor of human interests.

21. The issue posed is similar to the question, mentioned in Chapter 4 at note 66 and accompanying text, whether an individual should violate moral norms if he can do so with impunity. Of course, the simple answer to that question is that the violation is morally wrong. But if the true basis of morality is reciprocal advantage, why *should* an individual not do what is morally wrong if he is confident it will be to his advantage? The moral norms themselves cannot provide an answer to this deeper question of "should."

22. One might think that any manifestation of anger is wrong; in that event, breaking a twig in anger might be wrong, though not because of the interests of the twig. (Whether the "wrong" would be a moral wrong is a further question I need not explore.) Compare the discussion in D. Regan, supra note 7, at pp. 205–6, of the importance of the attitude of the last person alive were she to consider destroying the Grand Canyon.

23. See generally R. Attfield, supra note 14, at pp. 142–47. The possibilities enumerated in the text are not exhaustive, nor are they necessarily distinctive. R.G. Frey, for example, in *Interests and Rights: The Case Against the Animals* (Oxford, Clarendon Pr. 1980), suggests that language is necessary for self-consciousness and having interests. The view that language is necessary for self-consciousness and

interests is effectively criticized in T. Regan, supra note 5, at pp. 38–49, and P. Miller, supra note 2, at pp. 322–29.

24. Of course, we cannot be certain that when an animal reacts to a burn with physical manifestations that resemble our own that he is experiencing pain in the way that we do, but the conclusion that he does feel something similar is not much less secure than a similar conclusion we draw about what other human beings feel. For a careful and persuasive discussion of animal awareness, see T. Regan, supra note 5, at pp. 1–81.

25. See P. Singer, supra note 17, p. 96, describing the strategy by which a chimpanzee seeks to get a banana.

26. Quoted in P. Singer, id. at p. 50, and in T. Regan, supra note 5, at p. 95. Regan makes the interesting point that not all pain involves suffering and considers Bentham to be astute if making his claim in terms of suffering. For a defense of sentience as the critical standard for moral consideration, see L.W. Summer, *Abortion and Moral Theory*, pp. 124–60 (Princeton, N.J., Princeton Univ. Pr. 1981).

27. What follows could be put as an aspect of the balancing of interests rather than the borderlines of consideration; I place it here because the balancing in which I am interested is between human interests and animal interests, and this inquiry involves a comparison of interests of similar animals.

28. P. Singer, supra note 17, at pp. 94–105.

29. T. Regan, supra note 5, at pp. 207–11.

30. See R. Attfield, supra note 14, at pp. 145, 154, 157.

31. Id. at p. 154.

32. Donald Regan, supra note 7, at pp. 197–98, suggests that this way of talking confusingly leads us to think of the tree as having a good of which it is conscious.

33. Of course as valuable property, oak trees are protected against damage from nonowners, and one can certainly imagine owners themselves being restricted from destroying trees on aesthetic grounds. But neither of these forms of protection is based on the inherent worth of the trees.

34. See, e.g., T. Regan, supra note 5, at pp. 370–71.

35. *One* way of defending this egalitarianism *among* human beings is that most human beings have roughly equal capacities and societies should not get in the business of judging comparative capacities.

36. Bruce Ackerman does suggest that any animal who crossed his threshold of ability to question allocations of power and wealth would qualify for equal consideration, including equal material resources and a right to a liberal education. See B. Ackerman, supra note 3, at pp. 80, 169. This result follows from the rule that citizens cannot make arguments that depend on their conception of the good or their intrinsic superiority. We might imagine that most animals in a species were capable of attaining the quality of a life of a normal three-year-old human being. According to Ackerman, each ordinary member of this species would be entitled as a matter of justice to roughly the same shares of goods as ordinary human beings. Many people will, like myself, find this conclusion strongly counterintuitive, so much so that Ackerman's rigorous notions of neutrality and constrained dialogue

will seem plausible only as rules for a community of rough equals in which superiority of persons and of notions of the good are highly debatable.

37. R. Attfield, supra note 14, at p. 169.

38. It may be doubted whether physical pain can be related to the pain of sullied memories in any coherent way.

39. T. Regan, supra note 5, at pp. 266–400.

40. Regan, like other animal rights advocates, strongly contests the factual plausibility of such an assumption, but the implications of his claim about moral rights is as indicated.

41. Id. at p. 285.

42. Id. at pp. 324–26.

43. Regan might respond by saying that defective humans have no right to be protected from natural hazards or that *in this respect* being a member of our own species appropriately makes a difference. However, if membership in the human species matters for this sort of positive right, it is not clear why it cannot matter for negative rights against human harm as well. For a defense of some kind of species principle, see P.E. Devine, *The Ethics of Homicide* pp. 46–73 (Ithaca, N.Y., Cornell Univ. Pr. 1978).

44. See B. Norton, supra note 12, at p. 132 (1984). Of course, what constitutes an individual entity and what constitutes a more inclusive category of being is not itself a matter of sharp distinction, but I shall assume that a river or mountain is not an individual entity.

45. Noting the tension between the view that value depends on fairly sophisticated consciousness and the intuition that people have duties to preserve natural objects like the Grand Canyon, Donald Regan argues that what is intrinsically valuable is a complex consisting of the Grand Canyon, people's knowledge of it and their pleasure in their knowledge. D. Regan, supra note 7, at pp. 195–202. Though Regan claims that his account renders the value of the Grand Canyon not wholly instrumental, id. at pp. 202–4, for my purposes the duty not to destroy it still depends on what we owe to other human beings.

46. See B. Norton, supra note 12, p. 132, for an analysis cast in terms of the long-term interests of human beings.

47. See Watson, "A Critique of Anti-Anthropocentric Biocentrism," 5 *Environmental Ethics*, pp. 245, 253 (1983).

48. See A.S. Gunn, "Why Should We Care About Rare Species?" 2 *Environmental Ethics*, pp. 133–53 (1980).

49. *A Theory of Justice*, at p. 512.

50. See A. Lovejoy, "The Great Chain of Being," cited in Attfield, supra note 14, at p. 149.

51. Johnson, "Humanity, Holism, and Environmental Ethics," 5 *Environmental Ethics*, pp. 345–54 (1983).

52. This is the view of Aldo Leopold as reported in Attfield, supra note14, at p. 158.

53. S. Hampshire, *Two Theories of Morality*, p. 91 (Oxford, Oxford Univ. Pr. 1977).

54. See Donald Regan's resolution, briefly described in supra note 45.

55. See A. Brennan, "The Moral Standing of Natural Objects," 6 *Environmental Ethics*, pp. 35, 40 (1984).

56. An attractive aspect of Donald Regan's approach, see supra note 45, is that it gives effect to the intuition that destruction of the environment is wrong apart from instrumental reasons but denies that intrinsic value exists in the absence of advanced consciousness. From Regan's point of view, the notion that we owe the environment anything apart from our consciousness of it is mistaken.

7

Borderlines of Status II: Abortion

Induced abortion is the most controversial social issue as to which religious views figure prominently. It is also a tragic problem for our society. Some people sincerely regard the more than a million and a half abortions performed in the United States each year[1] as murders; others see them as exercises of a fundamental human right. The level of mutual understanding is very low and confusion abounds about the proper place of religion. Many of those who favor abortion see the pernicious influence of religious views on the political process; others respond simplistically that abortion is a moral, not a religious, issue.

My aim in this chapter and the next is decidedly not to make one more contribution to the proper legal treatment of abortion, how the existing Constitution should be interpreted, what legislatures should do, or whether a constitutional amendment should be adopted. My own personal positions, based on complicated grounds including the appropriate role of courts in interpreting the Constitution, are that *Roe* v. *Wade*, the case establishing a woman's general constitutional right to an abortion,[2] was wrongly decided but that, were they free to decide, legislatures should adopt a permissive approach to abortion, that a constitutional amendment requiring restrictive laws would be gravely misconceived, and that even an amendment allowing such laws would be undesirable. If the tenor of the remarks that follow is more sympathetic to the "pro-life" position on abortion than is typical for those whose own position is "pro-choice," the explanation is not a desire to promote covertly adoption of the "pro-life" perspective, but my belief that that position has often been mistakenly equated with the naked imposition of religious views.

The nub of the question whether a restrictive abortion law can be justified turns on when a fetus warrants significant protection from society. One traditional argument for proscribing abortion concerned the health of pregnant women, but no one seriously argues that with modern medical technology this argument is sufficient to justify a wholesale ban on abortions. Another traditional argument is based on the claim, especially associated with the Roman Catholic Church, that the openness of the sexual act to procreation precludes any artificial means, including contraception as well as abortion, to prevent the generation of life. Though purportedly based on a rational analysis of natural law, this particular claim presently has limited appeal to ordinary Catholics,[3] much less to most others. Yet another argument for laws restricting abortion is that permitting abortions causes a general lowering in the value assigned human life. In fact, little empirical evidence exists that permissive attitudes toward abortion lead to loosening of concern generally for human life.[4] *A priori*, one would suppose that the likelihood that permissiveness as to abortion would lead to a devaluation of human life would depend on whether many people regarded aborted fetuses as having a status similar to that of entities that are undoubtedly human lives. If many people did regard the fetus as like a human life, the legal right of a pregnant woman to have the fetus destroyed might represent a cavalier attitude toward the protection of innocent life; but if fetuses were generally thought to have no intrinsic value, their destruction would have little bearing on the sanctity of life of developed human beings.[5] Thus the worry about devaluing life turns substantially on the status that should be, or is presently,[6] assigned to the fetus.

The abortion issue is so intractable because of the sharp divergence over the moral status of the fetus. Those who think, for example, that at the moment after conception a fetus, or more precisely at this early stage a zygote, has moral rights as full as those of a newborn baby tend to take a very different view of the morality of abortion from those who think a fetus is only a potential life and that moral rights arise only at birth or at some later point in time.

If shared moral premises and common forms of reasoning are to resolve public policy about abortion by themselves, they must either resolve the stage of development at which the zygote, conceptus, embryo, or fetus[7] warrants protection or show that the propriety of various legal regimes can be answered independently. Adopting the common simplified terminology of referring to the fetus, whatever the stage after conception, I shall briefly examine the second strategy first.

I am assuming that if the fetus as such does not warrant any protection, the legal permissibility of abortion follows.[8] The claim that the permissibility of abortion can be settled without resolution of the status of the fetus depends on the claim that a permissive law is appropriate even if the fetus has a significant moral status.

Arguments for Permissive Laws That Concede a High Moral Status to the Fetus

One frequent argument in favor of permissive laws may at first glance appear to be independent of the moral status of the fetus, but it is not really so. That argument is that most aborted fetuses would have been born into exceedingly difficult life situations. Unless this argument rests on an assumption that the lives of most aborted fetuses would not have been worth living at all,[9] the argument presupposes that the fetus does not warrant significant protection.[10] Society does not allow parents to kill newborn babies who face difficult life situations, and it preserves the lives of children and adults who are locked into such situations. Further, as with unwanted babies actually born, adoption is a possibility for most unwanted fetuses who could be brought to term. Thus, the quality of life argument for permissive abortion is not in its usual formulation truly independent of some judgment about the moral status of the fetus.

At least two basic arguments for permissive abortion laws do not rest on assigning the fetus an intrinsic moral status that is less than that commonly thought appropriate for newborns. One is associated with Judith Thomson's famous analogy to a violin player who can only survive if connected to another's body.[11] The assertion is that since one individual has a right not to have his body used against his will to sustain the life of another individual, a woman cannot be required to use her body to sustain a fetus even if the fetus is valued as highly as a living human being. This basic argument has been developed with great subtleness and persuasiveness by Donald Regan, who asserts that the result in *Roe v. Wade* can be defended on equal protection grounds. Since people generally are not required to be good samaritans, he argues that it is unfair discrimination to require women to be so with regard to the fetuses they carry.[12]

Although an unvarnished act utilitarian might doubt the premise that an individual cannot morally be required to use his body over a period of time to save another, I shall assume that the premise is sound. The analogy between it and abortion applies closely to the woman who is raped and becomes pregnant as a result. She should not be required to carry the fetus to term if she does not want to. Of course, if her right concerns the use of her body, she could not object if the fetus could be removed and grown in another woman's body or in a test tube.[13]

In ordinary pregnancy, the woman is something other than an unwilling victim and a more complicated analysis of her responsibility is needed. If she has voluntarily performed an act, sexual intercourse, that she is aware carries some risk of pregnancy, she bears some degree of responsibility for the creation of the fetus.[14] Perhaps the degree of responsibility leading to pregnancy is so slight, especially if reasonable precautions against pregnancy have been taken, that the woman does not lose a right she would otherwise have to free her body of the demands of the fetus. That view will seem especially powerful if periodic, relatively frequent sexual intercourse is regarded as a part of virtually every healthy life. From that perspective, insisting that someone choose abstinence as the price of avoiding the risk of pregnancy brought to term would unfairly harsh.[15] But neither that view of sex nor the conclusion that the pregnant woman is effectively freed of responsibility is obvious. Remember, we are assuming now that the fetus counts as much as a full human being. On that assumption, the pregnant woman has voluntarily acted in a way known to risk creation of a dependence relationship between her and a new human being and she has in fact helped produce that relationship, a relationship that a great many women welcome when it arises. Believing that a woman who has chosen to take the risk of giving life to a new human being should have a moral duty not to terminate its life within her body is not unreasonable.

A different argument in favor of permissive abortion laws starts with present social reality. The essential claim is that even if the fetus intrinsically warrants as much protection as full human beings, enforcing a restriction on people who do not believe in its bases and will not comply is inappropriate. Though nonbelief and noncompliance are often joined in practice, we can separate them analytically; and the degree of strength of an argument against a restrictive law depends on both elements.

A shipwreck deposits Beth in a society in which infanticide is widely practiced and accepted, people generally believing that a baby becomes a person entitled to rights only when it acquires a capacity to communicate with others. The society is ruled by a monarch who is susceptible to new ideas, and birth records are adequate, so that examples of infanticide are easy to establish and would be easy to punish. Were infanticide outlawed and adequate enforcement efforts invested, the law would be generally observed and the rate of infanticide sharply reduced. Having been persuaded by Beth that infanticide is morally wrong, the ruler asks her advice whether the practice should be prohibited. Beth recognizes that if predictable discontent with a change would be intense enough, she might recommend waiting until the population was better educated about the intrinsic value of infant life, but given her view that each infant is intrinsically worth as much as every other human being, she thinks a prohibition would mean a great saving in human life. Not being an extreme proponent of the view that law should conform with popular sentiments, and not believing grave indirect negative consequences would flow from a prohibition, she advises in its favor.

If because of inadequate records and enforcement, the law would predictably have little effect on actual practices, Beth would approach the problem differently. Considering that the law should not often forbid practices that will continue unabated and be regarded as matters of moral right by most who engage in them, and believing that blatant disregard would undercut any positive education value the law might have,[16] Beth would then advise against a prohibition.

The application of this illustration to abortion is straightforward. Many women believe they have a moral right to have abortions and many will have them whatever the law says. Abortions will be less safe on the average if they are illegal. These difficulties should properly give one pause about a prohibition even if one is convinced that the fetus is morally entitled to the protection of a full human being, as is evidenced by Mario Cuomo's thoughtful explanation of why he is presently opposed to a more restrictive legal treatment than exists, though he accepts the Catholic Church's moral teaching about abortion.[17]

If a fetal life definitely counts as much as an ordinary human life, however, a legal prohibition on abortion, with minimal enforcement efforts, almost certainly will save some lives; the number of fetuses who will not be aborted that otherwise would have been aborted will be greater than the number of pregnant women who will die because abortions are less safe. Such a law may well exercise some influence on moral attitudes in the direction of protecting fetal life. The Supreme Court's implicit declaration that abortion is a moral right and its decision that early fetal life does not deserve the same protections as full human life may have encouraged the attitude that destruction of fetal life is morally acceptable; a switch back to general legal prohibitions of abortion might have the contrary effect on adults of uncertain view and on some young people considering the question for the first time. To the person persuaded of the full moral status of the fetus, the prudential arguments in favor of a permissive law, cast in terms of the practical limits on what a restrictive law can accomplish, may not seem powerful enough to eschew the modest benefits that could be achieved by a restrictive law.

A related but different version of the argument from present social reality asserts that so long as many people regard abortion as a moral right, forbidding it is inappropriate in a liberal democracy. This contention, implicitly rejected for a monarchy by Beth in my illustration, is addressed in respect to a liberal democracy and answered in the next chapter.

I have suggested some substantial arguments against restrictive laws, but these fall short of establishing convincing reasons why a believer in the high moral status of the fetus should support permissive laws. The person convinced that the fetus is morally entitled to full protection may reasonably believe that legal prohibition is warranted to save fetal life in the short and long runs.

Though I have concluded that the appropriateness of a permissive legal approach to abortion cannot be demonstrated if one makes the concession that the fetus is intrinsically entitled to as much protection as an ordinary human being, that assumption is not a requisite for what I want to claim about reliance on religious convictions. If, contrary to what I assume, publicly accessible arguments can establish the ill wisdom of a *prohibition* of abortion regardless of the moral status of the fetus, other questions of law and policy will make that status crucial. Should public financial assistance be given for abortions? Should methods of terminating pregnancies that will destroy possibly viable fetuses ever be allowed when other methods might produce live births? Once technology permits, should the fetus of a woman who wishes to discontinue a pregnancy be grown outside her womb[18] even if her wish is that it be destroyed?[19] These questions may not be resolvable without attention to the status of the fetus even if the right to end a pregnancy can be established independently.

And what of the timing of the basic right to terminate a pregnancy? Present constitutional law permits severe restrictions on abortion after the sixth month of pregnancy, and many states impose such restrictions. So long as a woman has ample opportunity to have an abortion prior to this period, the impairment of a right to control her body that a third trimester restriction involves is much less than the impairment if abortion is forbidden altogether. But even the lesser impairment may not be warranted if the fetus properly has no moral status prior to birth. Thus the modest restrictions of the present permissive legal regime may themselves be supportable only if one makes a judgment that the postviable fetus deserves protection.

The Moral Status of the Fetus

If the status of the fetus is critical for appropriate legal protection, shared premises and forms of reason could resolve the issue by indicating what the moral status of the fetus is at relevant stages, or by showing what the law should do in conditions of uncertainty. Stated baldly, my conclusion is that shared premises and publicly accessible reasons cannot resolve the points at which a fetus is entitled to particular degrees of moral consideration or what should be done in case of uncertainty. Though I cannot, of course, demonstrate that each argument about these subjects is inconclusive, I sketch the grounds for my beliefs in this and the following chapter.

We need initially to put aside two red herrings. The first is whether the fetus is alive. What one can uncontroversially say is that the fetus is a living, growing, entity with the genetic composition of a human being but one at the early stages of pregnancy that is incapable of independent life. That appraisal does not settle whether the fetus deserves moral consideration. The second red herring is the hope that science can resolve the moral status of the fetus. Science, as an empirical discipline, can tell us what are the characteristics of a fetus at each stage of its growth and the possibilities for independent life. Science in the form of improving technology can actually advance the point at which a fetus can survive outside the womb. But neither factual knowledge nor technology can establish how much consideration the fetus deserves.[20] Two people can agree exactly on how much a three-month-old fetus factually resembles a live baby and disagree radically about its moral status. Those who think only very advanced fetuses deserve protection are not likely to have their opinions altered by a new technological advance that permits a five-day-old fetus to be extracted from a pregnant woman and grown in another womb or in a laboratory. Understanding of fetal life and new technologies may very well affect judgments about the moral status of the fetus, but science cannot settle the moral issue.

Stages of Development and Inherent Worth

Our society lacks any shared decisive moral principle that establishes when an entity that will grow into an ordinary human being deserves protection, and rational thought may be incapable of settling upon one among the plausible candidates.

Initially I explain briefly why, as far as abortion is concerned, the critical issue concerns likely development and moral status, rather than what characteristics of fully developed entities are by themselves sufficient to confer moral status. Let us consider first a single cell zygote. The zygote, formed when the female ovum is fertilized by the male spermatozoon, has the genetic structure of a human being, and some have spoken of any entity conceived of human parents as being human.[21] But imagine that for some reason a particular zygote could survive as a single cell, but could not develop further. Supposing that a stringent duty exists to preserve the zygote in that form is almost unthinkable, since we believe that the undeveloped zygote has no feeling or other capacity that would set it apart from a plant or single cell animal. As the fetus develops, the conclusion becomes less obvious, and the exact characteristics at any particular stage less certain, but let us imagine that midway through a pregnancy a fetus, now possessing the limbs of a full human being, has a minimal capacity to feel pain but no self-consciousness or other mental powers.[22] If, for some reason the growth of the fetus was stunted but its present existence could be continued, perhaps we would owe *some* consideration for the preservation of life of this minimally sentient being. But the consideration owed would be far less than that accorded to ordinary human beings, and a conflict between preservation of such an entity and a strong interest of the pregnant woman carrying the fetus should certainly be resolved in favor of the pregnant woman. Although the moral status of the early fetus would seem most powerful if one believed that it had been given a soul by God, even then an early fetus incapable of further development might not appropriately receive the kind of protection afforded full human beings.[23] Though I have certainly not countered every possible contention that an early fetus deserves protection because of the capacities it presently possesses, I have said enough to suggest that most concerns for fetal protection rest heavily on what the fetus is highly likely eventually to become if it is not destroyed, a human being with ordinary human capacities.

Our culture, in its struggles over the status of the fetus, starts with a relatively firm consensus that we do not owe anything to individual entities that might be brought into being and that, for most purposes and on most occasions, a newborn baby has a moral status equivalent to more developed human beings and should have equivalent legal protection of its life. I explore these assumptions briefly, before turning to the special problem of the fetus. Attention to that problem will show that some of the possible bases for denying full moral status to the fetus cast into doubt the assumption that newborn babies have full moral status.

Neither the traditional doctrine of the Roman Catholic Church that artificial methods of birth control are unnatural, and therefore sinful, nor the idea that society owes something to successor human beings is at odds with my claim of a consensus that we do not owe anything to entities that might be brought into being. The Church's position on artificial birth control is not grounded on some notion that the rights of beings that might have been created are denied by prevention of pregnancy; the Church accepts the "nonartificial" rhythm method as a means of forestalling pregnancy. The idea of obligations to future generations, and more particularly the sense that a given generation has a moral duty to perpetuate the human race, are widely accepted, but almost all agree that no particular potential entity is denied some right when couples intentionally avoid pregnancy.[24] This is the consensus that I mean to capture roughly with the idea that we do not owe protection to potential fetuses before they are conceived.

Some troubling questions arise about newborn babies. Among the most sensitive are the steps that should be taken to keep severely handicapped babies alive. At least some people draw certain distinctions in this respect between newborn babies and developed human beings, believing that if the prognosis for a decent life is very discouraging, a newborn baby should be allowed to die even though a mature human being who suffers an equally gravely impaired future should be kept alive. Such a distinction might be based either on a theory that how developed human beings are treated more gravely affects the sense of security of healthy, developed persons, or, more directly, on the view that once someone becomes a developed human being society simply owes him more in the way of preservation than it owes a newborn baby. A related qualification about the full status of newborn infants concerns those who almost certainly will never reach a stage of self-consciousness; they may deserve less protection than human beings who have acquired self-consciousness or probably will acquire it. Though the experiment might have been justified in any event as a necessary step for saving other human lives, the transplant of a baboon's heart to Baby Fae raised this issue, given the prognosis that Baby Fae would almost certainly not live beyond a few months.[25] On a view that the predictable quality of actual spans of life is critical, six months of life for a mature baboon might be valued more highly than six months of life for a human infant who will never reach a stage of development as advanced as that of a mature baboon.

These controversial questions are enough to expose some uncertainties and paradoxes in our regard for newborn infants; but they do not undercut the basic conclusion that newborn infants with a potential for an ordinary mature existence are widely thought in our culture to deserve as much protection as fully developed human beings.

If infants warrant full moral consideration and legal protection and potential zygotes warrant none, how are the moral consideration and legal protection of the fetus to be determined? As far as proper moral consideration is concerned, one can distinguish a "sharp break" approach from a gradualist one. A "sharp break" approach posits one or more particular points in time at which the moral status of the fetus changes drastically. There could be one point in time, often cast rhetorically as the time at which one becomes a human being or a person, at which the change is from no moral consideration to the full consideration owed ordinary people, or two or more points at which the amount of consideration owed increases dramatically. To accept a "sharp break" position, one would not have to be certain exactly when in the life of a fetus each shift, say the initial acquisition of sentience, occurred, but one would have to believe that certain discrete factual changes had great moral significance. A gradualist approach would conceive the moral status of the fetus as increasing slowly and steadily over time until it reached that of the newborn infant. In each successive period the balance of contrary considerations necessary to override those of the fetus and to justify an abortion would increase.

The law of abortion should not directly embody a gradualist approach, since if it is to limit at all, it must indicate clearly what choices by pregnant women, doctors, and other interested adults are permitted at what stages of pregnancy. The criminal law should be reasonably precise about these matters and constitutional standards must mark off which areas of choice are preserved from legislative restriction. One can imagine a general proscription of abortion with an exception for "justified abortion," with those applying the standard using a gradualist approach to the status of the fetus, but such a regime would represent a very unfortunate approach if many abortions were to be permitted because it would give such unclear guidance to pregnant women. A law that itself is expressed in terms of discrete stages could, of course, be justified in terms of a gradualist theory of moral consideration, it being recognized that the law could only crudely reflect the more subtle moral reality.

Among the possible stages of significance are conception, the end of the period in which the fertilized egg may split to form twins, the beginning of development of face and limbs, brain activity, sentience, "quickening" (when the woman first experiences the movement of the fetus within the womb), viability, and birth itself. As the fetus passes through the stages up to birth it becomes more and more like a newborn baby.[26]

To many people the most obviously significant stage is birth; at that point the fetus becomes physically independent of the mother and is socially visible.[27] Complex social practices, including many legal rules, make birth a critical point in the life of a developing human being.[28] But to say that the fetus is owed no moral consideration prior to birth is troublesome.

What basis is there for valuing the fetus less than the newborn baby? Many people, including myself, have an intuitive sense that as the fetus approaches fuller development its moral claim to protection increases,[29] but how does one defend this intuition or decide at what stages the sharp breaks of a valid claim to protection and a claim to full protection are reached? On the latter question, suppose that a woman's obstetrician has advised that labor should be induced for a pregnancy that has already proceeded beyond the usual length, and that hours before the scheduled delivery, the pregnant woman has the fetus's life terminated. Many would regard this as just as wrongful as killing a newborn baby. But if birth is not the obvious place at which full protection should attach, no other stage in the development of a fetus has even that plausible a claim.

For some legal purposes, quickening has been regarded as significant, but in a more advanced scientific age, the idea that the moral rights of the fetus depend on the pregnant woman's sense that the fetus is moving within her body is not cogent.

The Supreme Court has fixed on a chance of life outside the womb as being critical for possible legal protection of the fetus,[30] but that stage also is far from being self-evidently crucial in respect to the moral status of the fetus. If the basic point about abortion were the unfairness of imposing on the pregnant woman, then viability would be obviously significant. One could reasonably say that once viability is reached the woman should attempt to deliver the fetus in a manner that it may survive. The point about viability, so understood, would concern a limit on how the rights of the woman over her body may be exercised; it would not describe a stage at which the moral status of the fetus is radically altered. This argument against abortion, however, would not explain why a woman could be required to maintain a viable fetus in her body rather than receiving induced premature labor if that is her wish. Viability may precede the point at which a fetus could actually *be delivered* and survive.[31] And since doctors will not induce premature labor without strong medical indications, the import of laws that forbid women from having abortions in the last trimester in the absence of strong medical reasons is that most women are required during the period of viability to carry their fetuses to term. This restriction tends to confirm that viability is thought to affect the fetus's moral status, not just the liberty of the woman,[32] and we are left with the question whether that view is sound.

A minor problem with the claim that viability is a critical threshold is the percentage of fetuses who would actually be capable of surviving, if prematurely born. Suppose five percent of fetuses could survive at a given stage. Why should all fetuses at that point be protectable? Is the point *really* that only the five percent that would survive warrant protection but that all need to be protected to safeguard the five percent? This question presses the general doubt that survivability outside the womb is so important to having substantial moral rights.

A further anomaly of the viability threshold is that the rights of the fetus depend on changing technology. If a one-day-old zygote could be transplanted into a test tube and could grow to maturity, in some sense virtually all fetuses would then be viable. Would that mean they would all be apt candidates for protection? One might say that only viability in a free environment counts, but the moral distinction between being a fetus growing in a test tube and being a newborn baby kept alive in an incubator with the aid of expensive medical equipment is not strikingly apparent.

The weakness of this possible distinction suggests a more pervasive doubt about the idea of independence. A newborn baby cannot survive by itself. Birth involves a kind of organic independence and alters the way in which the fetus is dependent, but survival still depends on the existence and care of others.[33] When the fetus becomes viable, it moves from being necessarily totally dependent in one way to being conceivably able to be totally dependent in another way. Does this shift mark a sharp distinction in its moral rights against society and against the pregnant woman on whom it has been totally dependent in the first way? Perhaps the stage of viability increases imaginative links with the fetus because we can conceive of it, but for "bad luck," being outside the mother's womb, a separate being;[34] but it is still not easy to understand why the capability to be totally dependent in a different way gives the fetus a right to remain dependent organically until natural processes end that dependence and begin another dependence.[35]

One important difference between the nonviable fetus and a baby is that prior to viability only the pregnant woman can actually provide the necessary aid; after birth others may save the baby without the mother's help. Although this difference relates more directly to possible moral rights of the pregnant woman than to the comparative moral status of the fetus and helpless baby, inquiry about who provides aid shows how difficult it is to think of the moral status of the fetus independent of the rights of the pregnant woman. In theory we can conceive of clashes of independent rights, but in actuality we are loathe to acknowledge that millions of beings with a moral right to society's protection can be terminated because of exercises of will by women with rights not to have their bodies employed against their wishes.[36]

The Relevance of Potential Capacity

The attempt to fix the moral consideration owed the fetus shares with the problem of animal rights the effort to determine what characteristics give entities inherent value. What differentiates the inquiry about the fetus is the special puzzle about potential capacity and its significance. How far does an entity's potential capacity bear on its present inherent worth?

Perhaps it is fair to say that the intuitive moral sense of most people in our culture is that both potential capacity and present or past characteristics matter. I have suggested that many people feel that a graduated approach or a multistage approach appropriately reflects the moral worth of the fetus. The only respect in which the *potential* capacities of the fetus change over time is that the likelihood of its surviving to birth increases somewhat; but this hardly explains the sense that the moral consideration that the fetus is owed increases substantially. Thus, present characteristics are felt to be relevant; the more a fetus is like a baby, the more consideration it is owed.

Yet, as my imaginary examples of fetuses whose growth is completely stunted have suggested, it is improbable that present characteristics alone are determinative of moral status. One reason why newborn babies and late fetuses are thought to have so much value is because of what almost all of them will become.[37] If the great majority of babies never developed capacities beyond those that newborn babies have, and the members of this majority were identifiable at birth, giving them much greater care and protection than is given mature higher animals, who have greater present capacities, would be a striking form of specism; and it seems unlikely that in such radically different conditions of life, *all* newborn babies would be regarded as having the inherent worth of developed human beings.

Perhaps because this mix of present characteristics and potential capacity is not a very neat way to assign value, various theories have been advanced that avoid its anomalies. Classic utilitarianism makes potential capacity ultimately critical. What is morally good, it asserts, is a maximization of happiness and minimization of unhappiness. Given the aim to achieve the maximum happiness possible, one's *present* capacity to feel pain and pleasure confers no special status; what counts are one's future possibilities for experiencing pleasure and pain and how one's treatment and actions will affect others. If a present early fetus is capable of experiencing more happiness and less unhappiness in the future than an existing person, then, other considerations aside, its interests should be preferred.

Both this conclusion and the broader implications of the exclusive emphasis on potential capacity are strongly counterintuitive. The utilitarian view that entities should be valued only as potential receptacles for pleasure and pain yields the startling conclusion that one has as much intrinsic reason to bring into being potential entities as to protect existing entities. People might have a moral duty to increase population to the level where, over time, total maximum happiness would be enjoyed; or, alternatively, to regulate the level of population so that average happiness would be maximized. Were it possible that some all powerful individual might increase happiness by wiping out all existing people in favor of a new race of beings, that would be the morally appropriate thing for it to do.

The idea that destroying all existing people could be morally best would be a paradoxical outcome for a philosophy that begins with people's desire for happiness and urges that their maximum happiness be the appropriate aim of most actions.[38]

A utilitarian might respond that in assuming that he would count fetuses and even potential fetuses as much as existing human beings, I have disregarded a crucial human characteristic mentioned in the last chapter, the capacity to feel fear and anxiety. A critical distinction exists between fetuses and mature people. If one fetus is destroyed, another fetus does not experience fear and distressing anxiety; if mature human life is treated as cheap, everyone will feel insecure. Social institutions should be established to minimize fear and anxiety and it is sufficient for these purposes mainly to protect entities that have those feelings.

One objection to this response is that it still does not make replacement of human beings wrong if an all powerful individual could destroy the human race without creating human fear *and* could substitute new entities who would not suffer anxiety because of the previous destruction of human beings. More importantly for our purposes, if fear and anxiety are the critical capacities, newborn infants are indistinguishable from fetuses; future development is needed before they warrant the protection accorded to more mature human beings. If the capacity to feel fear and anxiety is critical to protection *because* these painful experiences should be avoided, destruction of babies in a way sure to avoid these feelings is not precluded. Perhaps a utilitarian can come up with an explanation that supports present moral views by stressing the sense of identification between mature people and babies, but the explanation will not do justice to the feeling most people have that babies in their own right deserve protection.

To avoid these difficulties, a utilitarian might suggest that the aim should be maximizing the happiness of entities that now exist or that will exist in the future. On this construction, no protection would need be given in respect to potential beings becoming realized. Such a principle, however, affords no standard to decide when the threshold is crossed between potential being and existing being. The utilitarian might, of course, simply respond that nothing counts as an entity until it is born or viable, but neither of these lines can be drawn out of utilitarian premises.

In contrast to exclusive emphasis on potential capacity, some authors have argued that until actual capacity is acquired, moral status, or at least full moral status, is inappropriate. As with the similar conundrum about the "rights" of animals, at one level the claim is terminological, but typically the claim is also seen as having important substantive implications. The terminological claim is that the fetus cannot be the subject of moral rights or justice because it lacks the necessary capacities. Michael Tooley, for example, argues that a thing cannot have a right to life unless it is capable of having an interest in its continued existence, that it cannot have such an interest unless it is capable of conceiving a continuing self, and that, therefore, neither fetuses nor newborn babies have a right to life.[39] Others suggest that only moral agents can have claims of rights and justice.[40] The substantive conclusion that is explicitly or implicitly drawn is that killing a fetus, or a newborn baby, is either not inherently wrong at all or is less wrong than killing a mature human being.

The discussion of animal rights indicates why neither the conceptual claim nor the substantive conclusion is very forceful. Terms are used in a variety of ways, but there is nothing odd in thinking of entities that lack present moral capacities or the ability to conceive a continuing life for themselves as having a moral right to life. Suppose that Calvin, an adult, is in a coma that predictably will last three months, after which he will regain the capacities of a normal person. We certainly think that Calvin has a right to life though he cannot now presently conceive his own continued existence or act as a moral agent. Of course, Calvin did previously have these capacities, but that alone cannot be determinative if Calvin is thought, as commonly is the case, to have greater rights than someone who is in an irreversible coma. Many people regard a choice by relatives to turn off life-sustaining medical support as morally permissible if someone is in an irreversible coma, and many states permit that choice. Neither morally nor legally is the choice treated as permissible if the coma is judged temporary. If Calvin's combination of past capacity plus potential future capacity is plainly sufficient to confer rights, the supposed impossibility of future capacity conferring rights cannot be based on some straightforward conceptual bar.

In any event, the critical point is acceptable moral behavior by those who lie under duties. A coherent moral view can treat as wrongful some things human beings do to entities that are incapable of having rights. Once this much is granted, a possible candidate among duties is that people should not intentionally destroy the life of a being that is potentially sentient, and a fetus might warrant protections as stringent as those given mature persons though it is not deemed a holder of rights. Of course, someone can assert that the same incapacities that render the fetus an inappropriate subject of rights also make it less deserving of protection, but substantive argument, not conceptual analysis, is needed to reach that conclusion. We then revert to the problem of the moral relevance of present characteristics and potential capacities.

The notion that moral capacity is, in some sense, critical to moral status is less clear in its implications for this issue than is classical utilitarianism and is no more helpful in lighting the way to a convincing resolution. For both Rawls and Ackerman, the attainment of moral personality, the ability to make moral claims and to understand the claims of others,[41] is crucial for being a subject of rights and justice. Having suggested in the last chapter the implausibility of any view that entities that are incapable of entering into practices of morality are owed *no* moral consideration, I shall suppose that the claim rather is that entities participating in moral practices are owed a much higher degree of consideration than are other entities.[42]

One way of understanding the basic idea would be that membership in the particular moral community is what counts; another interpretation would emphasize one's participation in moral practices, whatever the community involved. This distinction can be illustrated by a variation on the fable about space travelers that Ackerman uses to develop his theory of justice.[43]

> Travelers from earth land on a distant planet. They discover inhabitants who appear to have developed highly complex patterns of life, apparently evidencing a degree of intelligence and concern for others that exceeds that of most human beings. Though the travelers are confident that the inhabitants have these characteristics, communication between the two groups proves presently impossible. The travelers suppose with enough time and effort they might learn to communicate with the inhabitants, but they think their own lives would be made more convenient if they simply exterminated the inhabitants. They would not hesitate in the circumstances to exterminate beings having the characteristics of other animal species on earth, but they wonder if they would be doing anything wrong by killing these highly developed creatures.

If one adopted the strong position that present capacity to communicate with members of the moral community is a condition of substantial moral consideration, the extermination would be justifiable. One is hard put to understand how such a position could plausibly be defended, how it could be that rational liberal morality must, or should, take as a starting point the idea that only beings who can communicate *with us now* deserve substantial moral concern.[44]

The illustration contains two lessons. It suggests that capacity and intelligence have independent significance; a duty not to take innocent life has at least some application to beings with capacities as great as those of human beings even if communication with them will never be possible. The illustration also suggests that insofar as ability to communicate moral claims to these constituting the relevant society *does matter*, ability to communicate at the present moment cannot be the only relevant consideration. If the expectancy based on past space travels is that communication can be established in a matter of weeks, and all agree that in that event equality of consideration would be appropriate, the travelers should not frustrate the possibility of this occurring by now treating the inhabitants as they might a lower order of beings.

The inhabitants in the illustration do differ significantly from fetuses, who presently engage in *no* moral practices and now totally lack communicative and moral capacity. Were present moral capacity itself what counts for substantial moral status, fetuses would still be denied protection given to the distant planet's inhabitants. So also would infants until the age of two or so. The conclusion that young babies do not intrinsically warrant full protection is not only strongly counterintuitive in our culture,[45] its grounding is dubious. If present *reciprocity* is not determinative, why should not a culture accord protection to entities capable of developing future moral capacity that will lead to reciprocal relations? Though Ackerman assumes present capacity to be critical to full protection, Rawls supposes that newborn babies will be protected under a principle defining moral personality "as a potentiality that is ordinarily realized in due course."[46] Once potentiality of existing entities to engage in future moral interactions is regarded as relevant, no clear basis exists for drawing the line at birth and not extending protection to fetuses.

Like utilitarianism, a moral capacity approach could be understood in a way that yields a definite answer to the relevance of potential capacity, but both answers are offensive to present intuitions. The most straightforward version of utilitarianism offends ·by making potential capacity all that matters; a strict present moral capacity approach offends by making potential capacity count for nothing directly. Understood in other ways, neither the moral capacity approach to moral status nor utilitarianism resolves whether a fetus warrants protection, because the theories do not themselves provide the standard for when entities begin to count.

We may tentatively conclude, subject to the deeper theoretical examination in the following chapter, that commonly accessible reasons do not settle the status of the fetus at various stages. No doubt, these reasons can show that some conceivable positions about fetuses are unreasonable on their faces; one might say this, for example, about the position that inherent value declines as the fetus develops or the position that fetal value is dependent on the prospective mother's hair color. But ordinary forms of reasoning leave open a number of possibilities about how far potentiality should count for the inherent worth of a being already living in some form, and thus leave open the way a fetus should be valued as it progresses.[47]

If this conclusion is sound, then people must resolve the status of the fetus on grounds that go beyond commonly accessible reasons. If this is inevitable, the religious believer has a powerful argument that he should be able to rely on his religiously informed bases for judgment if others are relying on other bases of judgment that reach beyond common premises and forms of reasoning.

In the next chapter, I test this conclusion against a more extensive analysis of the general issues.

Notes

1. See "America's Abortion Dilemma," *Newsweek*, Jan. 14, 1985, p. 24.

2. 410 U.S. 113 (1979). More precisely, what mainly was established was the constitutional right of a woman, with the consultation of a doctor, not to have the state forbid an abortion through the sixth month of pregnancy.

3. See, e.g., M. Novak, *Confession of a Catholic*, pp. 118–23 (San Francisco, Harper & Row 1983), who indicates his own dissent from the church's position and says that studies show that nearly 80% of Catholic married couples use contraceptives at some time during their married lives. See also C. Curran, *Transition and Tradition in Moral Theology*, pp. 29–30 (Notre Dame, Ind., Univ. of Notre Dame Pr. 1979).

4. See D. Callahan, *Abortion: Law, Choice and Morality*, pp. 127–28 (N.Y., Macmillan Co. 1970). See also P. Singer, *Practical Ethics*, p. 157 (Cambridge, Cambridge Univ. Pr. 1979).

5. See id. at p. 199. It is possible that acceptance of permissive abortion would contribute to acceptance of less than rigid protection for others whose status as full human beings was subject to doubt, e.g., those who have suffered irreparable impairment of all mental capacities, even if it did not dilute regard for those whose status as full human beings was undisputed.

6. It would not be illogical for someone to support a restrictive abortion law on the theory that because many people (wrongly) assume the fetus has great intrinsic value, the permissive law might compromise respect for life generally. This position would not be illogical, but given the widespread disagreement about the status of the fetus in our society, such a severe restriction on a woman's privilege to control her body could hardly be warranted by vague disquiets about possible indirect effects deriving from the misconceptions of some citizens.

7. Joel Feinberg, in his "Introduction" to J. Feinberg, ed., *The Problem of Abortion*, 2d ed. (Belmont, Calif., Wadsworth Pub. Co. 1984), at pp. 2–3, provides

a succinct account of the significance of the terms and of the times at which passage occurs from zygote to conceptus (about twenty-four hours), conceptus to embryo (about two weeks), and embryo to fetus (about seven weeks). See also D. Callahan, supra note 4, at pp. 365–77.

8. This assumption is not wholly uncontroversial. James Sterba has advanced an argument for the protection of the fetus that depends only on the fetus being a potential person, not on its having yet acquired any special status. He claims that if it can violate a right *not to be born* to give birth to an infant known to be highly defective whose life will be miserable, then it must violate a right *to be born* to prevent from being born a baby that is presumptively healthy. See J. Sterba, *The Demands of Justice*, pp. 143–48 (Notre Dame, Ind., Univ. of Notre Dame Pr. 1980). The theoretical answer to Sterba's argument is that the born but predictably miserable baby becomes a person with a life to lead and can then make claims about events that would have avoided this misery. See, e.g., J. Feinberg, *Harm to Others*, p. 101 (N.Y., Oxford Univ. Pr. 1984). (I personally reject the position that legal damages are appropriate for the quality of a miserable life for someone whose alternative was no life at all; I do not think we know enough about the quality of life under extremely difficult conditions to say that the person involved was damaged by being born. See D. Callahan, supra note 4, at pp. 113–14.) The potential person who is never created never reaches the position of having moral rights. Sterba explicitly challenges this asymmetry, but does not do so successfully.

Related to this point is the consideration that most people have opportunities to generate large numbers of reasonably satisfied offspring. But the present consensus is that the world is considerably overpopulated, and no one asserts that we all have duties to create as many children as possible. Thus the failure to generate presumptively healthy offspring does not strike us as a wrong. Sterba recognizes that an argument that does not rest at all on a status the fetus has acquired casts into question the moral legitimacy of contraception on demand as well as abortion. Few regard contraception as a moral wrong to the potential life whose existence is foreclosed, and no one regards that wrong as sufficient to justify a legal prohibition on contraceptive use. (I put aside here arguments that some contraceptives actually function to abort already created zygotes.) Of course, in having a fixed genetic composition the fetus differs from the potential fetus whose development is foreclosed by contraception, but if that fixed genetic composition is significant, the point is precisely that it gives the fetus a status that a shadowy potential person would not have. Thus, any plausible argument for a legal prohibition of abortion does rest on the fetus having a status that is important rather than on its pure potentiality.

9. Society does not, with the possible exception of newborns suffering extreme physical defects, discussed below, allow itself to make such judgments about the lives of existing people.

10. I am oversimplifying a bit here. If one took the position that whether any human life should continue depends on a balance of satisfactions for all lives affected by it, one could conceivably give the fetus the same intrinsic moral status

as existing persons and support permissive abortion (though present possibilities for adoption threaten the factual grounds for this position). The attitude underlying this position would, in theory at least, severely cut back the protection now thought to be warranted for newborn babies, although the attitude could allow some differential treatment of fetuses and newborns in terms of the general effects of their deaths on other people. I assume here that the quality of life argument does not depend on such a radical alteration in the theory of protection for existing people.

11. J. Thomson, "A Defense of Abortion," 1 *Philosophy and Public Affairs*, p. 47 (1971).

12. D. Regan, "Rewriting *Roe v. Wade*," 77 *Michigan Law Review*, p. 1569 (1979). Regan does not himself endorse the freedom our law leaves to bad samaritans and makes clear that his argument starting from that freedom is one of constitutional law rather than moral philosophy. Id. at pp. 1645–76. He says, id. at p. 1646, that had he been writing moral philosophy he "would have made the argument in favor of abortion turn centrally on the proposition that a fetus is not a person."

In my own view, the equal protection argument, forcefully put forward as it is, is not ultimately convincing. I think the ordinary situations in which aid to others is not required are too far removed from pregnancy to ground an equal protection ruling, especially when pregnancies numerically dominate the other situations by a great order of magnitude and involve, as the other situations often do not, an absolutely clear indication of what aid is needed and who uniquely can provide it. I also find the analogy to conscription somewhat closer than does Regan, think there is difficulty in equating the active termination of the fetus with an omission to act (on this problem and various techniques of abortion, see S. Bok, "Ethical Problems of Abortion," in J. Feinberg, ed., supra note 7, at pp. 188–89), and am troubled by the quasi-voluntary aspect of most pregnancies. The problems are candidly recognized and carefully dealt with by Regan, and I can only report a sense of the balance of arguments that differs from his. In any event, insofar the issue is a constitutional amendment to permit restrictive abortion laws, the argument from moral philosophy is the more crucial one; an explicit amendment could clearly authorize what would otherwise be an equal protection violation. As an argument against such amendment, the gist of the equal protection argument could play some role if reformulated as an argument of fairness that restrictive laws should not impose burdens on pregnant women of a sort that society is not willing otherwise to impose.

13. See Thomson, supra note 11, at p. 66. See also S. L. Ross, "Abortion and the Death of the Fetus," 11 *Philosophy and Public Affairs*, pp. 234–38 (1982).

14. See M. Warren, "On the Moral and Legal Status of Abortion," in Feinberg, ed., supra note 7, at pp. 102, 106–9.

15. See, e.g., F. Kamm, "The Right to Abortion," R. Abelson and M.-L. Friquegnon, eds., *Ethics for Modern Life*, 2d ed., pp. 113–14. (N.Y., St. Martin's Pr. 1982).

16. If disobedience was certain to be widespread but those violating the law did not conceive themselves as having a moral right to disobey (these conditions may be met, for example, by the 55 MPH speed limit on highways), then modest gains in deterrence plus some educative value might seem ample to justify legislation despite its predictable ineffectiveness.

17. M. Cuomo, "Religious Belief and Public Morality: A Catholic Governor's Perspective," 1 *Notre Dame Journal of Law, Ethics and Public Policy*, p. 13 (1984); also published in *The New York Review of Books*, Oct. 25, 1984, at p. 32.

18. See, e.g., C. Curran, supra note 3, at p. 209.

19. Taking the view that the fetus is less than a person but significantly different from a mere "clump of tissue" because of its genetic relation to its would-be parents, Steven Ross argues that the woman should be able to destroy the fetus. See Ross, supra note 13, at pp. 237–45.

20. See, e.g., S. Hauerwas, "Abortion and Normative Ethics," *Cross Currents*, Fall 1981, pp. 406–09.

21. See, e.g., J. Noonan, "An Almost Absolute Value in History," in J. Feinberg, supra note 7, at p. 9.

22. Though no one is certain when sentience first occurs, one author suggests that it does so at some point in the second trimester of pregnancy. See L.W. Sumner, "A Third Way," in J. Feinberg, ed., supra note 7, at pp. 71, 87.

23. The text's conclusion follows most comfortably if one conceives of the soul as developing with mental and physical development. But even if one believes the fetus receives a full-fledged soul at conception, if it is clear that the fetus could not develop further physically or mentally, one might conclude that its "death" would not frustrate its spiritual development but allow that development to proceed in another realm of existence. I acknowledge that this conclusion is debatable and standing alone may have disturbing implications in respect to severely retarded babies, but I think those cases of "stunted growth" are distinguishable in that the entities involved have reached a physical stage for which the most stringent protections are ordinarily wholly uncontroversial and the entities are capable of at least further physical growth and usually at least some further mental development. I have, of course, not dealt with a possible religious position that God forbids any infliction of death, or even failure to preserve life, on any entity that has received a soul. But the notion that heroic efforts need not be made to keep alive ill people who have permanently lost all higher mental capacities suggests a common qualification to any such position.

24. But see supra note 8.

25. See generally "Baby with Baboon Heart Better: Surgeons Defend Experiment," L. Altman, *New York Times*, Oct. 30, 1984, pp. A1, cols. 2–3 and C3, cols. 1–6; "Baboon to-Human Heart Transplant Draws Mixed Reviews," D. Franklin, *Sci. News*, Nov. 3, 1984, p. 276.

26. Perhaps this may not strictly be true for the time at which twinning can no longer occur, which is significant mainly for settling the single identity of the entity to which consideration might be owed.

27. See J. Noonan, "An Almost Absolute Value in History," In J. Feinberg, ed., supra note 7, at pp. 9, 11.

28. See. L. Lomansky, "Being a Person—Does It Matter?" in J. Feinberg, ed., supra note 7, at pp. 161, 170; Potter, "The Abortion Debate," in D.R. Cutler, ed., *Updating Life and Death: Essays and Ethics and Medicine*, p. 117 (Boston, Beacon Pr. 1969).

29. In his concurring opinion in *Thornburgh v. American College of Obstetricians and Gynecologists*, Justice Stevens, talking about the closely analogous question of the state's interest in protecting the fetus, suggests that this position is "obvious" if one limits oneself to secular interests. 106 S. Ct. at 2188 (1986).

30. Finding a constitutional requirement that abortion must even then be allowed if the health of the mother is at stake, the Supreme Court apparently supposes that a viable fetus has less status than a newborn baby, though its rule might be grounded in a woman's right to preserve health that would permit detaching even an entity valued like a full human being.

31. See A. Zaitchik, "Viability and the Morality of Abortion," in J. Feinberg, ed., supra note 7, at pp. 58–59, pointing out the viability does not mean deliverability, but that a fetus, if born prematurely, might be able to survive with the best medical assistance.

32. I should acknowledge a possible position that the status of the fetus has not changed, but that, since a woman with strong reasons for an abortion has already had ample time to get one and the risk of a live but severely handicapped baby is great with premature deliveries, the law should treat most abortions after viability as impermissible.

33. One possible line for a shift in moral status would be when a baby reaches true independence, the capability of surviving by its own efforts. What exactly this would amount to is hard to say. Would a child have to be able to contribute productively or would the ability to beg be sufficient? And if begging is enough, why would not the capability passively to create caring sympathy be enough, a capability that a newborn baby does have? If that capability is enough, it may also be possessed by the fetus. In this society most pregnant women do feel some concern for the potential human being they carry, and outsiders would often be willing to make some sacrifices to save the life of a fetus if they could. If the outsiders are willing and able to force women not to have abortions, then the fetuses would have this passive capability to survive. Capability of survival in this understanding provides no independent standard for moral protection because to a large degree it reflects present social morality. If no one cared if fetuses survived, then they would lack the capacity to survive; if almost all people thought fetuses had a right to survive, then even early term fetuses would have the capacity.

If capability to survive by one's own efforts were to mark an independent standard for moral protection, the relevant efforts would have to involve some more positive ability to bring about one's survival. Certainly no child would reach this stage until he had a rudimentary command of the language, so that infants up to the age of two or so would certainly be excluded. I shall not speculate about how much more would be necessary because the whole position is so at odds with present moral notions that beings that we can communicate with, beings that can indicate their needs to us and demonstrate their affection for us, are morally entitled to protection though not able to survive independently.

34. See A. Zaitchik, supra note 7, at pp. 60–61.

35. See P.E. Devine, "The Scope of the Prohibition Against Killing," in J. Feinberg, ed., supra note 7, at pp. 21, 39.

36. It is partly for this reason that the fantasy of the violin player attached to another's body yields such an insecure grasp of a moral situation that arises continually in everyday life. The difficulty of distinguishing the strength of the woman's claim from the moral status of the fetus is displayed in Justice White's dissenting opinion in *Thornburgh v. American College of Obstetricians and Gynecologists*, 106 S. Ct. at 2192–97. Not only does Justice White say the state's interest in protecting the fetus is compelling, he also asserts that the woman's interest in choosing abortion is not a fundamental liberty and that abortion legislation accordingly requires only the "most minimal judicial scrutiny." Id. at p. 4630.

37. See J. Noonan, supra note 21, at p. 12, suggesting how probabilities of development affect our moral outlook.

38. If, as Chapter 6 indicates, a utilitarian counts the pleasures and pains of other sentient beings, it will not always be appropriate to try to maximize human happiness; but most moral choices involve other sentient beings little, if at all.

39. See M. Tooley, "In Defense of Abortion and Infanticide," in J. Feinberg, ed., supra note 7, at pp. 120–34.

40. See, e.g., B. Ackerman, *Social Justice in the Liberal State* (New Haven, Conn., Yale Univ. Pr. 1980). Donald Regan suggests that only with respect to moral agents can a terminology of rights add significantly to an analysis of moral relations cast in terms of duties. D. Regan, "Duties of Preservation," in B. Norton, ed., *The Preservation of Species*, pp. 195, 197 (Princeton, N.J., Princeton Univ. Pr. 1986)

41. See J. Rawls, *A Theory of Justice* (Cambridge, Mass., Harvard Univ. Pr. 1972); B. Ackerman, supra note 40. There is a subtle distinction between simply making and acknowledging claims and the more advanced stage of comprehending a moral dimension of life, but we need not pause over which point might be critical.

42. To be significant, this higher degree of consideration would need to reach matters like the protection of innocent life, as well as matters that obviously depend on reciprocal interaction.

43. B. Ackerman, supra note 40. Ackerman's own treatment of a similar example, pp. 72–73, ends inconclusively in the comment that the earthlings *might* treat the inhabitants as if they were citizens.

44. The defender of the strong position might cliam that the example I have given is unfair, that in fact we could never know that beings are intelligent and possessed of moral capacity without our being able to communicate with them. Whether moral positions can fairly be tested by wholly artificial factual assumptions is a troubling question. Though I believe this illustration, however artificial, does suggest that mental and moral capacities themselves have significance inde-

pendent of the present ability to communicate with those who make the moral judgment, I also want to resist the challenge of artificiality.

Is it so implausible to suppose that we might discover creatures so different from us physically that we could attain a fairly high degree of confidence about their substantial capacities without their being able to communicate with us? Is it not even possible that such a conclusion might be reached about some animals on earth, such as dolphins? In earlier eras of this world, explorers landing on unfamiliar shores were initially unable to communicate very much with natives. No doubt, common physical characteristics made possible a degree of immediate body communication, but that alone may not have been sufficient for the putting of moral claims. Did not the explorers owe the natives substantial moral consideration at that point, if they recognized the natives as human beings possessed of intelligence and almost certainly also possessed of moral capacity?

45. The conclusion is courageously endorsed by Bruce Ackerman, supra note 40, at pp. 128–31, 145–46, though he relies on less direct reasons to protect healthy newborns from infanticide.

46. J. Rawls, supra note 41, at pp. 505, 509.

47. See R. Wertheimer, "Understanding the Abortion Argument," in Feinberg, supra note 7, at pp. 43, 49, 52–54; Sumner, supra note 7, at p. 76.

8

Borderlines of Status III:
Religious Convictions and the Limits
of Publicly Accessible Reasons

This chapter draws together the common themes of the preceding two chapters and analyzes in greater depth the claim that religious bases should not be relied upon by good liberal citizens. Though for clarity of presentation, I focus at points during this discussion on either animal rights and environmental policy or on abortion, I believe that my comments have application to both sets of problems and, indeed, more generally to other borderlines of status. Further, as I suggest at the beginning of Chapter 6, much, though not all, of what I say about these problems is closely similar to what I regard as the proper analysis for other troubling questions of value and difficult questions of fact. Thus, the treatment here is not only a culmination of the previous chapters but lays the basic analytical groundwork for what follows. At stages of the later discussion, I refer back to arguments made here, rather than fully readdressing fundamental points as they bear on issues closely analogous to the ones dealt with in this chapter.

Near the ends of Chapters 6 and 7, I suggested that people must reach beyond commonly accessible reasons to resolve difficult borderlines of status, and that a good argument exists that a person's reliance on religious grounds should be regarded as appropriate if everyone must inevitably use "nonpublic" reasons of some sort or other. I do not rely on any claim that depriving public decisions of religiously based understandings will result in bad laws and policies, impoverish political dialogue, or undermine the stability of law and government. Rather my argument is based on simple notions of fairness and tolerance for diverse beliefs and on what can reasonably be expected of people with deep religious convictions, the holding of which has never been assumed to disqualify someone from being a good liberal citizen. If all people must draw from their personal experiences and commitments of value to some degree, people whose experience leads them to religious convictions should not have to disregard what they consider the critical insights about value that their convictions provide.

In this chapter I test this tentative conclusion against a range of alternative possible positions. These consist both of proposals for the total exclusion of reliance of religious convictions and of proposals that would admit some reliance in certain circumstances and exclude other reliance. The five alternatives I consider are the following: (1) that since publicly accessible reasons do really resolve animal rights, environmental policy, abortion, and other practical issues, reliance on religious convictions or on personal bases of decision is inappropriate in a liberal democracy; (2) that because religiously based grounds are relevantly distinguishable from other "personal" bases of decision, either inherently or in terms of a healthy political life, reliance on religious convictions is improper even if reliance on more personal nonpublic grounds is proper; (3) that implicit reliance on general religious roots of common moral judgments is appropriate but that explicit reliance on religious convictions about particular moral issues is not; (4) that reliance on religious convictions and other personal bases of decision is appropriate only if they are supported by a consensus; and (5) that when claims conflict, a claim grounded fully in publicly accessible reasons must take priority over a claim that depends critically on evaluations that reach beyond such reasons.

I treat each of these possibilities in turn, explaining more fully what each consists of and analyzing the force of the reasons supporting it. Because this chapter undertakes the most thorough defense of the basic thesis of the book against the richest versions of opposing views, it is in many respects the most important chapter of the book. As I have said, it sets the framework for analysis of issues other than borderlines of status. And though I am still concentrating on the citizen's responsibilities to decide, what I conclude about that substantially influences my remarks about public dialogue and the responsibilities of public officials.

The Domain of Publicly Accessible Reasons

An advocate of the exclusion of reliance on religious convictions might argue that in the relevant sense publicly accessible reasons are not really inconclusive and that therefore everyone should aim to rely on these reasons rather than any other bases for decision. My discussion of animal rights, environmental policy, and abortion shows clearly that ordinary rational arguments do have something to say on all the problems. Not only do these arguments exclude many logically conceivable possibilities, say that worms have a higher moral status than dolphins, they speak with some strength to the possibilities that remain plausible. So long as publicly accessible arguments speak at all to one or both sides of an issue, perhaps the liberal citizen should follow the balance of those arguments, wherever they lead.

Such an approach would not necessarily bar some reliance on conservative or radical premises, or on moral authority. By conservative premises, I mean assumptions that in the light of uncertainty it is usually better to stick with present institutions. Such assumptions would be warranted if experience showed that human beings often abandon practices that later prove to have had a value they did not recognize. If experience showed that human beings often overestimate the value of present practices, contrary "radical" premises might be justified. And a sophisticated view might indulge premises more or less conservative or radical depending on the kind of issue involved.

I have indicated in Chapter 3 roughly what I mean by reliance on moral authority. If someone has proven in the past to have had a high degree of moral insight that I did not initially grasp, and that person is firmly of the opinion that factory farming is deeply immoral, his view might be a reason for me to oppose factory farming even though I am not independently persuaded by the arguments against it. As unpalatable as this idea of moral authority may initially appear to strenuous advocates of moral autonomy, no sensible model of how citizens should make political decisions would wholly exclude possible reliance on the judgments of moral authorities.

A denial that publicly accessible reasons are inconclusive could take a straightforward or a more complicated form. The straightforward form of denial is that the force of the public reasons now employed is fairly clear and that people should be able to make their decisions on the basis of those reasons. Of course, it is possible that on some questions, the competing reasons will be closely balanced; but some choices just are commensurately difficult because there is about an equal amount to be said on each side, and this fact of life is not a sufficient basis for flying from publicly accessible reasons to private sources of decision. Indeed, it may be said that I have set unrealistic standards in asking whether publicly accessible reasons resolve matters clearly. Inevitably there will be some disagreement about close questions, but this hardly shows that public reasons are inadequate bases for decision even for those questions.

Much of the point of the last two chapters is to rebut this thesis by example. Despite the range of publicly accessible reasons that bear on the questions of status those chapters address, my own sense is that these reasons are still radically inconclusive. It is not that the arguments in those terms are fairly evenly balanced, rather they seem not really to get to the heart of the problem. Some critical and very important judgment is needed, and the arguments seem of only slight help.

The reader can test his or her own sense of these social problems against my own. Some evidence for my view is provided by the fact that most people do not seem to regard the moral justifiability of abortion as a close question in the same way they may regard the question whether the United States should send technologically sophisticated airplanes to Saudi Arabia as a close question. Many people think the abortion question is quite clear one way or the other and those in the middle feel a deeper perplexity than that involved in choosing between nicely balanced arguments—they wonder how to get a reliable handle on the issue and they worry about being tragically mistaken about what is relevant. Writing on abortion, Daniel Callahan has commented that "we share no single, coherent, value system,"[1] and that in justifying normative principles, we "break through [the] circularity of infinite regress (in practice if not in theory) by an existential choice."[2] Reviewing Callahan's book and one by Germain Grisez, Stanley Hauerwas has suggested that the problem of abortion exposes the conceptual limitations of normative theories, and that such problems "are finally not susceptible to intellectual solution."[3] He talks of the arguments for and against abortion as often passing "one another as ships in the night."[4] Alasdair MacIntyre says more generally that in our society competing moral positions are put so that conclusions follow from premises, "[b]ut the rival premises are such that we possess no rational way of weighing the claims of one as against the other."[5] This difficulty helps explain the apparently interminable character of moral argument: "if we possess no unassailable criteria, no set of compelling reasons by means of which we may convince our opponents, it follows that in the process of making up our own minds we can have made no appeal to such criteria or such reasons. Hence it seems that underlying my position there must be some non-rational decision to adopt that position."[6]

The conclusion that the competing publicly accessible reasons seem radically inconclusive for problems like abortion and animal rights should not be too surprising. Borderline questions of status have proved among the most intractable for those developing comprehensive moral positions. Many questions of this sort are not susceptible to the techniques that permit rational moral judgment in other respects. Publicly accessible reasons can say a good deal concerning the conditions of a moderately peaceful joint social life, and the choice of means to accomplish valued ends.[7] Such reasons also have powerful implications for how we should treat other beings we recognize to be like ourselves. If we acknowledge that another human being is like us, but we fail to show him the respect we ourselves demand, we may be demeaning him, and perhaps ourselves, in a way that is at odds with a basic principle of morality (universalization) that is perhaps not logically compelled but is rooted in our notions of what is rational. Finally, when moral positions are tested by a standard of coherence with other moral positions, reason can often establish whether or not one position is out of line with other positions an individual or culture takes.

What is significant about many borderline questions about moral consideration is that they simply do not yield easily to these approaches. Ordinary reasoning can show the implications of various positions and it can show how well a position on one borderline question coheres with a position on another borderline question, but it fails to supply the determinative value judgment. The issue typically is how we are to count the ends and welfare of entities that are in some ways like us and in others not like us. The question is not one of means and ends, or of the conditions for mutual existence of entities already assumed to need to exist mutually. We must decide who we will recognize as beings like us, or somewhat like us, not what the implications of such recognition are. And many different positions on borderline questions will fit comfortably with otherwise similar moral positions, as is shown by the fact that people who agree across a wide spectrum of moral issues may disagree strongly over the moral status of the fetus and what is owed to nonhuman animals.

Before proceeding on the assumption that publicly accessible reasons cannot straightforwardly resolve the political questions involved in abortion, animal rights and environmental policy, I need to consider briefly the possibility that if accessible reasons cannot establish the moral status of fetuses, animals, and the environment, they can instead indicate what should be public policy in conditions of uncertainty. Unfortunately, there are competing responses to such possible uncertainty. The first would be that in cases of doubt, people should be regarded as morally permitted to do what they think is *probably* morally permissible,[8] especially if powerful reasons support their actions. Thus, for example, absent confident conclusion that the fetus has a right to life, a woman with strong reasons would be morally warranted in having an abortion, and a permissive legal approach to abortion would be called for. The contrary response is that the taking of innocent life should not be risked, at least barring the most extreme sort of justification, so that abortion, and perhaps killing of those animals with the highest capacities, is morally unwarranted and should generally be forbidden.[9] A conceivable third response would be that whatever the moral propriety of "running the risk," the law should at least leave the choice to private individuals. The kind of "risk" involved here is so different from ordinary risks based on uncertain facts, I believe other moral practices provide unsure footing for resolving the question of how to respond to uncertainty. The aspect of uncertainty introduces an important additional dimension to discussion of abortion and animal rights, but I am skeptical that, in general, it brings us closer to reasoned resolution of the problems of legal policy.[10]

Henceforth, I shall assume that publicly accessible reasons cannot now standing alone resolve the problems dealt with in the last two chapters, that is, cannot resolve them in the sense of providing comprehensive sets of reasons whose comparative force is relatively clear.

I turn now to two more complicated, and somewhat related, forms of the argument that publicly accessible reasons are not really inconclusive. The first of these is that what may be uncertain if treated as the subject of ad hoc consideration may be resolvable at the level of more general systematic approaches. The second form of the argument is that what now seems incapable of being settled on the basis of publicly accessible reasons may look differently after further enlightenment. The forms of the argument can be joined if it is supposed that part of the present difficulty is uncertainty about the most valid comprehensive system, which further enlightenment will illuminate. I want to examine the force of each of these suggestions more or less in its own terms, then I turn to consider their relevance for the plight of the citizen making political decisions; what needs to be said on the latter subject is roughly the same for both suggestions.

Though individual problems like abortion and animal rights may seem rather intractable viewed alone, perhaps the search for a systematic moral approach may establish the superiority of one solution over another. That a particular systematic approach to morality, such as "maximum total happiness" utilitarianism, can provide an answer to one or more troubling borderline questions does not, of course, show that the approach, or its implications for the borderline questions, is necessarily sound. If the systematic approach has other grave defects, its claim to our attention will probably be undermined for all its applications. The proposal I am assessing here does not assume that a problem is resolvable because one comprehensive system gives a clear answer. Rather, it asserts that the test of a sound systematic approach is the way it deals with a wide range of issues, that common forms of reasoning can be used to test various approaches, and that reason tells us that the approach that is best overall is the one that should be employed, even when it yields results to particular questions that are strongly counterintuitive.

This proposal is strongly rationalistic in two dimensions—in its confidence that reason can settle the merits of competing comprehensive systems and in its claim that the best of such systems should be followed in preference to contrasting intuitions. Examination of the merits of competing moral systems is such a wide-ranging and complicated affair, one must despair of arguing convincingly that publicly accessible reasons can or cannot produce persuasive arguments for one system against plausible competitors. I shall simply indicate my own deep skepticism, hinted at in the previous two chapters, that publicly accessible reasons really are capable of adjudicating between a number of plausible overriding approaches to morality, any more than such reasons are capable of adjudicating directly between conflicting positions on narrower issues.[11]

I shall say a bit more about the recommendation that one should follow an application to a particular problem of the apparently best comprehensive system even if that application, standing alone, is deeply troubling. I have noted that the theories that provide the clearest answers to the status of the fetus yield other answers that are strongly counterintuitive, simple utilitarianism suggesting that present beings can be dispatched in favor of potential entities who could be happier, and one version of the moral capacity approach radically downgrading the inherent moral status of infants in comparison with that of mature persons. If one were to relegate the fetus to a nonprotected status on the basis of a persuasive rational argument for a comprehensive theory, one should accord the theory and the argument their full scope.[12] That means, for example, that if a fetus is denied protection *because* it lacks present moral capacity, the moral status of infants must be conceded to be much less than that of mature persons.

What is a citizen to do if what appears to be the most persuasive position on rational grounds about the status of the fetus is one that he *feels* is deeply abhorrent because of its broader implications? Moral philosophers debate the comparative weights of rational thought and reflective intuition[13] when they are not reconcilable, but it would take an extreme rationalism to assert that every good citizen must always give priority to the abstract reasoned arguments he finds most persuasive. In light of the tremendous shifts in human history over what people have thought was morally demonstrable, requiring people to deny some of their deepest feelings, ones that are not dissipated by reflection,[14] in fealty to their present perception about the balance of reasoned persuasion concerning systematic moral positions, would be to give rational argument in its most abstract embodiments, argument which many people believe is infected with pretension and likely error, a preeminence that is not to be derived from any basic premise of liberal democracy. Perhaps it would be illiberal to refuse to abandon a moral conviction that one thinks can be demonstrated to be patently wrong by rational argument, a subject explored in Chapter 11, but it is neither illiberal nor irrational to hang onto the basic starting point that the healthy newborn has a status equal to that of a developed human being when all one yet believes is that extremely complex, highly abstract, reasoned arguments seem to tip slightly in a different direction.

I shift now to the possibility that, whatever the capabilities of existing arguments in publicly accessible terms, further discourse and insight may make clear what is now debatable. The history of attitudes toward slavery might be presented as an example of why we should not judge the inconclusiveness of publicly accessible reasons by their present undeveloped state. I certainly do not wish to deny that development along these lines sometimes occurs, or that working hard at reasoned discourse about moral and political problems is partly worth doing because it may produce growing enlightenment. On the other hand, embracing this model as a general explanatory account of shifts in moral views would seriously underestimate the importance of inherent limitations of reasoned discourse and the inevitable role of other elements.

In any event, a sustained examination of this model is not required here because the model has little relevance to the problem at hand. A minor question concerns the status of religious convictions. Perhaps many more of them will also be apparently resolvable on reasoned grounds in the future. If the possibility of resolution on publicly accessible grounds in the future determines the legitimacy of present reliance for political decisions, the exclusion of religious convictions may not be clear. But the main difficulty is that such future prospects are essentially beside the point. The likelihood of future reasoned moral enlightenment is not much help for the person who must decide here and now. If that person rightly conceives the limits of his own reasoned understanding and that of others, is he to rely on other sources of guidance or not? What common reasoning *may* show to some future generation is irrelevant.

Essentially the same difficulty infects any claim that the possibility of settling problems like abortion and animal rights on the basis of comprehensive moral theories constitutes a powerful argument for actual citizens sticking to publicly accessible reasons. The most intelligent philosophers have great difficulty bringing to bear the range of understanding and conceptual skill needed to cope with systematic moral outlooks in a reasoned way. The relevant arguments are so complex an ordinary person is ill-suited to make a reasoned choice between, say, utilitarianism and some version of the moral capacity theory. Since philosophers disagree about the best comprehensive system, and whether indeed there is such a thing, the hope that one theory may, in some ideal sense, be demonstrably better than others has only remote bearing on how the average citizen should set about reaching his own political decisions.

Having responded to various forms of the argument that publicly accessible forms of reason reach much further than I have intimated in the preceding two chapters, I revert to my claim that for relevant purposes such reasons are radically inconclusive in some important instances. If that is so, it would be asking a great deal of people to expect them for political purposes to disregard what they believe are fruitful sources of establishing morally sound positions, particularly in a country in which most people have accepted religious perspectives and in which it has never been supposed that religious belief is incompatible with good liberal citizenship.

The basic argument that it is unreasonable to suppose that people should eschew all their religious convictions in making political decisions is strengthened by a more realistic understanding of how such convictions and other personal bases of judgment actually relate to publicly accessible reasons, a subject that brings us back to matters discussed in Chapters 3 and 4.

I have so far proceeded in this chapter as if people can generally distinguish the force of reasoned arguments from other bases of evaluation, such as personal intuition, nongeneralizable experience, and religious conviction, and as if the basic question is whether they should attempt to disregard those bases. The underlying assumption is in fact highly misleading, because of psychological impediments to detached independent judgment, difficulties in disentangling the threads of publicly accessible reasons from other considerations, and the inherent interrelatedness of the two sorts of considerations.

Let us suppose first that a person draws a clear distinction between religious convictions and publicly accessible reasons. He sees the general arguments for and against animal rights and he reads passages in Genesis as indicating a dominion for human beings. Unless he is extremely introspective, such a person will be disposed to find that the publicly accessible arguments consonant with his religious convictions are more powerful than their competitors. Even if he tries, it will be hard for him to assess the reasoned arguments detached from what he thinks is correct on religious grounds.

Often, a person will have a hard time even disentangling the threads of religious conviction from publicly accessible reasons. I have suggested, for example, that some reliance on moral authority is compatible with relying on publicly accessible reasons; if asked to defend one's reliance on the judgment of another, one would indicate the previous occasions on which that person's judgment had proved correct. Insofar as a church member relies on the judgments of church leaders and fellow members because of their excellent past moral judgment, he remains within the boundaries of commonly accessible reasons. Insofar as he relies on their judgments because they have religious authority or because his assessment of the excellence of their past judgments depends on religious premises, he goes beyond commonly accessible reasons. An individual believer would be very hard put to guess where legitimate reliance ends and illegitimate reliance begins if he is not to rely on religious convictions.[15]

The degree to which people are unable to separate the force of religious convictions from the force of other considerations certainly affects the degree to which religious convictions realistically can be eradicated as influences; but perhaps the problems concerning detached judgment and disentangling threads do not alone seriously compromise the ideal of shared reasoned bases of judgment. The proponent of that ideal may say: "Of course, the religious influence is pervasive and unavoidable, but my point is that citizens should try to decide on publicly accessible reasons; all we can ask is that they make a reasonable attempt and cast their justifications to themselves and others in these terms."

This response might be unexceptionable if the religious convictions or personal bases of evaluation were always separable in theory from the reasoned arguments and all that was involved was an attempt to try to assess the latter on their own merits. But the problem goes much deeper, to the frequent interrelatedness of the bases for evaluation. I shall make the point in connection with particular religious convictions and the status of the fetus, but the analysis would be similar for many nonreligious bases for evaluation and for other social reasons.

To decide the status of the fetus, a person must adopt one of a number of debatable perspectives about how to look at something, either a general philosophic overview or the narrow question of rights of existing entities that are potential persons. A person might think that either divine scripture or prayer revealed decisively the moral consideration owed to the fetus, but it is rather rare for Christians and Jews to suppose that the Bible contains a straightforward answer to the problem. Much more common, especially among ordinary practicing Roman Catholics, is acceptance of a position on abortion because of authoritative church pronouncements. Their conviction based on the Church's religious authority that the fetus is a person and that abortion is morally wrong, is highly likely to influence their assessment of the arguments of natural reason in the way I have indicated.

The place of religious conviction in other positions on abortion is more subtle and complex. If someone thought the only way to work out a religious morality regarding abortion was to first work out an appropriate natural morality and then to import the transcendental perspective, any religious convictions might seem to be redundant to resolution of the moral and political issue. At first glance, this may seem to be close to the manner in which the Catholic Church often defends its own position on abortion.[16] The Church begins with natural law ideas, claimed to be rationally persuasive independent of particular religious belief; these preclude artificial impediments to procreation and protect innocent life. Absent a determination when human life relevantly begins, those principles alone do not explain why abortion, or abortion at a certain stage, is a worse moral wrong than the use of contraceptives; but the determination when life begins also depends on naturalistic moral reasoning. One looks to see what is the most natural point at which to fix the beginning of human life, and one *then* concludes that in all likelihood it is the same point at which God ensouls the fetus.[17] That the Church's position has been so formed is evidenced by its shift since the Middle Ages, in response to altered scientific understanding, over when God ensouls the fetus and when human life begins.[18] On this so far simplified view, when God ensouls the fetus may have special religious significance, but the determination when this occurs is effectively dependent on a prior determination when the fetus warrants moral consideration. Thus the religious perspective does not actually affect resolution of the moral and legal problem.

On deeper examination, however, one can understand that the religious perspective is not wholly passive and dependent in this inquiry. The very notion that at a specific time God gives each human a soul may influence someone to look for a critical either–or point, a point at which a shift takes place from virtually no moral status to moral status equivalent to that of a full human being. The ensoulment notion itself is relatively inhospitable to a gradualist or multistage approach to the moral status of the fetus.

Relatedly, when considered with an absolute proscription on the taking of human life, the ensoulment idea is unfavorable to the claim that the pregnant woman's interests override those of the fetus. Not only does it make it harder to say that the fetus with *some* worth has less inherent worth than that of a human being after birth, it tends to undercut the attractiveness of the argument that the woman may extinguish the fetus in "defense" of her own body. The religious moralities with which we are familiar are more duty-based than right-based, and not impairing innocent life is one of the most stringent duties. No one doubts that the fetus is without moral guilt and finding "innocent aggression" in the natural process of fetal growth is especially difficult if one has decided that ensoulment takes place at a very early point in that process. Thus, even if the point of ensoulment is decided on the basis of purely naturalistic reasoning, the whole perspective that surrounds that notion will subtly influence how the moral status of the fetus and the permissibility of abortion are regarded.

Among Protestants and Jews, moral evaluations of abortion vary widely. Although some Protestants and some Jews believe a definite conclusion can be extracted from religiously authoritative materials, a more common approach is to consider abortion in light of more general religious under-standings about God, human nature, and ethical demands.[19]

To demand that many devout Catholics, Protestants, and Jews pluck out their religious convictions is to ask them how they would think about a critical moral problem if they started from scratch, disregarding what they presently take as basic premises of moral thought. Asking that people perform this exercise is not only unrealistic in the sense of impossible; the implicit demand that people try to compartmentalize beliefs that constitute some kind of unity in their approach to life is positively objectionable.

It remains here to make some brief comment on the fact that discussion about many political issues, including animal rights, is generally carried on in publicly accessible terms. What this shows in part is that the interweav-ing of bases for judgment that are not publicly accessible and those that are renders it possible for people to talk to each other in shared terms. It might be said that discourse in publicly accessible terms shows that the role of other bases for evaluation is relatively small. Such a conclusion is false, however, and its falseness is exemplified by the critical role of highly personal feelings in the formulation of people's positions on animal rights. Arguments may be formulated in reasoned terms, but personal intuitive sense largely determines which arguments people accept.

The fact of discourse in publicly accessible terms might be said to show that people can *try* to decide issues on the basis of publicly accessible reasons and to support the claim that they should conscientiously aim to decide on those reasons alone. Were this recommendation widely accepted, the result would be that many or most people would proceed pretty much as they do now, but citizens who have more than average self-awareness would engage in a psychologically taxing effort to discount all bases for judgment not sustainable on publicly accessible grounds. The suggestion that such a demand should be placed on citizens is subject to rejection for all the reasons I have indicated, including the inherent interrelatedness of many publicly accessible reasons with other bases for judgment.

A rather different response might be made to the supposition that dialogue takes place in publicly accessible terms, a response that concedes everything I have so far argued. On this view, it is precisely such dialogue that the liberal theorist can reasonably demand, not that people purge, or try strenuously to purge, other elements from their own political judgments. This substantive position turns out to be one I largely endorse, as Chapter 12 in particular reflects. The position might be offered not only as correct in itself but as what a sympathetic reading of liberal theorists like Rawls and Ackerman would suggest. It is certainly true that the nature of public discussion has a great deal to do with their arguments against reliance on personal ideas of the good and religious convictions. I have indicated in Chapter 4 my belief that their theories reach further, to the legitimate bases of political decisions by citizens; but if I am wrong about this, then their views are less far from my own than I suppose.

Religious Convictions and "Personal" Bases of Decision

Although I have concentrated mainly on comparing religious convictions with publicly accessible reasons, I have assumed that were a critical line to be drawn, it would be between, on the one hand, shared premises of liberal democracy (and perhaps other shared fundamental premises) plus publicly accessible reasons and, on the other hand, other bases of judgment, including both religious convictions and more personal idiosyncratic bases of decisions. All these latter bases of judgment would be illegitimate; only the fundamental shared premises and accessible reasons would constitute appropriate grounds for political decisions. That construction comes closest to the line that Rawls, Ackerman, Lyons, and Henkin suppose or imply.

In this section, I explore the question whether a relevant distinction can be drawn between religious convictions and what I shall call personal bases of judgment, a distinction that would render reliance on the former improper even if reliance on the latter is not. To understand this issue, it is necessary to repair briefly to points made in Chapters 3 and 4. I treat religion as having to do with beliefs or institutional embodiments that involve a number of the features of traditional religions; I do not count every moral judgment or even every ultimate value judgment as implicitly religious. Thus, in this conceptual framework there lies room for personal nonreligious moral judgments. What I am calling personal bases for decision are bases that cannot be justified, in the force they are given, in terms of publicly accessible reasons. These bases would include personal perceptions, intuitions, feelings, and commitments, and deferences to the judgments of others that cannot be defended by persuasive reasons of interpersonal force of the sort explained in Chapter 4. If a vegetarian says, "My feelings about this aren't religious and I realize more steers and cows are alive because people eat beef, but I just have a strong sense that killing animals to eat them is wrong,'' then he relies on such a personal basis of judgment.

I have already stated the powerful argument for not favoring personal bases of judgment over religious convictions. By definition, those judgments are not fully susceptible to critical appraisal and public discourse. Unless a society was actually hostile to religion or riven by religious strife, how could it be thought preferable for people to rely on nonreligious personal judgments rather than upon religious convictions? The basic argument in favor of equality here is strengthened by two relationships between religio s and personal bases of judgment.

Significantly, today's nonreligious personal premises are often yesterday's religious convictions. It has been suggested that Christianity was largely responsible for development of the idea that newborn babies were entitled to have their lives protected.[20] Whether or not that is true, it certainly is true in our country, which has a rich religious tradition, and traces its cultural roots to a broader civilization in which religion has been a major element, that even positions that are not consciously religious are often deeply influenced by religion.[21] This happens for individuals when persons with a religious upbringing abandon religious belief and practice but still make many personal judgments of value in terms that comport with their religious training, especially when they do not identify the particular value judgment as tightly linked to their abandoned convictions. This kind of residual effect also operates in a broader cultural way when premises once seen to rest on religious bases come to be viewed as axiomatic truths not derived from any outside source. Neither a liberal nor any other political view could plausibly purport to eradicate the role of all such premises in the determination of social policy. It would be anomalous to treat such premises as legitimately playing a role only when an individual consciously does not hold them on religious grounds or when their religious roots have receded far enough into the past so that for most people these roots are no longer recognized as the cause of present presuppositions.

A closely related point concerns the unrealism of a principle that would exclude religious convictions but not personal bases of judgment. I have suggested that it would usually be very difficult for the conscientious liberal citizen who has religious beliefs that bear on a political decision to disentangle the threads of religious convictions and publicly accessible beliefs, even when the two are separable in theory. But however hard that will be, it will be much harder to say what publicly accessible reasons *plus* personal bases of decisions would suggest if religious beliefs were disregarded. On most questions, a religious person does not have a set of personal intuitions and feelings detached from his religious beliefs,[22] and he will be incapable of putting those beliefs out of his mind while he considers what his personal sense would be in their absence. A line of legitimacy that distinguishes between religious and personal bases of judgment would ordinarily be wholly incapable of application by religious persons.

Despite these formidable objections, the notion of excluding religious convictions in particular remains attractive to some people. We can imagine two sorts of arguments, based on what I call inherent differences and political differences, for treating religious convictions less favorably than personal bases for judgment. What I mean by inherent differences are ones that relate to the essential nature of the grounds themselves and that show that reliance on religious convictions is less compatible with liberal democratic premises than reliance on personal bases of judgment. By political differences, I refer to the actual effect on the political process of reliance on religious convictions and personal bases of judgment.

Claims of inherent differences concern externality versus internality, and rigidity versus flexible openness to publicly accessible reasons. The typical religious argument relies to some degree on outside authority; a personal basis for decision comes from the character and experience of the person. Now, the first thing to be said about this proposed distinction is that it is overblown. A religious person who thinks that he is inspired by prayer may not evolve his ethical views very differently from someone who is committed to meditation as a nonreligious source of understanding; the Christian who forms ethical judgments in light of self-sacrificing love may not go about reaching judgments very differently from someone who has decided on nonreligious grounds to live for the sake of others. Even in terms of how a judgment is characterized, the distinction may not be sharp. A nonreligious judgment, as well as a religious one, may be felt to be "compelled" by some moral order outside oneself.

In any event, the critical point here is that whatever may be true about liberalism as an overall philosophic point of view, liberal democracy has never been assumed to rest on a rejection of all outside authority for moral judgments. Indeed, even the most rationalist of our forebears assumed that a Divine Being of some kind stood behind the moral order. The simple fact that religious convictions are typically thought to rest on outside authority in some sense is not in itself a basis for disqualification.

The more dominant worry is that religious convictions are more rigid than personal bases of judgment, effectively foreclosing the possibility of effective discourse and changes of mind in response to publicly accessible reasons. The idea roughly is that someone who begins with a strong personal sense on a moral question can be persuaded out of it with good arguments but that the person with a sense of a religious answer is beyond persuasion. Again, the distinction is considerably overblown. Some people whose feelings lead them to strong personal premises are really not open to contrary arguments, but what is critical for our purposes is that many people with religious convictions that bear on ethical issues have by no means foreclosed the relevance of ordinary arguments. I shall provide two examples in the context of abortion. Suppose that someone who believes in God and ensoulment thinks that the time at which the fetus acquires moral status depends on naturalistic reasons. Such a person may be influenced by his religious perspective but open to the force of every relevant naturalistic argument. And this may remain true even if he gives some independent weight to authoritative church statements, so long as he does not take those statements as definitively closing inquiry or dictating his present political position. Suppose that a Methodist believes that the basic ethical message of the New Testament is that we should show loving and sacrificial concern for others. The Methodist may be relatively unsympathetic to arguments that the abstract moral rights of pregnant women would justify the killing of beings that are or may be innocent persons, but the Methodist may not suppose that his religious perspective provides much help at all on the question when fetuses attain personhood. Further, his thought about a proper political resolution can be deeply affected by increased understanding of the tragic situations in which many women with unwanted pregnancies find themselves. In short, as Chapter 3 shows, on many religious views and many social issues, the ways in which religious belief influences judgment is much more subtle and complex than "I know X is wrong because scripture (or the Pope) explicitly tells me so."

It may be that, in gross, religious convictions leave less room for further reasoning than personal bases of judgment, but if the worry is openmindedness and sensitivity to publicly accessible reasons, drawing a sharp distinction between religious convictions and personal bases would be an extremely crude tool. (In Chapter 11, I discuss the possible exclusion of religious and other personal bases for decision that actually conflict in some important way with publicly accessible reasons.)

The political arguments for excluding reliance on religious convictions bear some relation to those just discussed. Because of relative rigidity and notions of external authority, but also because of the institutional organization of religious groups and the importance to people of their religious convictions, reliance on religious convictions may seem to pose a more serious threat to a liberal democratic polity than reliance on personal bases of judgment. Of course, one can imagine organization of political positions along the lines of personal nonreligious bases of judgment, but such organization is less likely to arise or continue than organization centered around religious beliefs. History affords ample illustrations of division along religious lines and of minorities feeling excluded by dominant religious groups. Still, as with concerns about the inherent nature of religious convictions, the connection between the political worry and all reliance on religious conviction is not very tight. Imagine someone who considers himself a Christian but who is not presently a member of any church, who believes that his general Christian perspective should inform his judgments on ethical and political issues, but who thinks that this perspective sets only the most general kinds of ethical directives. That person's reliance on religious convictions hardly threatens the quality of liberal politics more than the reliance of others on personal bases.

Assessment of the political argument for exclusion of religious convictions involves different stages of evaluation. The first stage involves a generalized assessment of the dangers of reliance on religious convictions against the psychological costs and unfairness of people conscientiously forgoing reliance. If the dangers are deemed great enough to warrant a principle of exclusion, then thought would need to be given to the relevant categorization for that purpose: should all kinds of religious convictions be excluded or only some? In making both sorts of evaluative inquiries, one might consider not only which principles would be soundest if faithfully followed, but also which principles would actually produce the best consequences if imperfectly followed.

The first stage of evaluation calls for an overall historical and sociological inquiry. I shall not attempt to make that here. I shall simply say that in this society religious divisiveness has occasionally been a serious problem, but not one that has overwhelmed the capacity of the society to work. It has never been widely assumed that religious convictions are impermissible grounds for political decisions. The dangers of religious divisiveness that do exist can be largely countered by firm adherence to principles of religious liberty, nonsponsorship, and separation of religious and political authority. Given all the strong arguments for not preferring other personal bases of decision to religious convictions, any general principle of nonreliance on religious convictions would be much too drastic a remedy for worries about the stability and fairness of the political process. Those worries are genuine, however, and more moderate recommendations about a constrained commitment to publicly accessible reasons in Chapter 11 and about public dialogue and the activities of religious leaders in Chapter 12 are in response to them.

If one reaches a conclusion contrary to mine at the initial stage of evaluation, and thinks that reliance on religious convictions poses such a threat to liberal political processes that their exclusion may be justified, one then faces the decision whether only reliances that are actually or potentially threatening are to be excluded on principle or whether all reliance on religious convictions should be considered improper. I shall not undertake this effort to determine whether some religious convictions might escape an otherwise general exclusion since I reject such an exclusion in the first place.

An evaluation that shifts from the import of principles faithfully followed to the actual political effect of advocated principles[23] is more troubling for me. Suppose someone said the following: "We all know that reliance on religious convictions will continue, but if it is actually approved or deemed permissible as a matter of liberal political philosophy, its extent will increase and many people will close their minds on issues. If we stand firmly behind a recommended principle of *nonreliance* on religious convictions, the result will be some desirable reduction in present reliance and increase in openmindedness." This proposal for evaluation, which calls on us to consider the actual effect of moral and political principles, raises deep questions about the nature of moral judgment and of an effort such as my own in this book.

The basic claim for adhering to a more sweeping principle than seems justified is easy to exemplify: Parents who thought it was really all right for a teenager to drink moderately might decide, given the child's need to assert his independence and peer pressure, that what would work best toward this end would be a parental injunction not to drink at all.[24] Such a determination by the parents would have to involve some estimate of the likely effect of alternative parental statements in respect to drinking and also some evaluation of the moral propriety, perhaps including the long term indirect effect on relations of the parents and child, of misrepresenting the parents' honest actual view of what the child should really do. Of course, the factual components of such an inquiry are of infinitely greater complexity if one asks what the effect of a general recommendation not to rely on religious convictions would be, and the normative issue concerning the integrity and honesty of the recommender may vary depending on someone's role. An author writing a work such as this, for example, would have to decide whether he should disclose that the best argument for a principle of nonreliance on religious convictions is that it will yield desirably moderate reliance.

Though I mention it here, for the most part I disregard this perspective of evaluation in the book, simply assuming that the principles that should be recommended are those that would be just and desirable if widely followed. In part, my reason is that in this area the factual foundations for recommending other principles are so uncertain. In part the reason is that my own effort, like most academic efforts, is mainly to clarify what is stake, not to engage in moral and political advocacy. My task, as I see it, is to explore the implications and fairness of possible principles, not to guess about the likely consequences of weak adherence to them or to urge principles that I believe are inherently not defensible because I think their actual effects might be beneficial.

Guidance from Religious Roots of General Moral Judgments Contrasted with Explicit Reliance on Religious Convictions About Particular Moral Issues

Someone who recognizes the deep influence of religious ideas on our moral heritage may acknowledge that the notion of extirpating all religious sources of political judgment is neither realistic nor appropriate. But he may draw some distinction between the operation of religious ideas at the level of fundamental moral foundations and their use in respect to particular moral issues.[25] This proposal has some immediate appeal, but on closer examination it is not quite clear what distinction is meant to be crucial. I shall briefly consider some alternatives in turn and respond to them.

One possibility is that religious convictions should play a role only if not consciously relied upon. People whose religious convictions somehow influence their assessment of publicly accessible reasons or their personal intuitions in ways they do not understand would be on safe ground, but no one would be permitted consciously to let religious convictions determine his or her political decisions. Such a proposal seems inapt for an obvious reason. If reliance on religious convictions is really improper, religious believers should make at least minimal efforts to identify their place and respond accordingly. Otherwise unreflective persons could blithely continue to rely on grounds barred to those who think more seriously. Political principles should not contain such incentives to unreflectiveness, and the "reward" given to the unreflective would be unfair.

A second possibility is that what is critical is whether the implications of the religious convictions are now rooted in common morality. If so, reliance on them would be warranted, whether conscious or not; if not, reliance would be inappropriate. I shall not pause to consider this possibility here because I consider in the next section a possibility that is nearly equivalent, namely that reliance on religious convictions is proper only if the moral positions they yield are supported by a consensus.

A third possibility is that the generality of the moral judgment produced by the religious conviction is somehow crucial, that reliance on a religious conviction that love is the ultimate ethical demand is all right but reliance on a conviction that abortion is wrong is not. Assuming that the *basis* for the religious conviction is similar in both instances, say an understanding of scripture or an authoritative church statement, the proposed distinction suffers two obvious defects. One is the virtual impossibility of identifying any appropriate level of generality that would make reliance appropriate. What, for example, of the view that the welfare of the poor is an important objective or that intentional killing of innocent persons is always wrong? The more important defect, however, is that there is simply no reason why, by itself, generality should be particularly important. The fact that a religious conviction broadly reaches many subjects is hardly, standing alone, a reason why reliance on it would be appropriate if reliance on a conviction with narrower import is not.

The fourth possibility is that the real distinction lies between convictions that connect to publicly accessible reasons and convictions that are essentially independent of those reasons, the idea being that when someone's convictions are related to accessible reasons, he is open to counterpersuasion cast in terms of such reasons. A distinction along these lines would do much to meet the concerns about rigidity and narrowmindedness discussed above. Here the practical significance of the generality of the moral import of the convictions reveals itself. A highly general perspective, like the love ethic, is not likely to foreclose the impact of publicly accessible arguments; indeed its application will probably demand consideration of many such arguments. A detailed prescription on a particular subject may leave much less room for such appeals. Whether liberal democratic premises should be understood to require that any religious convictions connect significantly to publicly accessible reasons is one of the most troubling problems for my analysis; I take up that subject in Chapter 11. If that is the essential point about foreclosing reliance on religious convictions that yield particular moral judgments, the question raised is an important one.

I now turn to the other plausible interpretation of a principle that would permit reliance on religious convictions that influence fundamental moral premises: the idea that judgments supported by a present consensus are appropriate subjects of reliance.

Judgments Based on Religious Convictions or Personal Bases That Are Supported by Consensus

One possible position in this discussion is that political decisions must either be made on the basis of publicly accessible reasons or on the basis of consensus. In that event, individuals could rely on religious convictions or personal bases of judgment so long as the moral premises they embrace or the particular positions they yield are generally accepted.[26] We have, of course, been supposing since Chapter 4 that a position that citizens should rely on publicly accessible reasons would also admit reliance on basic democratic premises, even if in some sense these reach beyond reason. Here, the idea is that if a consensus supports other fundamental moral premises or narrower value judgments, such as the assumption that at least from birth one is entitled to the protections of a full human being, then such premises or judgments may properly be relied on for political decisions. Though in his important lecture at Notre Dame, Governor Cuomo's arguments for a permissive abortion law were mostly ones of political prudence, he also said: "Our public morality, then—the moral standards we maintain for everyone, not just the ones we insist on in our private lives—depends on a consensus view of right and wrong. The values derived from religious belief will not—and should not—be accepted as part of the public morality unless they are shared by the pluralistic community at large, by consensus."[27] On this view, judgments not themselves grounded in accessible reasons could be relied upon, but only if they were very widely shared. A similar suggestion is offered by Frederick Jaffe, who says: "Both the First Amendment and a public policy of pluralism bar enactment of beliefs that are *predominantly* religious when an overwhelming consensus does not support those beliefs. . . . When there are irreconcilable differences on issues of morality it is impermissible in a pluralist society—legally or as a matter of prudent policy—for legislatures to enact into law one set of beliefs and impose them on those who conscientiously believe otherwise."[28]

An initial clarification is needed about the implications of the consensus view. Is the point that no one should restrict another's liberty except on the basis of consensus or that no one should try to change the law except on the basis of consensus? The latter view plainly places too much weight on what the law presently says when no consensus exists either way. It cannot be right that if a consensus must initially support a ban on factory farming, a contrary consensus must exist before repeal is warranted. Thus, we may take the position as one that concerns permissible restrictions of liberty. The claim is that a person's liberty should not be restricted unless the basis for that restriction is fully supportable by publicly accessible reasons or rests on a consensus about the values at stake.

The main interest of the consensus approach lies in its claim that actions of certain kinds are improper when a consensus is lacking. Its difficulties concern the meaning and significance of consensus or its absence. One reason why it is hard to give content to the idea that political positions must rest on a consensus is because so much depends on the particular way in which the relevant ideas are cast. Let us assume that publicly accessible reasons cannot establish how much consideration animals are owed. Suppose that Jennifer favors a legal ban on certain forms of factory farming. Her position might be cast as an attempt to give specific application to an already existing consensus that animals should not be made miserable to serve marginal human interests. In that event her disagreement with others appears to be over the implications of shared values, and we have been assuming that in such circumstances an individual properly promotes the position he thinks right although he is presently in a minority. On the other hand, Jennifer's position could also be cast as opposed to an overwhelmingly accepted, more narrow, view that factory farming does not amount to improper behavior toward animals. Finally, Jennifer's position might be understood as not endorsed or rejected by any existing consensus, since the relatively few people who are made fully aware of the facts of factory farming, and do not have a strong economic interest in its continuance, are deeply troubled over whether it is proper. What we may have, more precisely, is more than one statable consensus; numerous consensuses may be cast, and they may be at different levels of generality and in terms of differential degrees of aquaintance with the facts.[29]

The consensus approach also leaves a gaping hole for critical issues for which no present consensus exists. Must opponents of factory farming or abortion decline to try to change the law until, and unless, they are supported by consensus, say the views of 95 percent of the population? That is not how liberal democracy does, or should, work. The manner in which shared social views develop over time is by citizens pressing positions that are not initially shared by a majority.

The problem is not just a matter of when individual citizens should feel free to press political objectives; it also concerns when they are justified in overriding those who oppose them. When people perceive that some humans are being grossly imposed upon, it is unreasonable to expect them to await a consensus before seeking protection of the innocent victims. One need think only of slavery and racial discrimination in employment as apt examples. If 70 percent of the population regards these practices as vicious wrongs, they are plainly warranted in prohibiting anyone from engaging in the practice. The way that opponents of abortion understand that practice is not so different.

I do not mean to suggest that in a liberal democracy restrictive legislation against a practice is proper when only a minuscule proportion of the population holds the (correct) moral view supporting restriction, but in a liberal democracy those who do hold such a view can suppose they will not be successful in achieving legislation unless their position enjoys substantial support. When they perceive the legislative choice as whether to protect innocent beings with a moral status like that of full human beings, they need not await near universal adoption of their position before imposing on those who disagree. It would represent an unacceptable cramping of democratic processes to suggest that no political position should be taken unless it presently rests on a consensus or can be established by publicly accessible reasons.

The Possible Priority of Claims Fully Grounded in Publicly Accessible Reasons

I have thus far considered and rejected arguments that religious convictions should be excluded as bases for political judgment because grounds based in publicly accessible reasons should always be determinative, because personal bases of decision should be preferred to religious ones, or because personal and religious grounds should count only if based on a consensus. In the discussion that follows, I assume that religious convictions and personal bases should sometimes count. I ask whether, when two claims conflict, a claim grounded fully in publicly accessible reasons should take priority. What do I mean by a claim grounded fully in publicly accessible reasons? Ordinary notions of liberty establish that if a woman must carry an unwanted fetus to term, that is a significant restriction of her liberty; ordinary notions of satisfying preferences establish that if many people like to eat meat, that is *a* reason for having practices that allow them to do so. Now if, contrary to what I believe, all ultimate value judgments are really beyond reason, it might be said that even these claims do not rest *fully* on commonly accessible *reasons*. But they do definitely rest on premises that are virtually universal in this society and commonly accessible reasons, and that is what matters for the purpose of this inquiry. The question to be considered is whether claims that have this kind of undeniable weight should receive priority over claims that are not unanimously accepted and whose force rests critically on the religious convictions or personal feelings of many citizens.

Put in absolute terms, the asserted priority of claims based on publicly accessible grounds is implausible. Suppose it were admitted that a regime of protection for the remnants of a species rested on a nonrational judgment about the relation of human beings to the natural environment and that the desire to kill members of this species was based on rational economic reasons.[30] Given the minimal impairment of liberty of a protective law, the judgment beyond reason should be able to prevail over the indisputable economic reason.

The hard question concerns two competing claims of roughly equal power, roughly equal power in terms of the premises each asserts. One might so view the competing claims on behalf of pregnant women and fetuses; that is, one might think a woman's claim to liberty, if sound, is roughly equal in power to the claim that the fetus should be protected, if sound. In such a situation, the argument might be that the claim based on ordinary reasons should always take priority.

When the great majority of citizens agree about priority between two competing claims, liberal democracy does not require that citizens forgo use of the law to protect a claim that rests finally on bases that are not commonly accessible against a claim that can be supported exclusively on ordinary reasons. In a liberal society in which 90 percent of the people regarded an early fetus as having the same moral status as a newborn, legal implementation of that judgment by a restrictive law would be apt even if people recognized that a woman's claim to abort could be grounded on rational arguments alone, whereas belief in the moral status of the fetus required a critical judgment beyond reason.

Whether the claim based on ordinary reasons should take priority if it is roughly equal in power and if opinion is closely divided is much more troublesome. I am inclined to reject even that notion, believing that it assigns too high a place for the products of rational analysis as opposed to deep-seated feeling, but I do see that notion as a serious competitor to my own position, a competitor that might yield a permissive approach to abortion at this stage of our society's history.

Restrictions on Liberty

An important conclusion remains to be drawn about animal rights, environmental protection, and abortion, which is implicit in much of the preceding discussion and of wider relevance.

As I indicated near the end of Chapter 6, many legal rules protecting animals and the environment will constrain the choices of those who own and use animals and parts of the environment, and some of those constrained will believe their moral rights to exploit nature for human advantage are being infringed. At least if animals are involved, a reverse choice in favor of human dominion may also be understood by some people as violating rights, the rights of the animals whose interests are wrongfully denied protection.

Society cannot avoid deciding how far to protect animals and other natural entities within its domain. Although a decision to protect does not usually work a severe imposition on those of differing view, the restraints that result when individuals properly act on their religious convictions in these matters may curb liberty in a way that some people think is unjustifiable. Despite these possibly controversial restraints, the reliance on religious convictions is appropriate, because everyone must reach beyond commonly accessible reasons, and the *nature* of the protection is of a kind that is called for in terms of rational secular objectives.

These comments provide the basis for understanding the error in the claim that reliance on religious convictions to oppose permissive abortion laws violates the principle of liberalism that the religious convictions of one segment of society should not be imposed on the rest.[31] If most people in society think that a fetus is entitled to protection for religious reasons and vote for legal protection on that ground, it is true that those who do not believe in the entitlement are restricted in their actions. But in contrast to a prohibition of homosexual acts simply because they are deemed morally wrong, the religious perspective here informs a judgment of who counts as a member of the community. Once that judgment is made, the restriction on abortion is a protection of the most obvious and vital interest, life, that members of the community have. The restriction is not different in principle[32] from the almost universally approved prohibition on infanticide.

Political Issues and Claims of the Priority of Justice

Our review of general problems concerning borderlines of status and the particular issues of abortion, animal rights, and environmental protection permits a partial assessment of the thesis that in political life shared principles *of justice* can be employed to settle political issues. Writers on this subject have tended to assume that the basic issue is whether justice can take priority over ideas of "the good," not acknowledging or paying little attention to the need for a society to resolve matters of status as well. But we have seen that people who agree on what justice to "persons" demands may disagree radically about the minimum conditions of personhood or about whether "nonpersons" must be taken into account.

The defender of the priority of justice can respond to this concern by claiming that his principles in context resolve all important questions of status. He may think this can be done by rational argument; that apparently is Ackerman's supposition about the status of the fetus and infants, though he is less confident about the status of animals.[33] I have strongly suggested the limited powers of publicly accessible reasons to resolve these issues.

Alternatively, one might suppose that in a particular culture the status questions are effectively settled and can be taken as given for purposes of a theory of justice. In our culture that is certainly not true about the fetus, and if it is presently largely true about animals, it may be less true in the future.[34]

Finally, a theorist of justice may resolve the status questions by fiat. If one understands Rawls's theory, though I do not, as excluding indirectly the moral claims on behalf of animals by setting up an original position in which beings who know they will be members of human society stake out principles from a self-interested point of view, that would be an example of settling status by fiat. There is no reason to suppose that principles *designed to serve human interests* will be fair to animals and the limitation of the original position to human beings is, without justification, arbitrary—why not imagine an original position in which the participants do not know if they will be born as humans or animals?[35]

A different response by those who assert the priority of justice would be to admit that status questions are not fully settled, but to claim that the theory of justice deals with the range of interhuman moral problems and leaves relations with animals and fetuses to another inquiry. That approach is the one I understand Rawls to take about relations with animals. But there is a big empty spot in this approach that Rawls does not apparently recognize. No doubt many political issues do not implicate these debatable questions of status, but many others do. Just legal regimes for farmers and hunters depend on the moral consideration owed animals; the proper liberty of a pregnant woman turns on the moral status of the fetus. If the reigning theory of justice does not itself resolve the borderlines of status, it is patently false that every political issue, or every political issue involving important claims of *justice among full human beings*, can be dealt with, as Rawls seems to suppose, by derivations from the basic principles of justice plus empirical knowledge and common sense. Some very important political issues will require reference to the troublesome problems of status. If social agreement *does not exist about these*, even a shared understanding about justice will be incapable of yielding answers to these political issues.

Notes

1. D. Callahan, *Abortion: Law, Choice, and Morality*, p. 13 (N.Y., MacMillan Co. 1970).

2. Id at p. 317.

3. S. Hauerwas, "Abortion and Normative Ethics," *Cross Currents*, Fall 1981, at

pp. 399, 414. The Grisez book is *Abortion: The Myths, the Realities, and the Arguments* (N.Y., Corpus Books 1970).

4. Id. at p. 405.

5. A. MacIntyre, *After Virtue*, pp. 6–8 (Notre Dame, Ind., Univ. of Notre Dame Pr. 1981).

6. Id. at p. 8.

7. In this respect the question of the status of fetuses is, as I have already indicated in Chatper 7's discussion of fear and anxiety, sharply different from otherwise similar questions about the status of persons whose intelligence, moral capacity, and ability to communicate have been lost through accident or age. One relevant inquiry about those whose capacities have faded is what effect variant practices will have on the security of persons who now have full capacities but realize that they may some day lose these capacities. Barring reincarnation, none of us will ever again be fetuses or infants, so the treatment of these beings can affect our security only in some much more indirect way.

8. See, e.g., P.E. Devine, "The Scope of the Prohibition Against Killing," in J. Feinberg, ed., The Problem of Abortion, p. 34, 2d ed. (Belmont, Calif., Wadsworth Pub. Co. 1984), on the notion of probabilism, an idea whose applications are caustically and entertainingly attacked in Pascal's Provincial Letters.

9. On abortion see G. Grisez, supra note 3, at pp. 306, 344. See also C. Curran, *Transition and Tradition in Moral Theology*, pp. 17, 190 (Notre Dame, Ind., Univ. of Notre Dame Pr. 1979), indicating that probabilism is regarded as inappropriate for instances involving danger to the life of another.

10. The qualification "in general" is important here. Suppose that Nancy and Olive live in a society in which they both recognize that 80% of the people regard fetuses as having no moral status, that a restrictive law would not be effectively enforced, and that such a law would cause great social tension. If Nancy thinks the fetus demonstrably does have the moral entitlement of a person, she might reasonably still support a restrictive law. If Olive thinks the moral entitlement uncertain, the obvious reasons in favor of a permissive law might seem dispositive. Whether acknowledgment of the uncertainty of the status of the fetus will make resolution of *any particular issue* simpler from the standpoint of publicly accessible reasons will depend considerably on relevant facts and the strength of other arguments in context.

11. It would be a conceivable position to say that citizens could employ religious convictions to choose a comprehensive overall nonreligious theory of morality, but that they would then apply that theory without further reference to religion. Such a demand would display an unwarranted preference for systematic theories against the skeptical position that they are unreliable. Further no basis appears for giving religious convictions influence only at this most abstract level of choice.

12. In his article on the duty to preserve the environment, Donald Regan, by no means sanguine about the present state of development of general moral theories, writes, "If we had a moral theory that was satisfactory, or even reasonably

satisfactory, in other respects, but that failed to account for our supposed duties of preservation, then we would have strong reason for denying those duties." D. Regan, "Duties of Preservation," in B. Norton, ed., *The Preservation of Species*, p. 216 (Princeton, N. J., Princeton Univ. Pr. 1986).

13. See, e.g., P.E. Devine, "The Scope of the Prohibition Against Killing," in Feinberg, ed., supra note 8, at pp. 21, 27.

14. Ideally the comparison of abstract principles with concrete intuitions brings about a reflective equilibrium in which a match is achieved, but people are not always fortunate enough to reach that stage.

15. James Burtchaell, in "The Sources of Conscience," *Santa Clara Magazine* (Summer 1985), at pp. 25, 27, suggests that if someone had "true convictions" about abortion, he "would be unable to say how much they derive from faith or from the unbroken Christian tradition extending back to New Testament days, or from his own verification of that teaching, or from the inadequacy of arguments to the contrary, or from other sources of conscience."

16. See generally D. Callahan, supra note 1, at pp. 409–47.

17. See, e.g., J. Noonan, "An Almost Absolute Value in History," in J. Feinberg, ed., supra note 8, at pp. 9–14 and J. Donceel, "A Liberal Catholic's View," in J. Feinberg, ed., supra note 8, at p. 15. Though the authors reach variant conclusions, both employ the methodology suggested here.

18. See generally J. Noonan, "Abortion and the Catholic Church: A Summary History," 12 *National Law Forum*, pp. 85–131 (1967).

19. See, e.g., G.W. Sheek, *A Compilation of Protestant Denominational Statements on Families and Sexuality*, pp. 94–116 (N.Y., Office of Family Ministries and Human Sexuality, National Council of Churches 1982); Klein, "Jeshuvah on Abortion," in *Conservative Judaism*, p. 47 (Fall 1959); Margolies, "A Reform Rabbi's View," in R. Hall, ed., *Abortion in a Changing World*, vol. 1, p. 30 (N.Y., Columbia Univ. Pr. 1970).

20. See P. Singer, *Practical Ethics* p. 77 (Cambridge, Cambridge Univ. Pr. 1979). See also M. Warren, "On the Moral and Legal Status of Abortion," in Feinberg, ed., supra note 8, at pp. 102, 118.

21. See, e.g., G.J. Warnock, *The Object of Morality*, p. 140 (London, Methuen & Co. 1971).

22. There will be exceptions, as when a person accepts church authority that he knows conflicts with his own personal sense on a subject.

23. Although I consider such a shift in focus of evaluation in this context, a similar shift could be proposed to defend a principle that people should rely exclusively on publicly accessible reasons or to defend one of the other possible principles I discuss.

24. On some occasions, a standard *less* demanding than what one regards as ideal behavior may work best. See, e.g., P. Singer, supra note 20, at p. 180, suggesting that advocacy of a genuinely utilitarian standard of what people should give to the needy may be counterproductive because too demanding. See also B. Williams, *Ethics and the Limits of Philosophy*, p. 106 (Cambridge, Mass., Harvard Univ. Pr.

1985), discussing Sidgwick's perception that it is an empirical question whether people's thinking about the greatest good is likely to lead to the greatest good.

25. See, e.g., L. Henkin, "Morals and the Constitution: The Sin of Obscenity," 63 *Columbia Law Review*, pp. 391, 408–11 (1963), writing on the constitutional question of establishment of religion.

26. It would be a conceivable position that a consensus could be relied upon only if it is nonreligious, but for all the reasons suggested in this chapter, including the fact that most widely held ethical beliefs in this society have religious roots, such a line between religious convictions and personal bases of judgment would not make sense. I assume that if action on a consensus of moral beliefs is otherwise appropriate, the religious roots of the consensus would not disqualify that action.

27. See M. Cuomo, "Religious Belief and Public Morality: A Catholic Governor's Perspective," 1 *Notre Dame Journal of Law, Ethics and Public Policy*, p. 13 (1984), also published in *The New York Review of Books*, Oct. 25, 1984, p. 32.

28. See F. Jaffe, "Enacting Religious Beliefs In a Pluralist Society," *Hastings Center Report*, August 1978, at pp. 14–15.

29. The difficulties here resemble some difficulties involved in assessing legislative intent.

30. I am assuming that the economic reasons for killing relate to extra profits rather than the survival of individuals or of the way of life of some cultural subgroup.

31. Roger Wertheimer talks about religious premises as "inadmissible in the court of common morality," "Understanding the Abortion Argument," in J. Feinberg, ed., supra note 8, at p. 50. Whether he means only that such premises are not a basis for argument or that they are inappropriate ones for a citizen to rely upon when an issue of public policy is involved is not clear.

32. A ban on infanticide does not, of course, impose upon anyone in anything like the same degree as a prohibition on abortion imposes on pregnant women. If, as in some earlier eras, parents had duties toward newborn children that could not be shed by putting the children in the hands of the state, the analogy between the two prohibitions would in this respect become much closer.

33. See text accompanying Chapter 6, supra note 6.

34. That is, concern about the status of animals is likely, in my judgment, to increase.

35. The same sort of theoretical problem arises as to whether those in the original position are to be born human beings or be fetuses whose lives might be terminated under a permissive abortion policy.

9

Moral Standards, Evaluative Comparisons, and Facts: Welfare Assistance and Other Issues

In the last chapter about borderlines of status, I made a claim that a good liberal citizen could properly rely on his religious convictions and I answered a number of possible objections to that claim. Here the effort is to generalize the analysis further. I try to suggest why similar considerations apply to a broader category of moral standards that bear on public policy, to evaluative comparisons of competing objectives, to standards of right individual action, and to complex factual judgments. I illustrate the themes in connection with three broad social issues, welfare assistance, punishment, and military policy, and with one narrow question of legal choice, the ambit of the general justification defense. I concentrate mainly on the question of welfare assistance, which is a critical issue of distributive justice.

Welfare Assistance

One of the most troublesome and pervasive issues in liberal societies is the extent to which those who cannot provide adequately for themselves should be assisted by the government. That issue is central to modern theories of justice, and its examination not only illumines the proper place of religious convictions, it poses a critical test for any thesis that political issues of justice can be resolved on the basis of shared premises of justice.

Welfare policies, of course, involve complicated judgments about who will be recipients, what form assistance will take, and which level of government shall provide it, but I shall oversimplify matters by talking of more and less.

Distributive and Hands-Off Approaches

Secular morality presents two rather sharp theoretical extremes about welfare, as well as intermediate possibilities. One extreme is that the government should perform only minimal functions that private organizations cannot perform, protecting people from being preyed upon by force and fraud, correcting the effects of depredations when they do occur, but otherwise leaving resources to be distributed by private ordering.[1] The animating principle behind this position is that persons have some kind of natural right to their own bodies and talents and that this right extends to free exchanges that others are willing to engage in with them. In this view, the state has no responsibility to improve the lot of those whose laziness or incapacity leaves them poor. The opposite extreme is that, as the collective organization of the entire society, the government is responsible for the distribution of social resources, that in order to treat all persons with equal concern and respect, it should distribute resources equally unless people generally benefit from an unequal distribution.

The basic distributive view takes many forms. Among the most familiar are the Marxist formula, "From each according to his abilities, to each according to his needs," the utilitarian principle of maximizing average or total welfare, and the suggestion of Rawls that distribution should be equal except as inequality will increase goods even for representative members of the least advantaged economic group.[2] In different respects each of these views treats all citizens as equal. For Marx, each's needs count equally; for the utilitarian, each's capacity for happiness (or some surrogate) counts equally in the search for maximum overall welfare; for Rawls, each's entitlement to resources in a fundamental sense is equal and inequalities are allowed only if everyone is made better off.

A choice among these and other distributive approaches[3] will depend on some initial premise about proper notions of human equality and upon complex judgments about human nature and actual or potential social relations. By denying the contractors in his original position knowledge of the likelihood of anyone's chances of falling into an advantaged or disadvantaged group,[4] Rawls in his *A Theory of Justice* seems almost arbitrarily to define a veil of ignorance that will yield his "difference principle,"[5] since in such circumstances a chooser would especially want to minimize the chances of his being badly off.[6] Rawls's most substantial argument in favor of the difference principle and against utilitarianism is that people will feel resentful if they find themselves badly off comparatively and live in a society in which the prevailing principle is that gains in the welfare of the better off are thought to warrant making the less well-off even worse off.[7] The "strains of commitment" will be too great to support general acceptance of the utilitarian principle. Rawls assumes that were the Marxist formula adopted, incentives to work would be sharply reduced, the economy would be much less productive, and the level of resources would be lowered for even the worst off, in comparison with a society with a market economy governed by the difference principle.

A utilitarian may respond that Rawls overestimates the resentment people would feel in a society publicly wedded to utilitarian principles; the Marxist may claim that Rawls fails to see the resentment and envy the difference principle would generate and that he underestimates the willingness of people, freed of capitalist social conditioning, to engage their talents for the good of others.

From these standpoints, the value judgments that divide Rawls from utilitarians and Marxists are largely reducible to judgments of fact about how people will respond to social orders with alternative principles of justice. A similar conclusion can be reached about what separates all the distributive positions from the hands-off position, if the latter is defended as the approach that best promotes economic productivity and human growth. Though in conception these factual questions about the effects of principles of justice operating in society may ultimately be resolvable by publicly accessible, or rational, criteria, the relevant factual inquiries are extremely complex and their answers depend on counterfactual judgments that no sensible person can be confident about.[8] In competition are subtly different understandings of the springs of human motivation in variant and unrealized social orders.

Bases for Complex Factual Judgments

When a citizen's judgment about proper distributive theory or its applications depends on complex factual evaluations that cannot be proved or disapproved on the available evidence, what are legitimate sources for his determination? We might initially suppose that at least as far as facts are concerned, scientific procedures and common sense are sufficient, and these publicly accessible forms of reasoning should be relied upon exclusively by the good liberal citizen.

No doubt these forms of reasoning can demonstrate the unsoundness of extreme views; but how is the citizen to choose among plausible accounts when ordinary reasons cannot provide a solid basis for selection? A person's conclusions about likely facts in such settings will be partly determined by his personal experience, his peculiar sense of human life, and his fundamental judgments of value. In the last three chapters, in which I have urged the unwisdom of a principle that citizens should try to decide borderline questions of status exclusively on the basis of shared premises and publicly accessible reasons, I have argued that counsels of impossible perfectionism are not well suited to the standards of good citizenship, that the threads of publicly accessible reasons cannot be disentangled from religious convictions and personal bases of judgment, and that strenuous efforts to make the separation would carry psychological costs and impair people's sense of individual unity. I have also claimed that it would be unfair and impractical to disfavor religious convictions in comparison with personal bases of judgment. Essentially the same analysis applies in respect to complex factual judgments, but the context of disagreements that reduce to complicated factual appraisals is different enough from the borderlines of status to warrant independent examination.

No sensible person would deny that people are influenced by factors beyond shared forms of reasoning in reaching factual conclusions, but the thesis that good citizens should try to limit themselves to ordinary ways of determining facts, assessing the balance of evidence as they best can, is more appealing than any analogous thesis about issues that are irreducibly normative. Perhaps, in theory, if human beings were given full enough information that they were capable of storing and digesting, they could arrive at agreed-upon correct answers to factual issues that bear on practical political choices; but if much of the relevant information is never forthcoming, and human capacities to hold and process information fall far short of what is needed, even the people who devote a great deal of attention to particular complex questions of fact may fail to reach confident answers for whose soundness they can convincingly argue. Actual people, including those who are best informed, will inevitably rely on other assumptions to close gaps.

We can identify three major objections to any principle that citizens should debar themselves from relying to any extent on religious convictions in making factual judgments for political purposes. The first is the most obvious: that if ordinary reasons are seriously inconclusive, people should be permitted sources of insight that they believe improve the chances for accurate and confident judgment, unless a powerful argument exists for excluding those sources. I have expressed strong skepticism that any such argument exists for excluding religious convictions in general. If some policy decision depends on what the world will probably be like two centuries from now, and everyone agrees that the present ascertainable facts yield only highly uncertain predictions,[9] there is good reason for thinking that citizens should be able to rely on what they regard as the most secure sources.

The other two objections to excluding religious convictions focus on difficulties in carrying out any program that recommends exclusive reliance on publicly accessible reasons. The first difficulty concerns the impossibility of knowing when the force of publicly accessible reasons runs out; the second difficulty involves the embedding of those reasons in debatable perspectives. Both kinds of difficulties will have a familiar ring because my discussion draws from points made earlier. I shall use as my main illustration here the factual thesis that people are irreducibly selfish: that different forms of social training, or techniques of common production, or a more equalitarian class structure would not make people basically unselfish. (Were such a factual thesis to be debated seriously, much more conceptual precision would be required, but this sketch of an idea adequately serves my illustrative purposes.)

Suppose that Janice is deciding whether to support a political movement urging a Marxist principle of distribution, and she thinks the critical issue is whether people are irreducibly selfish. She has surveyed some of the relevant literature in psychology and social science, has reflected on her own personal experience, has weighed the judgments of other people she respects, and has considered the relevance of her religious perspective. Insofar as she independently understands and assesses the empirical literature and can formulate her assessment of it in publicly accessible terms, her reliance on that literature is clearly within the range of publicly accessible reasons. But, as Chapter 4 powerfully indicates, she cannot be told to stop there. To some extent, she will have digested her own personal experience and be able to formulate it in publicly accessible reasons. If, for example, she feels that a strong element of selfishness is a powerful component of her identity, if she has witnessed a lot of selfish behavior by other people, and if she has found that in roughly similar situations people she knows in Marxist societies are about as selfish as those in capitalist ones, this all amounts to some modest and inconclusive but explicable evidence for the thesis that selfishness cannot be eradicated. What Chapter 4 indicates, especially with its discussion of the intuitive insights of the lawyer and the person who recognizes another's voice, is that people often know more that is actually defensible in terms of publicly accessible reasons than they can at that moment explain in those terms. Presumably Janice should not be denied the fruits of understanding based on experiences that *could be translated* into forcible public reasons even if she is now unable to make the translation. But if this is admitted, it will be impossible to deny her the force of personal experience that is more idiosyncratic. If Janice is not in a position fully to explain and defend her sense of her experience, she will not be in a position to know how much of it is publicly defensible and how much depends on her own subjective reactions that would not be shared by others. If she has relevant religious convictions, these, of course, are bound to affect her sense of her experience, as well as her sense of the weight of the obviously relevant external evidence.

Chapters 3 and 4 indicate that people making political judgments can properly rely on authority. The role of authority is much more obvious for facts than for value judgments, because many factual questions are highly complex and the differences in levels of understanding are usually easily identifiable. No one is capable of mastering a wide range of factual issues with a high degree of confidence, and comparatively few people may be capable of mastering some particular issues.[10] Certainly in assessing the social science literature, Janice is warranted in giving some weight to an author's reputation as an expert, even if to her untutored eye his arguments seem no more powerful than those of someone widely dismissed as shallow.

Unfortunately on most critical and debated factual judgments, the ordinary citizen, with limited time and energy, is hard put to know on which authority to rely, since those with special competence to appraise the facts themselves disagree. What are the likely effects of large budget deficits. Will preferential hiring of minorities increase or reduce racial hostility? Those who are best qualified and think hardest about these problems disagree sharply and only arrogance or deceit permits any of them to speak with assurance.

When complex factual questions are critical, people almost inevitably end up accepting the account of the facts adopted by people they know and like or with whom they are in general political sympathy. How many people, for example, who have views on whether civilian nuclear power is justified in light of its risks have themselves either formed a considered judgment about the risks in light of available factual information or made a solidly grounded rational judgment about whose opinion can be relied upon? We may wish for a society in which all citizens could sensibly form judgments about relevant factual questions, but that wish is a wish for a golden age in which all were on a roughly equal footing of relative ignorance. In a modern society, on troublesome issues we must expect that most people most of the time, conscientious citizens as well as lazy ones, will have to rely on factual judgments of others and will lack even the basis for deciding in a considered way whose judgments are trustworthy. The practically insurmountable confusion that overwhelms most citizens when considering complex factual questions leads them to find their factual authorities for critical political decisions on grounds that they would find hard or impossible to justify fully on publicly accessible grounds.

No doubt a distinction exists between accepting someone as a factual authority on nonreligious grounds and accepting a written text, religious leaders, or the church community as factual authorities because of religious premises. In practice, however, the distinction is thin. Religious perspectives, as I have said, typically include a comprehensive picture of the universe and people's place in it. Some factual elements of the perspective, say human selfishness, will seem confirmed by objective facts that are independently ascertainable.[11] Other factual elements may seem correct because they are linked to establishable facts in an account with intrinsic coherency, a coherency one might uncontroversially find in the best works of history and social science. Still other factual elements may seem plausible only because of particular beliefs about religious truth. A person's belief in many particular factual elements may draw support from all three sorts of bases, that is, direct objective confirmation, linkage with other objectively supported truths, and religious faith; a believer will usually draw no neat lines among the grounds for belief in these factual elements.

Similar difficulties of separation arise in connection with reliance on more personal authority. People's factual judgments are influenced by those with whom they have closest contact, including associates at work. If it is all right for Janice to say self-consciously, "I really don't know what version of the facts is correct so I am going along with the judgments of my close associates," then similarly she might defer to those she happens to be associated with at church. Were reliance on religious grounds disqualified, Janice would have to disregard the judgments of fellow members insofar as they rested on religious premises, and she could not give the judgments special weight because she is joined with the other members in a religious community. But Janice would be hard put to pinpoint the source of judgments of fellow members or to distinguish deference that follows from personal affection and general respect from deference to those she thinks possessed of special *religious* insight. The artificiality of such an attempt helps confirm the more fundamental conclusion that liberal democracy does not preclude some reliance on religious authorities as sources of factual insight.

I have talked so far as if religious convictions and personal bases are sources of judgment parallel to publicly accessible reasons and the basic problem is disentangling the various elements. But, as the discussion of abortion indicates most fully in respect to borderlines of status, the problem is still deeper. One approaches evidence and reasoned argument about facts with certain dispositions. A person who initially thinks that human

beings are irreducibly selfish will approach the scientific literature differently from someone who holds out greater hopes for socialization. Thus,
the second major difficulty with any program to preclude reliance on
religious convictions or personal bases of judgment is that a person who
tried to extirpate these sources of insight would be left to decide factual
questions without the fundamental framework with which he ordinarily
approaches such questions. He will have difficulty deciding what to put in
its place.

When we begin to understand just how difficult it would be for the
religious person to try for political purposes to decide factual questions
without reference to his religious convictions, our sense that such a
principle would be unfair and is not entailed by premises of liberal democracy is strengthened.

Were this conclusion challenged as at odds with our country's basic
traditions, the short answer is that the enlightenment philosophy that all
social questions can be resolved without reference to transcendent sources
of truth has never enjoyed general acceptance.[12] The theory that citizens
should divorce religious convictions from social assessments exceeds any
widely agreed upon idea of the separation of politics and religion, and the
proposed divorce is one that has been implicitly rejected over and over
again in countless American pulpits over the last three and a half centuries.

Any worry about the divisiveness of reliance on religious convictions for
factual determinations is met tolerably well by recognition that, throughout
the history of this country, many religious people and their leaders have
self-consciously viewed social facts through the prism of their religious
insights, and that has not proved a source of irrevocable social division.

A more serious concern, closely related to one explored in Chapter 8, is
that religious perspectives encourage disregard of ordinary factual evidence
and rational argument, which constitute the shared bases of factual appraisal in the society. If one believes scripture is inerrant and that scripture
provides an unambiguous answer to a factual question, one may perceive
little need to look further. In Chapter 11, I treat the perplexing problem of
reliance on religious conviction that in some manner contradicts common
forms of reasoning. Here it is enough to note that the major religious
traditions in the United States have never supposed that religious authority
provides fixed answers to the immensely subtle questions of social fact that
bear upon serious choices about public policy. Because certain fringe
religious views may actually be inhospitable to some ordinary examinations
of the facts is hardly a reason to prefer all nonreligious convictions to
religious convictions as sources of factual insight when ordinary evidence
and publicly accessible arguments are inconclusive.

Normative Alternatives

The fairly general analysis of complex factual questions just undertaken began with the possibility that competing positions about principles of distributive justice might be reducible to factual disagreements; but competing positions may instead, or in addition, differ over ultimate normative premises. The point can be seen most clearly if the hands-off position, that people are entitled to the fruits of their talents, is defended in a manner that does not challenge the factual premises of a distributive position. The defender of moral entitlement may concede that overall welfare might be higher were a distributive theory adopted but argue that other people simply do not have the moral right to treat the fruits of one's talents as up for general distribution. In this event, the basic disagreement between a distributive and a hands-off approach is over ultimate categories of moral desert.[13]

Commonly accessible reasons do bear on this fundamental disagreement. A defender of a distributive position may appeal to the social character of human beings and to the ways our very talents depend on social benefits. The extreme advocate of moral entitlement can rely on the premise that each person's mind and body is one's own in an important moral sense and argue that to view each person as having a right to all or part of the fruits of one's talents is a sensible extension of this basic right to one's person.

If compelled to choose between the most appealing version of a distributive view and the extreme hands-off position, most people would prefer the former, finding the implications of the latter too harsh to swallow. Publicly accessible reasons powerfully suggest that "hands-off" should not be a practical standard for public policy. In light of the state's unique capacity to coordinate, the idea that the state simply has *no* responsibility to care for those who would lack food and shelter if left to private ordering is in tension with ordinary moral standards concerning reciprocal support. Though the hands-off position does treat people equally in the sense that all are equally privileged to acquire resources by voluntary transfers, the conception of equality is too negative given the social character of human beings. Moreover, unless past wrongs are to be rewarded, the practical significance of the hands-off view should take hold only if an initial just distribution of assets is achieved, and how that could be accomplished is not clear.

Though the hands-off view is unappealing in its pure form, *some* moral right to the fruits of talents has much more attraction as a reason for settling between the two extremes. Many people do feel that the fruits of people's talents are not *wholly* up for social distribution in the way of some common benefit that miraculously drops on society like manna from heaven. A person may believe that it requires a very strong reason to take away the fruits of someone's talents, or that, at least once the minimal needs of others are met,[14] a person is entitled by moral right to a substantial percentage of the fruits of his talents. Neither of these intermediate positions is theoretically as clean as an unqualified distributive or unqualified hands-off view, but each allows endorsement of the welfare state without disavowal of the idea that people have moral rights to the fruits of their talents.

Common reasoning cannot settle whether individuals have *any* basic moral right to the fruits of their talents and if so exactly how far that right should be curbed or qualified in the interests of general welfare. As with other issues we have examined, premises beyond public reasons must determine choices among a number of plausible competitors.

The Place of Religious Convictions

What is the role of religious convictions in the resolution of these basic issues over welfare? The Christian and Jewish traditions strongly emphasize duties to care for the less fortunate. As Jurgen Moltmann says, "From the beginning of Israel's history, Yahweh was known as the God of the poor."[15] According to Gustavo Gutierrez, the liberation theologian, the biblical tradition's preference for the poor is not "social analysis, or human compassion, or the direct experience of poverty", but God, who "loves the poor by preference, not because the poor are good persons, better than others, or good believers, better than other believers, but because God is God."[16] Though others would explain the grounds for the tradition differently, the biblical concern for the poor is incompatible with any extreme version of the hands-off position that denies private as well as state obligations to help the poor.[17] Conceivably a person within the Jewish or Christian tradition might think that private charity is the only proper way to help the poor, although such a position plainly lacks biblical warrant.[18] In any event, the consensus that an extreme hands-off position is implausible derives partly from wide acceptance of religious duties of care.

Among the distributive models, "to each according to his needs" may come closest to the Christian ideal of universal loving concern and to the actual organization of early Christian communities. A Christian perfectionist might think we should try to live our lives accordingly. On the other hand, traditional Christianity has a powerful strand of realism about the depths of human selfishness and the limits of social organization; most Christians believe that large modern political societies should be organized on principles other than gospel perfectionism. For at least some of them, a position like that of Rawls represents a reasonable compromise between an ideal of loving concern and the social reality of self-interested behavior.

The American Catholic bishops proposed in 1986 that social resources should be more equitably distributed than they are at present.[19] Some have criticized aspects of the bishops' proposals as too insensitive to the values of liberty and a market economy.[20] In this fairly contained dispute we can see the dual operation of religious conviction. On the one hand, conviction may affect judgment about what is factually possible. A person convinced that a society is basically unfair from the perspective of transcendent justice may be inclined to think that alternative principles of distribution will work effectively. Religious conviction may also affect one's value judgment if the choice between two alternative courses can be reduced to helping the poor or helping the average member of the society. A person imbued with the strong biblical sense that our first social job is to aid the disadvantaged may opt for helping the poor.

Once we understand the limits of common forms of reasoning and the subtle role of religious conviction in factual and normative judgment, we will be unlikely to say, for reasons explored in the last chapter and the previous part of this one, that liberalism somehow requires individuals to try to forego all reliance on religion in developing their positions about appropriate levels of welfare.

The Limits of Shared Principles of Justice

These comments about welfare assistance expose a deep difficulty with any view that problems of distributive justice can be addressed solely by reference to shared fundamental notions of justice plus shared grounds for reaching factual determinations. I shall concentrate here on John Rawls's extensively elaborated and highly influential theory, but what I say has much broader implications.

Were Rawls's theory dependent on the notion that one set of principles, derivable from a rational decision procedure like that of the original position, is rationally best from a transcultural perspective, my criticism would be that no unique set of principles can be established as rationally best. As Chapter 4 indicates, Rawls's writings after A Theory of Justice make clear that his more modest aspiration is to develop principles of justice that best capture the underlying premises of liberal democratic society.[21]

Recognizing that in a liberal society citizens have highly variant religious beliefs and ideas of the good, Rawls hopes to start with premises that are widely shared by people who disagree on many fundamental questions to draw out of these premises principles of justice whose acceptance allows political decisions to be made without reference to the fundamental religious and metaphysical beliefs that divide citizens. As Richard Rorty puts it in a paper aptly titled "The Priority of Democracy Over Philosophy,"[22] in which he explicates and defends Rawls's approach, our concentrating on questions of social justice will allow subjects such as the "point of human existence, the meaning of human life" appropriately to be "reserved to private life."

Contrary to what he supposes, Rawls does not provide a theoretical basis for thinking that this ambition is realizable or desirable. I have already suggested some of its limits in respect to issues that turn on controversial assignments of moral status, but the problem of welfare assistance lies much closer to the heart of Rawls's theory of justice. If his theory does not successfully permit resolution of that problem without reliance on religious and metaphysical beliefs, there will be few, if any, genuinely controversial matters as to which the relegation of these beliefs to the private sphere will be called for.

The critical question for this purpose is the status of Rawls's difference principle, that inequalities must work to the advantage of the worst-off group. Passing over the complexities of defining the worst-off group, I assume that with that principle as a guide and the facts reasonably in hand, one could settle what is a just program of welfare assistance. Why should a citizen feel constrained to accept the difference principle?

Rawls's principles of justice are based on what he takes as the "basic intuitive ideas that are embedded in the political institutions of a constitutional democratic regime and the public traditions of their interpretation."[23] The relevant troubles for Rawls's theory arise in the transformation of those shared intuitive ideas into the more precise principles of justice. Rawls supposes that "familiar intuitive ideas" can be organized by a more fundamental intuitive idea, "a system of fair social cooperation between free and equal persons."[24] The principles of justice that are developed are ones "that can serve as a basis of informed and willing political agreement between citizens viewed as free and equal persons."[25] Though Rawls tries patiently to explain the process by which these shared intuitive ideas are transformed into his more precise principles of justice, one has the feeling of missing something.

Let us suppose, as Rawls does, that the notion of "a system of fair social cooperation between free and equal persons" does organize shared intuitive ideas in a liberal society. Many of those who accept that notion think that all people have some basic moral right, however qualified, to the fruits of their talents; others accept the idea that the fruits of talents are to be distributed as is best for all. Holders of these opposing views can join in agreement on the organizing intuitive idea about fair cooperation of free and equal persons. Lawyers and politicians are familiar with the way in which agreement on some common verbal formulation can in fact obscure divergent answers to important questions, and agreement on the basic organizing idea here can unite those who have contrary views about entitlements.

The difference principle at which Rawls himself arrives takes a purely distributive view about the fruits of talents. But he presents no sound argument why someone who has begun with a contrary sense of a moral right to talents should abandon that position when practical decisions must be made about redistributive transfer payments. I shall address three possible responses to this difficulty that might be given within the context of Rawlsian theory; the last of these is the one I take to be Rawls's own.

One conceivable position is that I have simply missed the point, that Rawls's theory is about an ideal society in which people all happen to agree on the principles of justice.[26] If so, it is silly to ask why someone who may not agree should be guided by the principles. That response would both understate Rawls's ambitions and condemn his theory to irrelevance. Rawls plainly thinks that his principles of justice are the best he can now come up with for modern liberal societies.[27] Since in no society will there actually be widespread understanding of and agreement upon principles as precise and specific as those of Rawls, why someone should accept those principles must remain an important question if the theory is to have practical significance.

The second possible response is that the person with the intuitive sense that people have some moral right to the fruits of their talents is out of step with prevailing liberal notions. At least at a simple level, this response seems both factually wrong and beside the point. Probably most Americans, at least, do not presently accept an undiluted distributive view. They retain, in however qualified form, *something* of the traditional Lockean, natural rights view that people have a basic right to enjoy the benefits of their labors. Even if I am mistaken about this, people are free in a liberal society to urge shifts in prevailing conceptions and to work for political programs that are in some opposition with those conceptions. Since the promotion of such programs is a major way in which controversial ideas are presented and developed, the citizen may properly support a program that could not be justified under the difference principle, even if that principle is presently accepted by a majority. Perhaps one would have a duty to tell one's fellow citizens how far the program one supports is out of line with prevailing conceptions, but liberalism does not *freeze* any particular notion of justice or demand that all practical choices derive from it.[28]

The third possible response to the citizen who now believes in a moral right to the fruits of talents is that the pure distributive view represented by the difference principle should be accepted because it is derivable from, or fits better with, the most fundamental notions that liberal democrats, including the citizen, accept. If this showing could be made, each liberal citizen would truly have a good reason to accept the difference principle as the starting point for welfare assistance. Given the extent to which Rawls conceives his theory as involving an imaginative construction, this third response seems clearly the one he would make.[29]

That response, however, is implausible. Within the loose umbrella of the premises of liberal democracy, there is more than one rationally sustainable theory of justice. If, as Rawls acknowledges, his principles of justice cannot be shown to be *rationally superior* to certain nonliberal principles, it is unlikely that they can be shown to be *rationally superior* to every other liberal set of principles. Certainly derivation from the original position does not demonstrate the rational superiority of the distributive view over a qualified moral rights view, since the conditions of the original position already embody the distributive view.[30] Nor does the elegance and clarity of Rawls's principles establish their rational superiority. I have acknowledged that once the hands-off view is abandoned, any suitably qualified version of the moral rights position is hard to formulate; we should not reject it on that ground alone. Relevant moral considerations may be exceedingly complex and difficult to formulate, and, as I suggested in the last chapter, it is not always unreasonable to cling to deeply held intuitions that conflict with the abstract arguments one finds most convincing. Rawls does undertake a sophisticated analysis of the social psychology of human beings, and this lends some support to the difference principle, but it is highly doubtful that any psychological analysis can show the untenability of a suitably qualified view that people deserve the fruits of their talents. Insofar as Rawls rest on the simple intuition that it is morally arbitrary that people with more talent acquire more, the answer is that others have equally strong intuitions that productive free exchanges are fair. One might, of course, write off a qualified moral rights position if it was actually at odds, or did not cohere adequately, with fundamental and uncontroversial liberal assumptions or was in severe tension with the social character of people, but I do not believe either showing can be made.

When one reviews the inadequacy of each of these possible responses, one understands the difficulty of arguing that liberal citizens should unite behind a single set of principles of justice. Perhaps a more realistic view is that citizens to a large extent apply different sets of principles of justice, but ones that can largely be captured by the same general concepts and that have critical overlapping parts. When decision falls squarely within the overlapping areas, no reference outside shared principles is required; but when a matter is one for which the truly shared premises do not provide an answer, citizens will revert to their own preferred theories, including whatever religious and metaphysical convictions underlie them. Religious convictions, therefore, have an appropriate role even for some questions of distributive justice in a society that has some important shared ideas about justice.[31]

Punishment, Military Policy, and the Justification Defense

What follows in this chapter are brief comments about how the insights already suggested apply to some other public issues. With the exception of an intriguing wrinkle concerning the justification defense, no novel theoretical problems are considered, but the illustrations show how religious convictions can bear on a range of normative and factual questions.

Punishment

Typically, the desirability of various proposed regimes of punishment will depend partly on their likely effects.

> A law that would drastically increase the use of probation over imprisonment is proposed. Supporters of the measure claim that it will mitigate the harmful influence of prison as a breeding ground of hardened criminals, without significantly affecting the danger convicted offenders pose to the populance and without weakening the general deterrence of criminal prohibitions. Opponents urge that reduction in the levels of incapacitation and deterrence will work harm that outweighs any benefits of the proposed change.
>
> Richard and Sara have reviewed the relevant psychological and sociological studies of punishment and understand the substantial arguments that the greater use of probation would or would not reduce future criminal acts among convicted offenders and the general population. Richard belongs to a religious group that is extremely pessimistic about human nature, believing that human beings must in this life be largely constrained and frightened into acceptable behavior. Sara's religion teaches that people are basically good, that love and mercy can draw out the best in them. Richard's view about human nature leads him to believe that the present practices are preferable to increased probation; Sara thinks the contrary.

Richard and Sara do not introduce into the balance any new interests or values that a nonbeliever would not recognize; rather they have developed opinions about how best to serve the values accepted by all. Since they think that the policies they choose will best serve those secular values, no question of their imposing their religious convictions on nonbelievers arises, or at least no *simple* question of the sort considered in connection with sexual acts arises. For reasons given earlier in this chapter, Richard and Sara should not be precluded from giving their religious convictions the weight they think they intrinsically deserve.

Using the stark problem of capital punishment, I turn now to an essentially normative question about punishment, the respective places of utilitarian, or consequentialist, and retributive perspectives.[32] The latter include notions about the inherent rightness of punishing criminal behavior, the severity of punishment that certain acts deserve, and equality of treatment among equally blameworthy offenders.

A person's views about capital punishment will depend not only on factual appraisals but also on a mix of attitudes about the legitimate aims of punishment and any constraints on the pursuits of those aims. Seeing how religious convictions may affect these attitudes is not difficult.[33] A person who believes in a God that punishes evil severely and who expects human agents to act similarly will likely support a retributive approach to punishment; if he thinks God approves punitive killing in authoritative scripture, he will probably perceive no principled barrier to capital punishment. A person who understands God as mild and forgiving will be more hesitant to accept any punishment justified primarily on retributive grounds. Considering any formal punishment as a kind of compromise with a less-than-ideal world, he may regard a punishment that irrevocably cuts off its victim from the human community as absolutely foreclosed.

Though no straightforward correlation exists between believing in life after death and accepting or rejecting capital punishment, views about an afterlife may also influence one's assessment of it. Belief that this world is a preface to another existence will incline one to regard death as less of a harm than it seems for someone who thinks human life does not extend beyond the grave. Such a view might lead one either to more willing acceptance of capital punishment or to acknowledgement of strict limits on what humans can do to offenders in pursuit of social objectives.

The respective merit of retributive and utilitarian perspectives toward punishment and the moral acceptability of capital sentences are the subject of reasoned argument in nonreligious terms. Because substantial arguments can be put forward about whether retributive or utilitarian perspectives fit better with other moral views and will best promote social life, the domain of common reason has a considerable reach here, and since the major competing views about punishment are each supported by substantial rational arguments, a religious believer is particularly likely to suppose that he would still come out with the same conclusions if he put aside his religious convictions. Nevertheless, the ultimate premises that divide retributivists from utilitarians either are not in principle establishable by reasoned argument or rest on such fundamental and complex factual assumptions about human nature and social existence that convincing resolution between them on publicly accessible grounds is not practically possible for real human beings. The consequence is that people will inevitably choose their starting premises on the basis of intuition, personal experience, and commitments. For all the reasons already given, people who are sensitive enough to understand the way in which religious convictions affect their view of punishment should not have to disregard the implications of those convictions.

Military Policy

Disagreements over military policy arise that are closely analogous to disagreements about forms of punishment.

> The Republican candidate for the presidency says she will urge increased military spending to deter Soviet adventurism. The Democratic candidate says he will bring about a sharp reduction in arms, agreeing to terms for arms control that his opponent regards as too unfavorable to American interests, and will increase trade and cultural ties with the Soviet Union. A substantial consensus exists among Richard and Sara and other voters about overall objectives: the avoidance of all-out war, preservation of the security and independence of the country, and a world in which other people are free to choose to govern themselves as they wish. Disagreement exists over the likely effects of relatively mild or harsh military postures, and these reduce to a rather fundamental divergence over the efficacy of threat and accommodation. Members of Richard's fundamentalist church believe that any superpower whose government is based on militant atheism cannot be counted on to exercise reasonable restraint and is bound in the long run to be hostile to another superpower most of whose citizens are religious. Sara's much more liberal church thinks that people and governments, even militantly atheist governments, are reasonably trustworthy when one acts with a good spirit toward them. Disagreement over how the Communist government of the Soviet Union will respond to various sorts of initiatives from this country leads Richard and Sara to differ over whether the Republican or Democratic candidate's military program is preferable.

Divergences of value can also affect one's view of desirable military postures. Is intentionally killing, or even threatening to kill, innocents always morally wrong? Is a slightly added risk of all-out war worth a substantial chance of helping another country avoid oppression? In regard to such questions of absolute limits or trade-offs among goals, discussion in publicly accessible terms can clarify the issues and show some extreme positions to be untenable, but among a number of plausible options, one can hardly say that one stance is rationally better than the others.

Religious conviction certainly affects people's judgments about these matters. For some, the transcendent perspective, and confidence that life on earth is a passing phase, establish that death should be risked to avoid suppression of freedom and religious truth. Others draw from the New Testament pacifist themes with radically contrary implications for military policy. Some people are persuaded that religious principles establish an absolute prohibition on the taking of innocent life, or forbid not only using but any threatening to use military means that are disproportionate to objectives; they will likely reject out-of-hand some kinds of nuclear strategies that others will find acceptable. Citizens being guided to some extent by their religious convictions is as proper with respect to military policy as with respect to the other issues I have discussed.

The General Justification Defense

The narrow issue that I have chosen to analyze about the general justification defense in criminal law is whether the law should absolutely refuse to authorize the intentional taking of innocent life. One's opinion about this is likely to be heavily influenced by whether one thinks that the intentional taking of human life is ever morally acceptable, and that is a judgment on which religious convictions may bear.

The general justification, or "necessity," defense exempts an actor from criminal liability although his behavior violates a specific section of the penal code. A person, for example, could invoke the defense if he broke the speed limit in order to get someone dangerously ill to a hospital. Most of the present statutory provisions in American criminal codes are consequentialist and focused on the immediate context of choice. The influential formulation of the Model Penal Code,[34] for example, grants a privilege to an otherwise criminal act when "the harm or evil sought to be avoided by [the actor's] conduct is greater than that sought to be prevented by the law defining the offense charged . . . ." Under this and other formulations,[35] one would apparently be justified in intentionally killing one innocent person to placate an angry invading general who would otherwise wipe out an entire village.

Someone who believes that intentionally taking an innocent life is always morally wrong will regard such killing as unethical and may suppose it should not receive legal authorization.[36] The absolute rule against intentional killing might be defended as the one that will produce the least taking of lives in the long run, but the factual premise of this defense is certainly debatable. Other arguments within the domain of ordinary reasoning are that one should never choose against a basic good, that one should never use people as mere means, and that one should never yield to extortion. I shall not attempt the analysis here, but I think it can be shown that none of these arguments are particularly compelling ones in favor of the absolute rule.[37]

Another commonly held opinion is that people are unauthorized to intentionally take innocent life. Now, one might give such an opinion a nonreligious twist, but its most obvious form is that God does not authorize us, God's creatures, to take innocent life. Suppose a person recognizes that such a religious view is at the root of his belief that the intentional taking of innocent life is always morally wrong. What I have said in other parts of this chapter indicates that a person may permissibly rely on such a belief, but there is a special problem here that warrants brief analysis.

The problem concerns the relationship between the intentional taking of innocent life and my claim in Chapter 5 that legislation must be based on some notion of protecting people, or other entities, from harm that can be understood in a secular way. Of course, if one is contemplating taking innocent life, there is a potential innocent victim, and the absolute rule may be said to protect his right not to have his life taken in these circumstances. However, the victim's right in context depends on the wrongness of the act; the victim might not have the right if the actor's intention were different (for example, if the victim's death were a certain but unintended conse-quence)[38] or he might even be about to lose his life anyway (perhaps unless one kills the innocent victim the angry general will kill the victim *and* all the villagers). Because the critical judgment operating here is about the wrong-ness of action rather than a right to protection, perhaps persons who perceive that the root of their position is particular religious belief should be more hesitant to impose its implications on others than when the critical inquiry is who really deserves protection. But because the judgment is an important part of an other-regarding morality and does *eventuate* in a notion of the rights of innocents not to be intentionally killed, I think that believers may justifiably rely on that judgment if it is shared by most of the population or if an absolute principle of nonkilling is supported by a good many people on different grounds.[39]

Value Judgments and Ideas of the Good

The general theme of this chapter, covering a fairly wide range of factual and normative judgments, is that the premises of liberal democracy do not entail any wholesale exclusion of religious bases for political decisions by citizens. I want now to comment briefly on the implications of my conclusions for the thesis that decisions about justice in a liberal democracy should not involve reliance on controversial ideas of the good.

None of the examples I have used have directly undercut that thesis understood in a certain way. If ideas of the good are taken to concern the best forms of life for an individual to pursue, judgments of that sort have not been involved in resolution of the social issues I have discussed. If all I have argued is correct, it would still be possible to argue that although religious convictions, metaphysical assumptions, and personal bases of judgment may be used to decide what we owe to each other, nevertheless a person should not treat his idea of the good life as a legitimate basis for public regulations. The proposal, roughly, would be that liberal democracy must be wholly open to competing forms of human flourishing.

Given all else I have said, I suspect that what people think is a good life for individuals is too closely attached to how they think people should behave toward others for this proposal to work. Although a liberal society should leave considerable latitude for people to pursue their own notions of the good life, I believe some political judgments about that subject are proper to determine the content of public education and the direction of public aid for cultural and artistic endeavors, and I further suppose that ideas of the good will properly influence beliefs about other-regarding aspects of morality that bear on desirable laws and policies. Thus, I presently suppose that the challenge I have made to any total exclusion of religious convictions or personal bases of judgment has implications for an exclusion of ideas of the good. But the reader should be aware that I have not made the argument against *that* exclusion. Rather, I have showed how many political judgments do not depend either on shared notions of justice or ideas of the good in the narrow sense, and I have strongly urged the unfairness and impracticality of any principle that religious convictions are inappropriately relied upon when citizens make such judgments.

Notes

1. See generally R. Nozick, *Anarchy, State and Utopia* (N.Y., Basic Books 1974).
2. J. Rawls, *A Theory of Justice* (Cambridge, Mass., Harvard Univ. Pr. 1971).
3. In his *Social Justice in the Liberal State* 169–80 (New Haven, Conn., Yale Univ. Pr. 1980), Bruce Ackerman proposes as an ideal an initially equal share of resources for each citizen reaching adulthood followed by free exchange. The ideal may not

be workable in actual social institutions but it should guide choices of "second-best" arrangements. Id. at pp. 23, 275.

4. See J. Rawls, supra note 2, at pp. 152–56.

5. See, e.g., B. Williams, *Ethics and the Limits of Philosophy*, p. 79 (Cambridge, Mass., Harvard Univ. Pr. 1985) R.P. Wolff, *Understanding Rawls* (Princeton, N.J., Princeton Univ. Pr. 1977); J.P. Sterba, *The Demands of Justice*, p. 34 (Notre Dame, Ind., Univ. of Notre Dame Pr. 1980); T. Nagel, "Rawls on Justice," in N. Daniels, ed., *Reading Rawls*, pp. 1, 11–12 (Oxford, Basil Blackwell 1975). Nagel questions other limitations of the original position at id. pp. 8–10.

6. Of course if he knew there was a high probability he would be among the worst off, he would be even more likely to want their position to be as good as possible.

7. See J. Rawls, supra note 2, at pp. 136–38, 145, 176–79, 498–500. Bernard Williams, supra note 5, at p. 77, suggests that Rawls's idea of strains of commitment helps make Rawls's the richest and most complex contractual account of moral and political philosophy.

8. For claims that people in something like Rawls's original position would, or might, choose not to adopt the difference principle, see, e.g., B. Ackerman, supra note 3, at p. 167; J. Fishkin, *Tyranny and Legitimacy*, pp. 108–13 (Baltimore, Johns Hopkins Pr. 1979); J.P. Sterba, supra note 5, at pp. 34–55, 121; R.M. Hare, "Rawls's Theory of Justice," in N. Daniels, supra note 5, at pp. 81–107.

9. See V. MacNamara, *Faith and Ethics*, p. 135 (Wash., D.C., Georgetown Univ. Pr. 1985), suggesting how a religious outlook can affect optimism or pessimism about scientific risks.

10. Having thought a fair amount about criminal punishment over the past two decades and having taken economics as a minor in college, I find myself unable to understand recent economic analysis relating to capital punishment.

11. A religious perspective too far at odds with rationally ascertainable truth would have little appeal.

12. See generally H.F. May, *The Enlightenment in America*, pp. xiv–xv, 322–24, 361–62 (N.Y., Oxford Univ. Pr. 1976).

13. Rawls defends his distributive view in *A Theory of Justice*, supra note 2 at pp. 100–4.

14. See M. Walzer, *Spheres of Justice*, pp. 75–78 (N.Y., Basic Books 1983).

15. J. Moltmann, "The Cross and Civil Religion," in J. Moltmann, W.W. Richardson, J.B. Metz, W. Oelmuller, M.D. Bryant, *Religion and Political Society*, p. 42 (N.Y., Harper & Row 1974).

16. *Harvard Divinity Bulletin*, June–Aug. 1984, quoted in Ball, "Obligation: Not to the Law but to the Neighbor," 18 *Georgia Law Review*, p. 911 (1984).

17. Richard B. Mouw speaks of the church's duty to "identify with the oppressed, especially with the economically oppressed." See E.L. Long, Jr., *A Survey of Recent Christian Ethics*, pp. 65–67 (N.Y., Oxford Univ. Pr. 1982).

18. In the Old Testament, which contains no clear distinction between community concern and private charity, public rules are used, for example, to require return of land, lending without interest, and giving part of one's harvest for public

distribution to the poor. The practices in medieval Jewish communities are described briefly in M. Walzer, supra note 14, at pp. 73–75.

19. U.S. Catholic Bishops, *Economic Justice for All: Catholic Social Teaching and the U.S. Economy* (1986).

20. Lay Commission on Catholic Social Teaching and the U.S. Economy, "Liberty and Justice for All," 4 *Crisis*, pp. 4–16 (1986).

21. See J. Rawls, "Justice as Fairness: Political not Metaphysical," 14 *Philosophy and Public Affairs*, p. 223 (Summer 1985); "Kantian Constructivism in Moral Theory: The Dewey Lectures, 77 *Journal of Philosophy*, p. 515 (1980).

22. R. Rorty, "The Priority of Democracy Over Philosophy," in M. Peterson and R. Vaughn, eds., *The Virginia Statute for Religious Freedom* (N.Y., Cambridge Univ. Pr. 1987).

23. Rawls, supra note 21, at p. 225.

24. Id. at p. 229.

25. Id. at p. 230.

26. Bernard Williams, supra note 5, at p. 100, suggests that Rawls's procedure assumes a degree of homogeneous belief that goes beyond minimum assumptions of liberalism.

27. Rawls admits the possibility that better principles may be discovered and, given what he says about levels of desirable simplicity in principles, *A Theory of Justice*, supra note 21, at p. 517, it is certainly possible that social changes would alter the best possible set of principles.

28. See M. Walzer, supra note 14, at p. 9, suggesting that social meanings are historical and change over time.

29. See especially J. Rawls, supra note, 21, at pp. 226–30.

30. Roughly, by positing persons in the original position who do not know their talents and who are to choose principles that will best serve their interests, Rawls treats talents as part of a public pool to be encouraged and employed for the benefit of all.

31. See, e.g., B. Mitchell, *Law, Morality and Religion in a Secular Society*, p. 129 (London, Oxford Univ. Pr. 1967).

32. Unless one thinks that criminals somehow place themselves outside the ambit of social concern, crucial normative problems about punishment do not involve borders of protection. No doubt, choices about punishment may sometimes turn on how substantially the interests of offenders are to be counted in comparison with the interests of innocent persons; to this extent the problem of choice resembles in degree the problems of weighting the interests of fetuses and animals once it is determined, if it is, they are entitled to some moral consideration.

33. See, e.g., C.F.H. Henry, *Aspects of Christian Social Ethics*, pp. 161–63 (Grand Rapids, Mich., William B. Eerdmans Pub. Co. 1964).

34. Model Penal Code, § 3.02 (1985). The Model Code is not itself law, but it has influenced formulations in revised criminal codes throughout the country.

35. See especially New York Penal Code § 35.05 (McKinney 1975), which has been followed in a number of other jurisdictions.

36. I explore this problem in considerable depth in "Natural Law and Political Choice: The General Justification Defense; Criteria for Political Action; And the Duty to Obey the Law," 36 *Catholic University Law Review,* pp. 1–26 (1986).

37. Id.

38. The absolute rule has traditionally been thought to apply only to purposeful killings. Thus if someone closes off a part of a mine to prevent a flood that will kill fifty people, knowing that the effect of the act will be to kill five other people, he is not guilty of intentional killing.

39. To be a little more specific, if 90% of society thought on religious grounds that intentional killing was always wrong, they could properly impose that rule by law; if 40% of society thought on nonreligious grounds that intentional killing was always wrong and 30% reached a similar conclusion on religious grounds, then the 30% could properly join the 40% to impose that rule by law.

10

Church-State Problems

The practical political subjects I have discussed thus far have not concerned religious belief and religious observance in the sense in which these are involved in obvious church-state problems. None of the available choices have involved direct promotion or impairment of religious belief or practice.[1] In this chapter, I consider three kinds of social choices that do present such possibilities: school prayer and public aid to religious institutions, both now highly controversial, and accommodations to religious conscience. Since these areas are ones of continuing Supreme Court involvement, let me reiterate that I am not here concerned with constitutionality in a strict legal sense; I am addressing the propriety of a citizen's developing his position about possible political choices in terms of his own religious convictions.

Organized School Prayer and a Moment of Silence

Various arguments for and against organized school prayer are compatible with the premises of a liberal society. The main argument against school prayer is that in a society in which church and government are separate, the state should not be sponsoring religious exercises. Given the widely accepted premise of our liberal society that the state should not be promoting any particular religious view, any school prayer is bound to be highly dubious. Either the state composes or endorses particular prayers itself, or it leaves formulations of prayers to individual students, thereby in effect bolstering majority views over time. Any prayer undoubtedly poses difficulties under the somewhat more debatable premise that I accept in this book, that the state should not promote religion over nonreligion.

Among the various claims in favor of group prayer in the public school, I shall focus on two: that since school occupies so much of the child's day, not to allow such prayer is to limit the possibilities of effective worship; and that if the schools shut off all opportunity for organized group worship during the school day, the implicit message that is conveyed is that God and religion are unimportant.

Whatever its relevance for soldiers and prisoners, the argument in favor of prayer that concerns the time students are in school is implausible, at least for those whose religion does not demand prayer at particular times of day. Students have plenty of time outside school to engage in prayer.

More disturbing is the argument that if in their most important social grouping outside the family, students are precluded from an opportunity of shared religious experience, the implicit message of this school time will be that religion is not important. This worry is softened, though not wholly eliminated, by the possibility that voluntary subgroups of students may be able to engage in group prayer outside of ordinary class time, say, during lunch. Since the liberal state should not be in the business of denigrating religion, practices that convey the message that religion does not matter much are not wholly consonant with liberal premises.

One's appraisal of the argument that students should have an opportunity for shared religious experience need not be directly determined by one's religious convictions. Many religious people do not accept the argument, believing that the place of religion can receive adequate emphasis elsewhere, in settings that do not put subtle pressures for conformity on those with minority views. On the other hand, some nonbelievers might be persuaded that fairness and neutrality indicate some place in school for voluntary prayer by interested students in the organized classroom setting.

In contrast with organized school prayer, which now is plainly precluded by Supreme Court doctrine,[2] a moment of silence at the beginning of the school day apparently remains a permissible constitutional option.[3] Most of the arguments for and against a moment of silence are similar to those applying to oral prayer, but their strength varies significantly. Though most people will understand that a silent moment is made available largely so that students who wish will have a chance to pray, the moment of silence constitutes a much weaker encouragement to religious practice and involves little or no imposition[4] on those with unorthodox religious beliefs. As with organized prayer, one's overall appraisal of the arguments for and against a moment of silence need not depend directly on one's religious beliefs.

If religious conviction does not dictate one's position on school prayer or a moment of silence, it can well affect how someone resolves the issue once he recognizes the competing considerations: that establishing prayers or silence may constitute some support to religion that trenches upon a principle of nonsponsorship, and that refusal to have prayers or silence may indirectly convey the implicitly secularist message that religion is not central to life. When one must squarely decide which horn of the dilemma to choose, one may be influenced by one's view of the value of public or silent prayers within large social groups that are not selected on religious bases. One's estimate of this value may well rest on religious convictions. If someone thinks religious beliefs are foolish and prayer a superstitious practice, the risk of indirect and implicit support of secularism will seem more tolerable than the state's relatively slight but direct support to religion involved in group prayer. If someone is persuaded that general group prayer or shared silence, largely employed for prayer, is important from a religious point of view and that religious practice is critical for human life, the tolerability of risks may seem reversed. Since shared values and common forms of reasoning themselves provide no answer to the intrinsic importance of various religious practices, a person should not be expected to estimate the acceptability of these risks without any reference to his own religious convictions. These would certainly affect not only which risk people would prefer to have run in respect to their own children but also their view of which risk the public as a whole could better afford.

My own position concerning organized public school prayer is that the argument against it, based on the directness of the state's involvement and on the subtle coercion of group prayer on children of minority views, is so clearly the stronger that such prayer should be regarded as inappropriate in a liberal pluralist society, and I think our Constitution has properly been interpreted to require that result. A moment of silence, properly instituted and practiced, is much less threatening to liberal premises, though its religious value is doubtful. In any event, my main point here is that liberalism does not demand that citizens attempt to resolve these questions wholly without reference to their own religious perspectives.

Claims of Conscience

Similar questions are generated by claims to grant exceptions from ordinary rules for those who have conscientious reasons for acting differently. The best known example is the claim that conscientious objectors should be granted an exemption from required military service, a claim that has relevance even in a volunteer army for persons presently under a commitment to serve. Another example is the claim that the government should require that employers make special accommodations in terms of days off or working conditions for those who conscientiously cannot work on certain days or under certain conditions. One issue that arises is whether any exemption from a particular rule should be granted; a second issue is whether an exemption should be cast in terms of religious belief and association.

Common forms of reasoning have a substantial bearing on the possibility of exemptions for those whose conscience forbids their conformance to ordinary requirements and on how such exemptions should be formulated. On the one hand, futilely demanding that people do what they regard as morally abhorrent is not the most productive use of rules and is bound to cause resentment among those whose conscience is burdened. On the other hand, creating exceptions may generate inequity, be difficult to administer, and weaken the force of a rule's general application. On the one hand, casting an exemption in religious terms might reasonably be thought to make more accurate administration possible, to identify a class whose feelings of conscience will be especially strong, and to represent a proper accommodation to a sphere of life that has long been thought to interpose demands that may conflict with state authority. On the other hand, any straight preference for religious conscientious claims over nonreligious ones may be regarded as an unjustified state support of religion, and religiosity may be thought an inaccurate or inappropriate basis either for recognizing those with especially strong claims or for simplifying administration. These arguments against religious categorization have generally been thought to have persuaded the Supreme Court in the *Seeger*[5] and *Welsh*[6] cases to interpret out of existence the efforts of Congress to limit the exemption from military service to distinctly religious objectors.

No uniform satisfactory answer can be given to the questions whether there should be any exemption from an ordinary rule or practice and whether, if so, the exemption should be cast in religious terms. As to the creation of any exemption, much depends on the degree of need for uniform observance and on the possibilities of fraudulent claims. As to the scope of an exemption, it will matter whether the conscientious objection is of a kind likely to be raised by nonbelievers and whether defining the favored class in religious terms is critical to accurate administration. I strongly believe that when feasible, a system of self-selecting exemptions, in which anyone is free to choose the alternative to what is normally demanded but the alternative carries burdens that would lead most people to choose subjection to the standard requirements, is far preferable to the state's deciding who is and who is not an eligible conscientious objector.[7]

However one resolves these issues, it is unlikely that one can, or should, try to approach them in disregard of one's own convictions about religious and moral truth. No doubt, it *would be illiberal* to look at these problems in terms of how best to impose or promote one's own religious views in society.[8] But if one believes that there exists an objective religious truth whose moral demands may well come into conflict with the state's requirements, one may be more disposed to think that conscience should be accommodated than if one does not believe in transcendent sources of moral truth. Further, if one believes that religious truth actually requires action that is contrary to what is demanded by present state requirements, as a religious pacifist would feel about a general conscription law, one would be likely to rate the need for accommodation very high. The pacifist who derives his views about war from religious premises is not required by liberal principles to put his religious convictions out of his mind when he thinks about whether pacifists should receive an exemption.

Aid to Religious Institutions Conferring Secular Benefits

Many religious organizations perform social services that confer an undoubted secular benefit. One thinks of religious hospitals, religious schools, and religious charities for the poor. If the state chooses to help finance private conferrals of such benefits, its failure to assist private religious organizations may compromise its efforts and constitute a discrimination against religion. If the state includes religious organizations, it may end up aiding the religions purposes of the organizations. At this time, financial aid to religious hospitals and charities for the poor is noncontroversial. As far as financial support is concerned, religious organizations are simply treated like other private organizations engaging in the same endeavors. Aid to religious schools, on the other hand, is marked by intense controversy and continuing constitutional litigation. The twofold explanation for the difference concerns the special place of the public school in the United States and the perception that in parochial schools a close connection exists between religious instruction and education in standard subjects.

Neither liberal principles nor constitutional clauses provide pat answers to the degree of acceptable support for religious organizations that make direct contributions to secular objectives. Assuming that a form of aid is constitutionally permissible, how is an individual to decide whether that aid should be given? Let us concentrate on private schools—if aid is to be given to all private endeavors, the vast majority of beneficiaries will be religious organizations. How one rates the importance of assisting the secular objectives of the private schools against the risks of assisting religious objectives will depend partly on how valuable one thinks private parochial education is. Can this judgment be made without reference to one's religious convictions? If a person believes that the best education for children is by religious organizations, a view that does not *by itself* run afoul of liberal principles, he will be inclined to suppose that giving state support to secular functions warrants any risk of oblique support for religious objectives. If one believes that religious training is misconceived and harmful or that attitudes necessary to maintain a liberal pluralist society can only be promoted in a state school environment, one is likely to take a rather different view of the harms and benefits of state aid. One's own religious convictions are bound to figure in one's estimate of the ideal place for religious education in a liberal society, as well as whether one wishes to have one's own children supported in religious schools.

With respect to school prayer, claims of conscience, and aid to religious institutions conferring secular benefits, we have seen that nonreligious arguments can be offered on both sides of the issues as they arise in particular contexts. Relying on religious conviction in the sense of favoring a result because it will promote one's own religious views or because it will directly embody one's religious conception of how a proper society is organized may be at odds with liberal democratic principles, but a good citizen could not and need not disregard his religious convictions in assessing the balance of the ordinary arguments.

Notes

1. A minor exception to this point is the discussion of military policy, where I mentioned the perceived gravity of the harm of suppression of religious truth.

2. See Abington School Dist. v. Schempp., 374 U.S. 203 (1963).

3. See Wallace v. Jaffree, 105 S. Ct. 2479 (1985), striking down moment of silence legislation because of obvious religious purpose.

4. Since the moment of silence has no specific content, the number of people who might be offended is obviously fewer; but if the moment is subtly portrayed as being mainly for prayer, it may cause some distress for nonbelievers.

5. United States v. Seeger, 380 U.S. 165 (1965).

6. Welsh v. United States, 398 U.S. 333 (1970).

7. These matters are explored in much more depth in K. Greenawalt, *Conflicts of Morality and Law*, pp. 311–36 (N.Y., Oxford Univ. Pr. 1987).

8. See C.F.H. Henry, *Aspects of Christian Social Ethics*, p. 78 (Grand Rapids, Mich., William B. Eerdmans Pub. Co. 1964).

11

Religious Bases That Conflict with Common Forms of Reasoning

Reliance on religious convictions is appropriate under any plausible model of liberal democracy much more often than is claimed by those who would have the good liberal citizen restrict himself in political decisions to shared nonreligious premises and common forms of reasoning. It does not follow, however, that such reliance on religious bases is always apt. I have already suggested some limits: liberal democrats should not promote illiberal outcomes or objectives; they should not try to prohibit behavior just because they believe it is wrong; they should assess programs in light of their capacities to serve secular objectives, not because they promote separable religious objectives.[1] In this chapter, I explore another possible qualification whose dimensions and proper import are harder to discern.

The qualification concerns religious bases of judgment that in some way conflict with the assessments that are or could be yielded by common forms of reasoning. As I shall indicate, such judgments are possible in the realm of value as well as fact. I treat two different sorts of situations. In the first, what the religious bases indicate is in conflict with a conclusion that common forms of reasoning strongly support. In the second, more troublesome, situation, the conclusion of the religious ground is not at odds with what common forms of reasoning might suggest, but the ground stands independently and fails to connect to those forms of reasoning.

203

Clear Conflicts in Conclusions

The most obvious conflict of religious conviction and publicly accessible reasons occurs if one's religiously based factual conclusions clearly contradict all rational estimates.

> Thomas concedes that common sense and scientific analysis yield no plausible basis to suppose that the earth will suffer a cataclysmic flood in three years; he acknowledges that all reputable scientists assert that a flood of the predicted dimensions is physically impossible, but he believes that authoritative inerrant scripture indicates the certainty of such a flood.

Without doubt, Thomas offends no principle of liberal democracy if he takes steps with cobelievers to minimize the effects of the predicted tragedy, but is he warranted in trying to engage the efforts of the government? Like Richard and Sara, the disputants over whether imprisonment or probation will work most effectively, Thomas believes that the government's following the truth as he sees it would produce overall secular benefits; but unlike them, his conclusions are effectively contradicted by common forms of reasoning, indeed would be regarded by those who rely on those forms as irrational.

The question whether Thomas should rely on his scriptural prediction for political purposes can be put more generally: does being a good citizen of a liberal democracy involve a limited commitment to shared forms of reasoning, a commitment that one will adhere to those forms at least insofar as they give clear answers? We might conceive of an otherwise liberal polity in which citizens with various religious and personal views sought to base policy upon determinations, like the predictions of an imminent flood, that would be deemed irrational according to common forms of reasoning, it being left to the political process to make necessary adjustments and compromises. But it is hard to imagine a liberal society working very well if shared bases for making factual assessments and predictions were frequently just disregarded and blatantly departed from. A plausible theory of liberal democracy probably does require that people follow ordinary modes of thought in their political judgments when these lead to solid factual conclusions; that degree of commitment to a common method of discourse and thought is owed to others of diverse convictions in a pluralist society. If this is granted, Thomas would not act in accord with the premises of our liberal democratic society if he tried to engage the state in a project that would be senseless given any rational secular assessment of the facts.

Value judgments can also conflict with the clear conclusions of shared forms of reasoning. Suppose that Norma acknowledges that gray cats have no scientifically ascertainable capacities greater than other cats and that they have less capacities than dolphins, but she believes that gray cats are sacred and should be protected above all other animals. She is, of course, perfectly free with her coreligionists to try to obtain as many gray cats as possible and to treat them with great respect and consideration, but if she urges a political program that would give gray cats more legal protection than other cats and than dolphins because they intrinsically deserve greater protection, she would depart from the spirit of liberal democracy.[2]

In defending my conclusion about a limited commitment to shared forms of reasoning, I need to explain a little more carefully how I understand the possibility of judgments conflicting with them. I shall concentrate here on Thomas's conclusion about the flood. In accord with what I said about religious beliefs generally in Chapter 3, it is not my position that common forms of reasoning play no role at all in Thomas's conclusion. He may think that there is historical evidence, about the Jewish nation or the resurrection of Jesus, that supports his belief in the inerrancy of scripture; he may use ordinary techniques of translation and interpretation to decide what the scripture predicts. I am assuming, however, that the inerrancy of the scriptures is not establishable by publicly accessible reasons[3] and that therefore Thomas's belief about the flood does rest critically on a premise that goes beyond those reasons.

Now, it might be argued that in some ultimate sense Thomas's belief is no less rational than that of the scientists. The scientists have methods of ascertaining what has happened and will happen in the physical world, and they assume that the regularities of the physical world consistently apply. All or some of these methods and the confidence that past regularities will continue in the future rest on nondemonstrable premises. Thomas believes, instead, in a powerful God, capable of suspending ordinary physical laws, who has chosen to disclose in advance some of the occasions when that will happen, and who has made such a disclosure in this instance. These premises of Thomas undoubtedly are different from those of the scientists, but they are no less rational in some absolute sense.

Is the supposition sound that Thomas and the scientists are just employing varying forms of rationality? The supposition strikes me as unsound. The scientists are relying generally on premises that have so far been confirmed by common human experience and by techniques of discovery that would be accepted as valid by those capable of understanding them intellectually. That does not mean ordinary human experience and indisputable techniques confirm that miracles never occur, only that up to now physical regularities obtain in the vast majority of instances and it is a part of "common sense" to believe that will continue. Thomas's premises are less securely rooted in common human experience and in techniques whose validity will not be contested by anyone capable of an intellectual grasp of them.[4] One can therefore say that the scientists' premises are "more rational" than those of Thomas in a sense that transcends culture.

Suppose I am wrong. I then revert to the more critical point that common sense and the techniques of science are the shared form of reasoning for this society. When we try to decide when it will be safe to launch another space shuttle, we examine what are the physical problems with "O-rings" and what changes are needed to assure their adequate performance in the future; we do not ask why God may be angry with us and when God might favor another launch. Thomas is not relying on shared forms of reasoning, the scientists are.

Thomas might reply that the usually shared forms are not shared on the question of the flood because he and others like him believe another technique is here more reliable. In the absence of shared forms of reason on this issue, he may claim he is free to rely on grounds he finds persuasive. This response does not avoid the reality that Thomas, on the basis of particular religious premises, is departing from a form of reasoning that he as well as everyone else deems generally applicable to just this kind of factual question. Were it not for the biblical passage, Thomas like others would assign a high degree of probability to the scientists' prediction that no such flood will occur.

Given the historical connection between the rise of liberalism and what are presently conceived as rational modes of thought, it may be hard to say whether liberal democracy could flourish in a society where the critical ingredients of factual judgment were something other than common sense and scientific procedures, but those are the methods commonly accepted in modern liberal democratic societies, including our own. If my earlier comments are right that such societies do need some shared premises for resolving factual issues, that is sufficient to suggest that Thomas would not act as a good liberal citizen if he employed his judgment about the flood to achieve a governmental response to the danger.[5]

Though I shall not work through the analysis here, any claim that Norma can rely on her judgment about the importance of gray cats because, given the nonrationality of all ultimate value judgments, her judgment is ultimately as rational as any other value judgment, is similarly unpersuasive. I believe there are some relevant transcultural standards of rationality in value judgments, and even if there are not, there are shared standards accepted by our liberal democratic society, which a good liberal citizen should observe. These standards include the notion that skin color, or fur color, has no bearing on one's intrinsic value.

If publicly accessible reasons decisively answer a question of fact or value, or limit the range of plausible answers, the good liberal citizen does not rely on particular religious premises to urge a political result that is at odds with the answer or range of answers that the publicly accessible reasons indicate to be sound.

Religious Bases of Judgment That Fail To Connect with Publicly Accessible Reasons

The example of Thomas's prediction about the flood combines three features: religious convictions that do not connect to publicly accessible forms of reasoning; disregard of the products of those forms of reasoning; and a factual conclusion that is at odds with the clear import of those forms. My claim that in these circumstances good liberal citizenship does preclude reliance on the religious convictions involves an important theoretical point about a constrained commitment to shared premises and ways of reasoning. But my claim is of highly limited practical significance, since it is very unlikely that in our society many policies or laws would be adopted that blatantly fly in the face of common sense and clear scientific understanding. What matters much more in a practical sense are instances in which shared forms of reasoning do not produce undeniable conclusions. I turn now to such instances.

Much of my discussion in the book has been about religious convictions that connect to publicly accessible reasons in some important way. One connection is the embedding of one's ordinary factual and value inquiries in basic presuppositions that derive in part from religious convictions. Examples would be someone's examining literature on probation in light of skepticism about human goodness or considering arguments about the general justification defense in light of a sense that the intentional infliction of wrong is very hard morally to justify. As to this sort of connection, I have argued that people cannot be expected to disregard the basic premises they employ for evaluating the data and arguments that are the common currency of the society. A second sort of connection involves parallel support for a conclusion, when disentangling the religious support for the conclusion would be virtually impossible. A person believes in the irreducible selfishness of human nature because of psychological literature, personal experience, and the Bible. He is unable to say how much weight the literature and the publicly accessible content of his experience carry and how much weight he gives to the idiosyncratic aspects of experience and the Bible. As to this sort of connection, I have argued that people should not have to try to slice their understanding into pieces, attempting to guess what they would think were it not for religious convictions, or were it not for religious convictions and personal bases of judgment.

The problem I address in this section is religious convictions that do not connect in either of these ways to publicly accessible reasons. Is it proper to rely on such convictions when publicly accessible reasons themselves provide no ready answer? I want to consider two variations. In the first, the religious convictions render publicly accessible reasons irrelevant; in the second they do not.

Suppose that Thomas believes that scripture authoritatively establishes that by the year 2050 a worldwide conflict will destroy the human race on earth. Social scientists regard that as a distinct possibility, but Thomas does not rely at all on, or even pay attention to, the reasons why they say such an event might happen. Norma believes that scripture gives members of the human species absolute dominion over every other species; she thinks that significant moral consideration would not be owed to members of other species even if it could be shown that their capacities exceed those of human beings and even if they became capable of full communication with human beings. The practical positions Thomas and Norma adopt, Thomas favoring space and earth policies that look toward likely extermination of human beings on earth and Norma opposing animal rights claims, are positions about which shared premises and common forms of reasoning are inconclusive, but Thomas and Norma treat ordinary reasons not only as inconclusive but as irrelevant.

Suppose, instead, that Thomas and Norma do not treat ordinary forms of reasoning as irrelevant, but give considerable weight to religious grounds that they perceive as quite independent. Thomas does not assume either that scripture is inerrant or that it is always correctly interpreted by him, but he thinks his interpretations of it have a significant degree of reliability for future events. Thus, despite his reading of scripture, he might acknowledge that a flood is unlikely *because* scientists say it is impossible, but when the scientists are uncertain, scriptural interpretation becomes for him an important independent basis for predicting one way or the other. Similarly Norma might say that scriptural passages suggesting human dominion have strong independent weight for questions of animal rights, but believe that significant ordinary reasons also support the human dominion view.

These reasons based on scripture, which may tip the balance for Thomas and Norma, do not connect significantly to ordinary forms of reasoning in either sense I have suggested. They are not basic premises in which ordinary reasoning is embedded nor are they so close to that reasoning that the threads are hard to disentangle. For Thomas and Norma the scriptural arguments are divorcable from the shared modes of assessing facts and analyzing normative questions.

What principles are appropriate for reliance on religious convictions when shared forms of reasoning are inconclusive and the religious convictions make no connection in the relevant forms of reasoning? With this question, we reach what seem to me among the most troublesome problems in the book. In addressing the question, we need to consider three possible positions: that reliance on religious convictions is always all right when the publicly accessible reasons are inconclusive, that reliance is never appropriate when the religious convictions do not connect to those reasons in one of the two senses I have mentioned, that reliance is only appropriate if the religious believer remains open to publicly accessible reasons. We need also to be aware that the best position for factual determinations may or may not be the best position for value judgments and that some further subcategorization may be called for.

I shall begin by considering Thomas and Norma when they rely on scripture in a way that treats publicly accessible reasons as irrelevant. In their *attitude* toward those reasons they are just as illiberal as if they disregarded some clear and conclusive answer to the question of fact or value that those reasons yielded. Their own political positions escape obvious illiberality only because each has the good fortune to be dealing with a question on which publicly accessible reasons are inconclusive. Perhaps we can say that a good liberal citizen must remain open to publicly accessible reasons, that Thomas and Norma are acting illiberally if they treat those reasons as irrelevant to their political decisions.

What is the practical import of this principle? Let us imagine that Thomas and Norma are persuaded and seek to act as good liberal citizens. They now acknowledge some responsibility in their political lives to consider publicly accessible reasons and to follow their direction if that direction is clear. Nevertheless, Thomas and Norma conclude, respectively, that these reasons are inconclusive about the end of the human race and the moral status of animals. Giving those reasons due consideration, they may still reach the same positions they presently do on the basis of their religious convictions, if some significant reliance on the convictions is appropriate. Their openness to publicly accessible reasons would be practically important for their stance on the immediate issues only if Thomas and Norma thought that the strong balance of these reasons was clearly contrary to their religious convictions or if those reasons established the uncertainty of any relevant judgment and the degree of certainty mattered.[6] Despite its limited practical significance for immediate political issues, a principle of openness to publicly accessible reasons bears importantly on the attitudes citizens should bring to public decisions and indirectly on the quality of public discourse.[7]

A principle that one should never rely on a religious conviction that is unconnected to shared forms of reason would have greater bite. In that event a good liberal citizen would not be expected to make strenuous efforts to disentangle the threads of complex assumptions and beliefs, but he would be expected to not act politically against what he perceived to be the balance of publicly accessible reasons.

The position that the good liberal citizen should not consciously rely on grounds for assessing facts that are utterly removed from ordinary forms of reasoning has considerable appeal. But, given the difficulty of saying just when religious convictions are connected to shared forms of reasoning, and the fundamental awkwardness of asking people to disregard sources of truth in which they have confidence when the publicly accessible reasons are inconclusive, I am inclined to reject the position that people should never rely on religious convictions that bear on factual determinations unless the convictions connect to shared reasons.

With respect to value judgments as to which publicly accessible reasons are radically inconclusive, as I have contended is the case with animal rights, the appropriateness of relying on "unconnected" religious convictions, such as Norma's reading of particular narrow passages in Genesis, seems clearer. It is unreasonable to suppose Norma should limit herself to admittedly sketchy publicly accessible reasons. When the value judgment mainly involves some sort of derivation from shared premises, and the ordinary rational arguments on both sides are powerful, the question is closer. The position that citizens should then rely only on *general* religious perspectives that inform their consideration of relevant public arguments and should not rely on convictions that are distinctly separable from those arguments has roughly the same appeal as the analogous position with respect to factual determinations. For essentially the same reasons I gave in that connection, I hesitatingly reject that position.

The complications, incomplete clarifications, and halting conclusions in this chapter are in part a reflection of the extremely complex relations between religious convictions and shared bases of reason. One of the fundamental messages of this book is that as a culture we have tended in our abstract rhetoric to oversimplify that complexity to an almost incredible degree, and that the result has been an impoverished picture of how religious ideas fit in the political decisions of liberal citizens. Whatever illusions I initially entertained about my ability to capture and categorize these complex relations are largely exposed by difficulties this chapter illuminates. They show that I have only scratched the surface, that a deeper account of how religious convictions properly figure in liberal politics will depend on a richer picture of how religious dimensions relate to ordinary forms of reasoning.

Notes

1. Supporting a military policy because it best conforms with one's sense of a divine command to convert atheists, or supporting a limited exemption based on religious conscience because it would promote conversion to one's religion would be to act upon separable religious objectives.

2. I should add significant qualification here. The argument that the gray cats *intrinsically* deserve more protection would be inappropriate. However, it would be appropriate to argue that other people should accommodate the strong religious beliefs of those who hold gray cats to be sacred by giving some protection to gray cats.

3. If a substantial number of other clearly made scriptural predications (comprehensible to nonbelievers) had undeniably proved accurate in the past and these earlier predictions had flown in the face of scientific evidence, one would have a basis in ordinary reasoning to give some credence to this prediction.

4. This assertion does depend on a view about the degree of clarity and ascertainable reliability of other claimed scriptural predictions. It assumes that few scriptural predications have been both precise and indisputably accurate.

5. Of course if the flood threatened general extermination, Thomas might reasonably decide that saving people was more important than adhering to liberal principles.

6. In actual planning, the probability of the end of the human race would be important. Suppose Thomas believes he has subjective certainty based on scripture that human life on earth will end before 2050. Ordinary forms of reasoning would establish that such certainty is not possible. Many policies would obviously be different if people thought that the end of human life on earth was not certain, but slightly more probable than not. If ordinary reasoning cannot conclude whether the end of human life on earth is probable, Thomas could rely on his religiously based judgment only in respect to policies for which that probability was the critical determination.

7. See R.J. Neuhaus, *The Naked Public Square*, pp. 15–16 (Grand Rapids, Mich., William B. Eerdmans Pub. Co. 1984), expressing concern over fundamentalists' lack of engagement with publicly accessible reasons.

III

DIALOGUE, OFFICIAL ACTION, AND CONSTITUTIONALITY

12

Appropriate Political Discourse
in a Liberal Society

In some important respects, all the previous chapters are mainly a prologue for this chapter and the two that follow. In these chapters, I discuss public justifications for political positions, the activities of officials, and the constraints set by constitutional law. These questions may seem to have a practical significance that the discussion of how individuals form political positions lacks. Even if liberal democratic theory has significant implications for how citizens develop views and vote, there is little anyone else can do about that; public discourse and official activity are more easily affected by shared, articulated understandings of the place of religion. Apart from this difference in the effectiveness of principles to influence behavior, some people believe that the premises of liberal democracy, properly understood, either do not reach at all to the actual decisions of individual citizens or set very few restraints on them; it is on this view when citizens enter the political process more actively by engaging in public justifications of their positions or by becoming officials that constraints derived from liberal democratic premises really matter.

Whatever their importance directly for the decisions and votes of citizens, the preceding chapters have immense bearing on the remaining discussion. The arguments and analysis advanced there are critical for the somewhat different topics now to be addressed; for these, a primary concern is some reasonable fit between how citizens reach decisions and what else takes place in the political process.

In the preceding chapters, I have urged that even though a model of our liberal democracy includes a limited commitment to shared bases of evaluation, it leaves considerable room for religious citizens to rely on religious grounds for moral judgments that affect law and public policy. If I am correct, any hope that all political issues can be resolved solely on the basis of commonly shared premises about values and commonly shared approaches to factual knowledge must be abandoned. To abandon this hope is to free oneself from a misguided illusion, not to forfeit any vital premise of liberal democracy.

I turn in this chapter to guidelines for public articulation of political positions and organization of political interests. Saying what liberalism implies is troublesome. Much depends on how the open discussion of religious grounds for positions will be taken, especially by those who reject the underlying religious convictions. For this reason, one must have in mind a particular stage which this and other liberal democratic societies have reached.

I believe that now in the United States there is (1) a substantial consensus on the organizing political principles for society; (2) a shared sense that major political discussions will be carried on primarily in secular terms; (3) a respect for religious belief and activity and a hesitancy to attack religious practices as nonsensical; and (4) an assumption that one can be a seriously religious person *and* a liberal participant in a liberal society. With these assumptions, we can develop some rough guidelines for political behavior for persons with religious convictions, though prudential assessments must largely supplant clear lines of principle.

A deeply religious person will want to work out the implications of his convictions for his political views and activities. He will rightly discuss political issues in those terms with coreligionists, seeking to gain insight and to persuade. Religious leaders similarly bring their religious convictions to bear when they address members of their faith; a Christian minister appropriately preaches about why the Gospels require pacifism or a nuclear freeze if he believes that they do. When persons of different religions share some common religious conviction, such as the idea that God commands aid to the poor, that conviction is properly invoked in discussions among them. A religious Presbyterian who thinks practical conclusions about welfare policy can be drawn out of that premise properly relies on it in a conversation with a Conservative Jew.

Open public discussion is more difficult. When a citizen writes a letter to a newspaper, should he try to persuade on the grounds of religious arguments? Very roughly, my answer is that he should not. The government of a liberal society knows no religious truth and a crucial premise about a liberal society is that citizens of extremely diverse religious views can build principles of political order and social justice that do not depend on particular religious beliefs. The common currency of political discourse is nonreligious argument about human welfare. Public discourse about political issues with those who do not share religious premises should be cast in other than religious terms.

This straightforward conclusion needs to be qualified in various ways. I want initially to introduce four exceptions. One concerns discourse that is one or more steps removed from ordinary political advocacy. An author writes an article about Jewish perspectives on nature for an environmental journal.[1] Most readers of the journal are not Jewish. But the article is not written in a manner that presupposes that most readers accept Jewish perspectives. The article serves at least two purposes for non-Jewish readers. It informs them of the implications of one important religious and cultural perspective in our society; by introducing a perspective that varies from their own, it may enrich their sense of the significance of their own perspective and of alternative possibilities. Even if the article is about Christian rather than Jewish perspectives, the nonreligious reader, or the reader from another religious tradition, is not likely to feel left out, in the way that he might if public advocacy over welfare assistance seemed to turn on whose interpretation of Christian doctrine was more sound.

The second exception concerns the discourse of religious leaders. Religious leaders are, in a sense, experts on religious perspectives; they may devote much of their time to figuring out the import of the basic religious convictions they accept. When they speak about public issues, their special competence has to do with their religious understanding. If, for example, a statement by Catholic bishops on the use of nuclear arms looks just like a statement that might be made by any secular political leader, we feel something is missing.[2] We expect a contribution that reflects the unique position of the bishops. Here a delicate balance must be struck. The Catholic bishops' statement should make some effort to root the positions it takes in Catholic understandings about war and military weapons, but if the statement is designed to have general influence, it should also contain language and ideas that have a broader appeal. In part, the effort should be to cast ideas that conform with Catholic understandings in as generalized a form as is possible.[3]

The third exception is already illustrated by the previous examples. Often there will not be a sharp distinction between how one reaches a general audience and how one reaches fellow believers. The bishops' statement on nuclear weapons is not only addressed to the community at large, it is also designed to enlighten Catholics about what their faith implies. A writer whose primary intended audience is Christians concerned with environmental problems may assume he will reach more of this audience in a general journal about the environment than in any specialized religious publication. Because there is no neat way to reach just the audience one intends the line between communication with cobelievers and the general public cannot be exact.

A fourth exception concerns proselytizing. Suppose a religious speaker's intended audience is a general one, but the main point of his discourse is not to promote a particular political program but rather to convert others to his religious beliefs. A person who is trying to persuade others to religious convictions may understandably wish to convey some of the moral and political implications of those convictions; these implications may affect the appeal of the religious convictions for nonbelievers. People generally are aware that many religious believers seek to proselytize in this manner. Discourse of this sort that develops connections between religious premises and political conclusions does not make nonbelievers feel left out, as does general political advocacy in religious terms.

My discussion of the last three exceptions leaves a discrepancy between church leaders and ordinary believers that is somewhat troubling. The problem is that what the second exception allows to religious leaders may seem to incorporate a hierarchical perspective that is at odds with the Protestant idea of "the priesthood of all believers." The third and fourth exceptions would permit an ordinary believer who is trying mainly to reach fellow believers or to convert others to his religious views to develop the theological underpinnings of his political positions; but only church leaders, under the second exception, would appropriately develop religious grounds for political positions when their main intended audience is nonbelievers and the purpose of the message is mainly political. Since the premises of liberal democracy certainly dictate no preferences for hierarchical conceptions of church authority, this discrepancy may seem anomalous. Roughly, the idea is that even within the most egalitarian church politics recognized leaders emerge, and the impact of other citizens is very different when these leaders speak in religious terms than when ordinary people do so. Nonetheless, conceivably the second exception should be expanded to embrace all those who seriously conceive of themselves as having a special expertness or vocation in religious matters, whether or not they are recognized leaders among their fellows.

Is there yet another exception to my general proposition that fully public political discussion should be carried on in nonreligious terms? Are there some religious premises that are *so widely shared* that they are properly a subject of such discourse? What I have in mind are premises like "God loves us all" or "Social justice is a duty to God as well as to other humans." Though interpretations differ, these propositions unite virtually all Christians and Jews, as well as adherents of many other religions. Since in the United States relatively few people consider themselves atheists or agnostics, such premises coincide with the religious beliefs of a high percentage of the national population. Are arguments in these terms an appropriate part of general advocacy? That may depend partly on how much of the population does not accept the premises, and that varies considerably in different sections of the country and among subgroups. At major eastern universities, where many students and faculty do not believe in God, a political argument cast on even such broad religious premises would be inapt. But one might reach a different conclusion about a civic speech in Utah or rural North Carolina. A separate reason to eschew reliance on these religious premises is their considerable indeterminateness; they are not likely to be much assistance in resolving genuinely difficult issues of public policy.

Why should it matter if religious premises are shared? Why isn't it all right to advocate political positions in terms of narrower religious convictions? After all, a public speech relying heavily on religious arguments might be expected to reach some coreligionists and others of like view. In a very religious but extremely tolerant society, public airing of particular religious views might work well, but in actuality such discourse promotes a sense of separation between the speaker and those who do not share his religious convictions and is likely to produce both religious and political divisiveness. If public argument is seen to turn on which interpretation of the Christian tradition is sounder, non-Christians may feel left out and resentful.

I have been discussing the use of religious premises to support controversial positions on public policy. I need now to enter an important caveat concerning other uses of explictly religious language and of imagery drawn from our religious tradition. Explicitly religious terms may be employed, not directly to support controversial political positions, but to enjoin divine assistance, to emphasize the fallibility of human efforts, to call people to act on conscience, and to remind us that all we do is subject to some higher judgment. Though even this employment of religious discourse may offend some nonbelievers, it does not involve practical choices being weighed in terms the nonbeliever rejects. Thinking of our country's strong tradition of reference to the divine, and eloquent examples like Lincoln's "Second Inaugural Address," I find this sort of use of religious terms appropriate even at the national level. Robert Bellah has referred to America's civil religion, "a set of religious beliefs, symbols, and rituals growing out of the American historical experience interpreted in the dimension of transcendence."[4] People may reasonably disagree about whether the benefits of a civil religion, including its unifying power and its call to higher purposes, outweigh its drawbacks—its homogenization of religion and its (sometimes) arrogant association of the progress of the United States with God's purposes. In any event, I am not proposing here that all reference to the divine and to transcendent understandings of this, or any other, country's destiny should disappear from public dialogue.

A closely related point concerns references to imagery that derives from our religious heritage. Ethical notions like the Golden Rule, stories from the Bible, and personal exemplars like St. Francis of Assisi are part of our general cultural heritage. These sources of understanding and appeal should not be extirpated from public discourse, especially since, as John A. Coleman suggests, this religious tradition may provide the richest source of cultural symbols for the perspective that people should care deeply about each other and for the common welfare.[5] Suppose that in a public address opposing a cut in welfare programs, a speaker, drawing from the story of Cain and Abel, said: "Am I my brother's keeper? Time and again that question presents itself to us as individuals and a society. The answer is yes. We cannot be true to ourselves and our traditions if we fail to cope adequately for the poor and needy." I do not mean to challenge this use of religious imagery and reference to a tradition with important religious roots. Suppose instead the speaker said: "The story of Cain and Abel as reported in Genesis clearly establishes that God wants us to take care of other people; other parts of the Old Testament (citing passages) and the continuous teachings of the true Christian church (citing authoritative church documents) reveal the minimum amount of care for the poor and needy that is required; the proposed cutbacks fall under those minimum standards and are therefore contrary to the will of God." That is the kind of explicitly religious support for a particular position that I claim (with the qualifications I have indicated) is inappropriate for general public dialogue.[6]

My basic thesis, that fully public discourse advocating political positions should not rely on explicitly religious arguments, is subject to two related objections. The most straightforward objection is that my proposal promotes a degree of concealment that is immoral and unwise. If citizens *rely* on religious grounds, shouldn't they say so and explain their reasoning?

I begin with the assumption that, apart from private conversations with friends and acquaintances and exploratory discussions in small groups like faculties, political discourse mainly involves advocacy of positions arrived at, not full revelation of all the bases by which a decision is reached. We do not expect a speaker to reveal all the personal judgments that have led him to his position; we expect him to put forward considerations that will appeal to others.[7] Effective argument appeals to grounds that the audience will accept. If the audience includes many people who do not share one's religious convictions, the most effective persuasion will rely on other than narrow religious arguments. Thus, the course I have suggested not only relates to liberal principles; it is also a maxim about effective advocacy for religious persons. Since most religious people cannot cearly identify where religious conviction leaves off and other values and factual judgments begin, they will *usually* suppose that the position they take will be the right one even apart from religious conviction, and they will not be insincere if they make arguments in nonreligious terms.

Even the most self-critical person will be likely to think that there are strong nonreligious arguments for his position, though perhaps conscious that his decision in favor of the position is determined by religious conviction. He does not act inappropriately by making strong arguments in nonreligious terms even if he does not believe they are ultimately dispositive.[8] In social life, as I have suggested, we are often in the position of making rational arguments for the position we think best, even if we are aware that our own commitment to the position may be determined by underlying premises that are really not subject to rational demonstration.

Despite what I have said thus far, these recommendations may seem to smack of something unwholesome, even dishonest. Part of my response to that worry concerns expectations. If people understand that as part of the liberal tradition, religious premises are not to figure prominently in ordinary political argument, they will not suppose that their omission signifies their unimportance for the speaker. Further, I am not suggesting that one actually try to conceal the place of religious conviction. Suppose that a speaker has urged protection of the fetus on nonreligious grounds. If asked by a member of the audience "Isn't it true that your religious beliefs inform your judgment that the fetus is entitled to life?", he should answer "yes" if that is the case. Indeed, he might even say at the beginning of his own speech that religious convictions undoubtedly have an effect on one's views of the topic, but that he is going to present an argument that does not rely on those premises. My supposition that the discourse in which social issues are publicly argued should be largely nonreligious is not an invitation for private people to conceal the grounds of their own conclusions.

One might still object that I have not gone far enough, that even if people need not engage in extensive argument cast in religious terms, they should state clearly their religious premises so that others may be more fully aware of the place these premises have in determining their positions. Initially, I shall assume that this challenge concedes the appropriateness of relying on religious convictions and is actually directed at fuller candor about that reliance. The first point to be noted is that the counsel of full candor would have to apply to all bases of judgment that reach beyond shared premises and common forms of reasoning. If a religious person should disclose his religious premises, a nonreligious person should disclose that what he finds ultimately persuasive on the subject of abortion are his intuitive feelings, not the rational arguments some have put forward. The idea would be that people should not try to deceive others into believing that positions are rationally demonstrable when they realize that they are not.

So understood, the argument for candor becomes a general one about the limits on a good citizen's persuasive advocacy, rather than an argument limited to religion. My own sense is that in private conversations and in small groups something like full candor is usually most appropriate. One really should try to lay one's own convictions on the table as fully as one can, thus avoiding manipulation of one's partners in dialogue and permitting a much more sincere and possibly productive exchange of views. I also have the sense that broader community discourse would be enriched were that example of forthright candor more commonly followed. A notable result might be greater tolerance for those who adopt varying nonrational premises. One cannot, however, draw out of the premises of liberal democracy conclusions about how far political advocacy may seek to persuade, without outright dishonesty, and how far it should rest on candor that is as complete as possible. Present practices permit much less than full candor about personal starting points generally,[9] and no reason appears to single out religious premises for some specially high degree of candor.

The argument for *full* candor might be turned around to mount a second objection, a challenge to my basic thesis that citizen *reliance* on religious convictions is proper. The claim would be that public dialogue should both provide a basis for reasoned resolution of social issues by all citizens *and* reflect actual grounds of individual decisions. Since discourse about religious convictions fails the first test, only arguments in terms of common forms of reasoning should be made publicly. Since discourse should reflect actual grounds of decisions, people should try hard to rely on such grounds for their own political positions. We can see now more clearly how assumptions about the quality of public discourse can be used to support the claim that shared premises and forms of reasoning should be the exclusive bases for citizens' decisions.

My response is to repeat that a viable theory of liberal democracy cannot demand the impossible. If shared grounds are radically inconclusive about major social issues, one cannot expect wholly reasoned resolution of those problems.[10] If liberal theory really requires that, then the poverty of liberal theory is shown, but I claim that the principles of liberal democracy are not so rigorously rationalistic.

Liberal democratic theory already contains assumptions by which judgments based partly on unshared premises may be accommodated. To oversimplify greatly, there are two competing models of how a liberal democracy should work: one is that citizens should, or will inevitably, seek to have their own preferences satisfied in the political process and that government should try to satisfy as many preferences as possible; the other is that citizens and governments should seek to advance political positions that are right for the general public. On the first, "accommodating preference," model, the proper political choice will often depend on actual preferences that are held; the preferences themselves, perhaps within certain limits,[11] are beyond rational scrutiny and discourse. Only on the second, "civic virtue," model does it seem possibly conceivable that choices could be examined without reference to one's own personal preferences. Closer examination reveals that even on that model, irreducible preference will sometime be critical to a proper decision.

We can see the point most easily if we imagine a small direct democracy like a faculty.

A law school faculty has decided to teach a month long summer program in American law in Europe. The decision must now be made exactly when the course will be held. The relevant facilities would be available at any time and attendance at the program will not be affected by the choice of dates. All agree that the only relevant consideration is convenience for the faculty itself. The meeting might proceed with each individual expressing a preference, and its basis and intensity. Or an initial show of hands, with an opportunity to express any specially intense preference, might constitute a first step. On either of these courses, a final vote might be taken in which each faculty member voted for what appeared to be the best dates overall. Alternatively, a vote, or a series of votes, with each voting his or her own preference, might be made dispositive; that vote could be by simply majority or with some weighted value[12] for specially intense preferences.

Since in a democracy an initial decision is typically subject to reconsideration, whether the dispositive vote itself involves preference expression or one's sense of what is best overall seems here to be not much more than a formality (unless, perhaps, it turns out that the order in which alternatives are voted upon is critical). Some reasons for wanting dates may objectively be stronger than others, but other reasons will resolve to conflicting desires for personal convenience that do not yield easily to rational weighing. Whether people vote preferences or overall desirability, the crucial determinant of a good outcome will be the number and strength of preferences for various dates; either these will not be subject to interpersonal rational analysis at all or the effort to undertake such analysis would not be worth the time of the group.[13]

A similar issue could arise for public government.

> A countywide vote is to be held on whether a wilderness area will be opened to skiers. Everyone realizes that some people who delight in skiing will not be able to ski unless the area is opened and that permitting the skiing will impair the enjoyment of the area by nonskiers. Within a radius of a few hundred miles, there are other wilderness areas and other ski areas, so county residents rightly feel they can concentrate on the needs and wishes of people presently within the county, not on the preferences of a larger populace or the needs of future generations.

Certainly among relevant considerations for the decision are how many people want to ski, how many nonskiers would suffer if skiing were allowed, and how intensely the members of each group feel. Not much can be said rationally about the comparative joys of skiing and of viewing woods that are not scarred by ski trails. Much more than the preferences among possible dates of an academic program, these preferences are irreducible. On the extreme civic virtue model, each citizen would have to weigh the interests of skiers and nonskiers, but doing so without any systematic sampling of opinion may be very difficult. Quite possibly, a better strategy for reaching the best decision here would be for each citizen to vote his or her own preferences. In any event, even if citizens vote to do what is best for the community, they will have to accept more or less as given the subjective preferences of their fellows. We have, even on this model, conflicts of preferences that cannot be resolved by the political process on shared grounds, except in the sense that people agree to the ideal of an appropriate accommodation of preferences.

Conflicts of judgments that reach beyond common forms of reasoning and lead people to different opinions about what social justice requires might be viewed similarly to the conflicts of nonrational preferences that are a staple of the preference accommodation model and that are, as I have illustrated, sometimes important even under a civic virtue model.[14] When analysis based on publicly accessible reasons runs out, all the political process can do is to accommodate the contending claims in the best way it can. Since any plausible model of liberal democracy must admit some areas in which resolution on shared bases is not possible, the existence of such areas is plainly not at odds with the operation of a liberal polity. I have shown that many political issues of justice are unavoidably among those areas.

I now briefly examine special problems that concern religious leaders and organizations. Critical questions for religious leaders are whether they should support particular candidates or urge that voters decide which candidates to support on the basis of single issues. The problem is not their indisputable right to take such actions but whether these actions are desirable and in harmony with the spirit of a liberal polity. In general, such involvement in the political process is unwise, since it tends to link religious leaders and organizations too closely to the government. The broad policy of major religious groups not to support particular political candidates reflects a wise prudential judgment not to mix practical religion and practical politics too closely.[15] But on a matter such as this, one cannot be absolute. If the government pursues a policy that is so abhorrent from a religious point of view that it dominates all other issues, or if a candidate strongly supports a set of values that is directly at odds with interests and values a religion takes as preeminent, then a religious leader may reasonably make an exception to ordinary principles of restraint. One could not fault religious leaders during the civil rights era if they urged votes against rabid segregationists. The controversy over abortion is more troublesome, but if a religious leader really believes that permissive abortion results in the murder of millions of human beings, the issue takes on an understandable preeminence that it does not have for most people.

The organization of political interests and positions along religious lines presents another question. Religious leaders urging political conclusions certainly may aim for coordination within a denomination to develop and disseminate appropriate positions. For example, the adoption of stands on public issues by Roman Catholic bishops and the direction that these stands be conveyed to Catholics in individual parishes are appropriate activities in a liberal society. Further, when a church or other religious organization has reached a definite position on a social issue, it appropriately states and urges that view before legislative bodies and in other public settings.[16]

Attempts to organize people along religious lines for overtly political purposes is much more dubious than interdenominational coordination and public urging of positions adopted by religious groups. Here, as with general political discourse, effective strategy and observance of the spirit of liberalism largely coincide. A minority religion that creates its own narrow political action group or political party is not likely to promote its political objectives with maximum effectiveness.[17] Such efforts will make its positions seem sectarian, leaving some outsiders indifferent and inducing hostility among others who wish to avoid dictation by religious views they do not accept.[18] Political organization that bridges religious divisions is likely to be more effective and is more consonant with the broad principle that religion and politics should remain roughly separate.[19]

When leaders of a religious group support political organizations that bridge religious lines, may they properly encourage their members to join and support these organizations? Ministers can appropriately preach against abortion; can they also promote particular "pro-life" organizations? Such urging imparts a degree of involvement with the political that is troubling, but it cannot be ruled out on principle if the leaders believe that the members can most effectively promote vital political aims in this way.

Related to the problems just discussed is the involvement of religious leaders directly in the political process. Obviously clergy and other leaders will be involved in teaching and discussion within the church about public issues, and they are appropriate spokesmen before a larger public for positions the church has adopted. The question here concerns further activities, such as leading major political movements (as those for civil rights or against abortion) and running for office.

An initial point that needs to be made is that in our society ministers are not necessarily locked into a life as clergy, any more than are the members of other professions. Although among some religious groups the minister or priest may have distinctive functions he is not to abandon, in many others someone who is once a minister may decide to engage himself in a secular vocation. There is certainly no premise of liberal democracy that would bar people who are once ordained from playing a full political role, people like Andrew Young and William Moyers who become identified predominantly as officials or political figures rather than religious leaders. Of course, if a person who is already an important religious figure makes a very swift transition, there may be some confusion of roles in public perception, but the problem I have mainly in mind concerns someone who is simultaneously an important religious figure and an important political actor.

Principles of church-state separation are severely strained when such a person has public office, especially executive office, or runs for office with any expectation of being elected. If someone simultaneously holds himself out as a political leader and a religious leader, say, running for office *and* maintaining a parish ministry or preaching on television, no amount of assurances by him that his political aim is not to promote distinctly religious objectives is likely to persuade those of different religious beliefs. Because a person running for executive office would make decisions for all the people, the concern in this respect is greater than when a religious figure seeks one of many legislative positions, but even in the latter case, constituents of various religious persuasions may feel substantially excluded if any active religious leader is elected.

Sometimes people run for office with no expectation of being elected, hoping to make some symbolic point and to move policies in a desired direction. This, I think, is a realistic appraisal of Jesse Jackson's candidacy for the Democratic presidential nomination in 1984. Such an effort for a religious leader (although I am not sure whether Jackson counted as a religious leader during that period) seems to me to fall somewhere between leading a major nongovernmental political effort and running for office with an expectation of being elected. In practical effect, it is very much like the former, but it resembles the latter in two important respects. Such a candidacy represents an implicit statement that one's own election would be appropriate, a conclusion that itself is in tension with church-state separation, and the realities of politics are such that the candidate is likely to encourage support by overstating his own electability. He addresses supporters as if he has a chance at election and as if his election would be highly desirable.

The leader of a major political effort, such as the civil rights movement or the Moral Majority, is not running for office, but is playing an important political role. In the instances of Martin Luther King, Jr., and Jerry Falwell we have two people who were undoubtedly major political and religious figures at the same time. If political efforts are directed at specific issues of conscience, a religious leader's involvement is less threatening to church-state separation than if he aspires to the reins of office, both because his efforts will remain at one remove from final political decisions and because he does not involve himself in the entire spectrum of political choices. Still, when a religious leader stands at the head of a movement not organized along explicitly religious lines, there is bound to be a blurring of his religious perspectives and the movement's political principles, which are meant to embrace those with different religious perspectives. Perhaps one can say that such a situation is generally unfortunate, that, other things being equal, political leadership would better be in the hands of someone who does not simultaneously hold himself out as a religious leader; but much depends on context. It will matter what other potential leaders are available, whether the religious leader's religious principles are embracive or exclusive, what is the degree of his tact and eloquence in including others of different faiths. Further, though such a conjunction may impose some strain on ordinary premises of liberal democracy, the blurring of religious and political aims may occasionally be highly productive in promoting social justice. Thus, while the occupancy of important and direct political roles by religious leaders is a cause for serious concern, such roles for a religious leader who also seeks to be a good liberal citizen cannot comfortably be ruled out as inevitably misguided.

The general themes of this chapter have been the following. The liberal ground rules for public political dialogue are more constraining than the principles relevant to how private citizens make political choices, and religious convictions should figure much less prominently in public justifications for political positions than they may in the development of the positions themselves. Political activities by religious groups and leaders are a healthy part of a liberal democracy, but a degree of self-restraint is appropriate to prevent dangerously close connections between religion and politics.

Notes

1. See S. Schwarzchild, "The Unnatural Jew," 6 *Environmental Ethics*, pp. 347–62 (1984).

2. See C.E. Curran, *Transition and Tradition in Moral Theology*, pp. 89–90 (Notre Dame, Ind., Univ. of Notre Dame Pr. 1979).

3. See generally National Conference of Catholic Bishops, *The Challenge of Peace: God's Promise and Our Response* (Wash., D.C. U.S. Catholic Conference 1983); C.E. Curran, supra note 2, at pp. 120–21. From a Protestant perspective, John Bennett has written of the importance of middle axioms, common moral convictions shared by Christian and non-Christians, from which specific policy implications can be drawn. See J.C. Bennett, *Christian Ethics and Social Policy* (N.Y., Charles Scribner's Sons 1946); P. Lehmann, *Ethics in a Christian Context*, p. 148 (N.Y., Harper & Row 1963). See also R.J. Neuhaus, *The Naked Public Square*, p. 125 (Grand Rapids, Mich., William B. Eerdmans Pub. Co. 1984).

4. R.N. Bellah, "Civil Religion in America," in D. Cutler, ed., *The Religious Situation*, p. 389 (1968). See also R.N. Bellah, *Beyond Belief*, pp. 168–72 (N.Y., Harper & Row 1970).

5. J.A. Coleman, *An American Strategic Theology*, pp. 184–98 (N.Y., Paulist Pr. 1982). In Coleman's view, liberal philosophy emphasizes the pursuit of self-interest, to the neglect of the tragic dimensions of life and the need for civic virtue.

6. Id. at p. 195. Coleman, having strongly argued for the use of a public theology, says "I am not, in fact, particularly interested in seeing that specifically formulated theological *arguments* enter societal debate about policy" (emphasis in original).

7. As Daniel Callahan points out in *Abortion: Law Choice and Morality*, p. 9 (N.Y., MacMillan Co. 1970), groups advocate their positions in a one-sided way in the public arena.

8. There is an interesting wrinkle here closely related to a point made in Chapter 3, about belief that arguments are ultimately dispositive. If a person employs exclusively rational arguments, but believes that religious premises cru-

cially supplement what is rationally discoverable or determine the perspective from which the rational arguments are viewed, he is making arguments that he does not think standing by themselves are fully persuasive. If the person instead believes that religious premises always confirm what rationality can discover, his position is subtly different. He may not fully understand the rational arguments he makes or may not find them convincing to his rational faculties alone; but he may *believe*, because of his religious convictions, that these same rational arguments are dispositive. A Roman Catholic who accepts the Church's teaching on abortion *might* find himself in this position when he employs natural law arguments for the status of the fetus.

9. See B. Williams, *Ethics and the Limits of Philosophy*, pp. 100–2 (Cambridge, Mass., Harvard Univ. Pr. 1985).

10. See id. at p. 117; V. MacNamara, *Faith and Ethics*, pp. 204–6 (Wash., D.C., Georgetown Univ. Pr. 1985).

11. I suggested earlier that preferences might be irrational if their satisfaction conflicted with the satisfaction of one's own more important preferences. Preferences might also be irrational if they are the consequence of defective preference-forming mechanisms of mechanisms that function inadequately. See J. Elster, *Sour Grapes: Studies in the Subversion of Rationality*, pp. 1–42 (Cambridge, Cambridge Univ. Pr. 1983). Some preferences, say to see other people suffer physical pain, might be thought unacceptable per se. Other preferences, say to subjugate racial minorities, may be barred by liberal democratic premises.

12. Such a self-selecting extra weighting of one's vote could work only in a small group with a high degree of mutual trust. Rawls suggests that the intensity of preferences is not relevant (*A Theory of Justice*, pp. 230–31, 361 [Cambridge, Mass., Harvard Univ. Pr. 1971]; "Justice as Fairness: Political not Metaphysical," 14 *Philosophy and Public Affairs*, pp. 223, 243–44 [1985]; "Kantian Constructivism in Moral Theory: The Dewey Lectures," 77 *Journal of Philosophy*, p. 545 [1980]), but I am doubtful he has in mind examples like this one. See generally J. Fishkin, *Tyranny and Legitimacy*, p. 14 (Baltimore, Johns Hopkins Univ. Pr. 1979), suggesting that on some issues for an apathetic majority to overrule a sufficiently intense minority would be tyranny.

13. Perhaps most preferences for dates are reducible to considerations other people could evaluate, such as other commitments, convenience for family members, reactions to warmer or cooler weather. If this is so, the major barrier to extensive rational evaluation of the relevant preferences may be that the issue does not warrant that degree of examination.

14. If a person adopted one version of the extreme civic virtue model about these matters, he might conclude that each citizen should try to figure out the best accommodation possible, treating all positions resting on judgments beyond publicly accessible reasons as of equal intrinsic merit. On this view, a person believing on religious grounds that the fetus deserves protection might have to accede politically to a contrary view that he reconigzed was accepted by the vast majority of fellow citizens. But even then, his religious convictions could count in the initial

stage of identifying claims to be accommodated. In any event, this version of the extreme civic virtue model would be inapt. Everyone agrees that when citizens think arguments from shared premises support their position, they are supposed to vote their convictions rather than count other people's noses. The intermingling of "personal" and religious premises and arguments based on shared forms of reason is too great to ask citizens to count noses as to one and vote convictions as to the other.

15. See, e.g., C. Whelan, "Religious Belief and Public Morality," 151 *America*, Sept. 29, 1984, p. 159.

16. See, e.g., D. Saperstein, "Jewish Perspectives on the Role of Religion in the Political Process," 1 *Journal of Law and Religion*, pp. 215, 218–20 (1983). There are some difficult issues that my single sentence passes over. One is the wisdom of relatively weak national religious organizations taking a political position when there has been little input from members and the position may be rejected by most members. Another concerns the kinds of lobbying tactics appropriate for religious, and other public interest, organizations. See J. Berry, *Lobbying for the People: The Political Behavior of Public Interest Groups* (Princeton, N.J., Princeton Univ. Pr. 1977). What I say in the text is barely the beginning of thought about appropriate roles for religious groups in our liberal democracy.

17. See, e.g., C. Henry, *Aspects of Christian Social Ethics*, pp. 142–43 (Grand Rapids, Mich., William B. Eerdmans Pub. Co. 1964).

18. See R.J. Neuhaus, supra note 3, at p. 52.

19. See id. at p. 107, pointing out that, contrary to what a good many liberals suppose, the Moral Majority does not portray itself as a distinctly religious movement.

13

Religious Convictions and Official Action

Conclusions about individuals form the starting point for assessment of the influence of religious convictions on official action. I have argued that, with certain qualifications, an individual acts consistently with the spirit of political liberalism when, in adopting a position on an issue of public policy, he gives weight to his religious convictions in resolving highly complex issues of fact and in making judgments of value that require some input beyond shared premises and forms of reasoning. The individual can appropriately vote on the basis of public policy judgments that are influenced by his religious convictions, and he can advocate these positions and organize to promote them. When speaking to an audience of those who share his religious premises, he properly urges the connection between those premises and his public policy conclusions; when speaking to a more general audience, he should ordinarily cast his arguments in essentially nonreligious terms, though he should not conceal the bases of his own convictions and should feel free to use cultural imagery that derives from our religious tradition.

This chapter asks how far officials may take religious convictions into account in performing their public roles. I shall concentrate on legislators and judges. In a liberal society, public officials plainly should not rely on religious premises to a *greater* extent than individuals making up their own minds,[1] so the two poles for analysis are that officials should not rely on religious premises at all and that they can rely to the same extent as can private persons.

Legislators

Legislators must vote on proposed legislation. Because they are also leaders of public political opinion and their political positions partly determine whether voters will approve their performance, they must formulate and advocate views on laws and policies in public.

I am going to make four simplifying assumptions. The first is that a prospective legislator running for office is in the same position as a present legislator. Whatever may be true of fringe candidates who have no hope of being elected but wish their candidacies to symbolize something, a person with a realistic chance of being elected should develop his positions on issues in a manner similar to that of legislators in office. However often such bonds may be broken, candidates do have some obligations of fidelity to their constituents to stick to positions asserted during the campaign, and they have duties of honesty not to misrepresent how they will decide issues once they are elected.

A second assumption is that we can disregard the extent to which legislators may compromise otherwise appropriate standards in the interests of idiosyncratic constituencies and electability. Suppose that we could somehow identify the extent to which legislators and an understanding citizenry imbued with the liberal spirit could reasonably expect a legislator to be guided by religious convictions. We might then imagine a district in which most citizens accepted a distinctly illiberal view of the appropriate role of religious convictions in the making of public policy and were unwilling to vote for anyone who disregarded their religiously based views. Perhaps a legislator for that district could reasonably compromise the ideal principles in the service of his own constituents and in the interests of being reelected,[2] especially if the likely alternative were the election of someone wholly indifferent to liberal principles. How far actors in the political world should adhere in their actions to "correct" standards and damn the consequencs and how far they should bend in terms of what is realistically possible is a pervasive and troubling question, but one that I avoid. I shall suppose that a legislator can persuade enough members of a constituency to accept what are the proper liberal principles for reliance on religious convictions so that his own continuance in office and his effectiveness will not be threatened by his adherence to those principles.

A third simplifying assumption is that we can disregard differences between the interests of a particular legislator's constituents and those of the entire body of citizens. How far a legislator should promote the particular welfare of his own district as contrasted with that of the general population is an important question, but it is not a central one for our purposes. (The related question whether a legislator should reflect his constituent's *views* is addressed below.)

My fourth simplification is to talk about legislators without discussing the role of political parties.[3] In many liberal democracies, party decision effectively determines how individual legislators vote. Parties are not nearly so powerful in the United States, but party influence and loyalty are still important factors in some votes. To a large extent, the questions I discuss in terms of individual legislative choice could also be addressed in terms of a proper position for those who control political parties.

Once we have eliminated these various complexities concerning what legislators should do, we are left with a rough cleavage in traditional theories of representation.[4] The "delegate" theory, which enjoyed considerable prominence in colonial America,[5] is that the legislator should reflect in his actions the views of those he represents; the "trustee" approach, associated with Edmond Burke's famous "Bristol speech,"[6] is that the legislator is empowered to make up his own mind about what is sound public policy.[7] Both views in extreme form are implausible. The more serious issues are precisely how much and when representatives should be guided by one perspective rather than the other.[8] For our inquiry about the role of religious convictions, we do not have to worry about how much weight in which contexts each perspective should have; we need only understand that legislators often should accord weight to constituency views[9] and often should try to determine for themselves what a sound decision would be.[10]

If appropriate deference to constituency opinion meant a completely passive reflection of citizens' views, either the views of the majority or the views that somehow carry the most weight, the question about reliance on constituents' religious convictions would answer itself: representatives' indirect reliance on religious convictions would mirror the direct reliance of relevant constituents. But I suppose that legislators, even when acting as "delegates," have some duty to screen out certain political views, or grounds for political views, that are at odds with liberal democratic premises.[11]

To revert to an example I used in Chapter 1, a legislator should certainly not vote against minority preferences because of constituent views if those views are based on desires to perpetuate racial subjugation. Or suppose that citizens rely on religious convictions in some way that is not consonant with liberal principles; they want to suppress actions just because they are sinful. A courageous legislator who considers liberal principles to be the secure foundation of our political order should refuse to go along. Rather, he should try to persuade voters that policy in a liberal democracy is not properly made on such grounds.

The serious questions arise when private individuals rely on religious convictions in a way that is consistent with the liberal spirit. Should legislators give views formed in this way any weight at all, and if so, should they give them the same weight as is given to positions formed in other ways, or less weight?

We have reason to start with an assumption that legislators may properly rely on positions formed in a proper manner. Saying that citizens can make up their minds on certain grounds but that legislators may not take the resulting conclusions into account would be somewhat paradoxical. The paradox is sharpened if one focuses on my conclusion that citizens can properly vote for candidates in accord with positions the citizens have arrived at on the basis of religious convictions. If legislators had to disregard these positions, a serious tension would exist between proper grounds for election and proper grounds for legislative decision. A further potential anomaly concerns direct votes by citizens on public issues. In many states, citizens must approve constitutional amendments; in many localities, they must approve certain taxes; and in many states and localities, referenda can override legislative decisions. It would be odd to think that what are proper bases for citizens' votes in these situations could not figure in legislators' deference to constituency opinion.

Against the conclusion that legislators may rely on all views formulated consistently with the liberal tradition, it might be argued that since public officials must represent the entire spectrum of religious views, they should not give weight to positions based on particular religious opinions. An adequate answer to this argument requires some preliminary clarification and a brief reprise of what I have stressed about citizens in the preceding chapters.

We can imagine a rough cleavage in defenses of the position that legislators should disregard religiously influenced constituency opinion that is not itself improperly formed. One defense would be that the implications of liberal democracy really only touch legislative decisions, that it is too much to expect that citizens will understand and restrain themselves according to any liberal democratic premises. Unless this defense treats all direct citizen voting on public issues as itself misguided, such voting is an embarrassment to it, for on issues on which citizens vote directly no legislative filter of raw opinions operates.[12] From the perspective of this book, the more fundamental answer to this defense of a gulf between principles applicable to legislators and those applicable to citizens is that most of the powerful reasons for accepting citizen reliance on religious convictions do not rest on the remoteness of citizens from actual political decision; the reasons are ones of inevitability, fairness, and unity of personality. I have argued that even the most public-spirited and conscientious citizens can properly allow their religious convictions to play a role in their political positions.

The second defense of the position that legislators should disregard religiously influenced constituency opinion acknowledges that liberal democratic premises reach citizens as well as legislators, but contends that the implications of those premises are different for the two groups. Even in respect to citizens, I have admitted that worries about the denigration of shared bases of judgment, a sense of exclusion for minorities, and political divisiveness are plausible reasons against conscious reliance on religious premises. But I have found the contrary arguments much stronger. Someone might say that the balance of the arguments as they affect legislators is quite different. The worries about reliance on religious convictions are much more serious when the behavior of legislators is involved, and since legislators are a relatively small number of the population and are professionally concerned with the making of political choices, the consequences of self-imposed constraint will be much less detrimental than if all or most citizens conscientiously tried not to take religious convictions into account.

In this form, a defense of excluding legislator reliance on constituency opinion influenced by religious convictions has an initial plausibility, but in addition to approving a paradoxical divergence between what can count for citizens and for legislators, the position still takes inadequate account of why citizens can rely on religious convictions and how they do so. I have emphasized how difficult it will be for a religious citizen to weigh the nonreligious merits of competing arguments and how often his employment of common forms of reasoning will be embedded in religious premises. If a person himself will often be hard put to know the degree to which religious conviction influences judgment, how much harder will it be for a legislator to make that assessment for the opinions of thousands of constituents. Further, I have urged that common forms of reason are radically inconclusive for many public issues; if a legislator is to defer to constituency opinion at all about these it would be unfair to defer to "personal" bases of constituency judgment and not to bases self-consciously related to religious convictions.

This conclusion is strengthened because, as I indicated earlier, many of the widely held personal feelings of today were earlier held as matters of religious conviction. If the evaluations based on such feelings cannot be established on reasoned grounds, legitimate legislative reliance should not depend on their religious origins being no longer recognized. Legislators must sometimes rely on constituency opinions that exceed the domain of common forms of reasoning; when legislators do so, the personal judgments of constituents should not be preferred to their religious convictions.

What of the possible argument that legislators should rely on the personal and religious judgments of constituents only when those judgments are supported by an overwhelming consensus? Even if, as I contend in Chapter 8, citizens need not await a consensus to promote political positions that go beyond shared forms of reasoning, perhaps legislators should not act until a consensus supports such a position. There are some obvious difficulties with this suggestion that closely resemble those explored in the earlier chapter. One concerns premises that are initially shared but begin to be challenged. Suppose that the full legal protection of newborns rests on judgments beyond reason.[13] Legislators are warranted in providing this protection so long as almost everyone agrees that it is appropriate. But if a substantial enough percentage of people, say 15 or 20 percent, starts to doubt that position, the consensus has disappeared. It would be odd to say that legislators must now disregard the belief of the great majority that protection should continue. A related difficulty is more general. Often no consensus will exist about a problem that cannot be settled on reasoned grounds. Legislators must choose to protect or not protect. Their decision is bound to reflect one set of judgments beyond reason in preference to another. As I have argued in Chapter 8, it would not make sense to say that in such circumstances, the law must remain unaltered; that principle would give too much weight to past practice and inertia. Nor would it make sense to say that in cases of division, legislatures should always refrain from legal prescription; application of that principle might demand that legislators sit by and allow what 80 percent of the people regard as the murder of innocent beings.

I conclude that liberalism does not require legislators to disregard constituent views grounded in religious conviction when these views are themselves formed in accord with liberal principles. Legislators may give some weight to such views whether or not there is a consensus behind them.

The matter of how much weight to give these is more troublesome. Suppose a legislator is considering two issues and the majority of opinions of his constituency are based on two very different grounds. On one issue, a substantial majority of constituents take a position that they think is implied by shared premises underlying the political order. On the second issue, the majority is as great but the constituents recognize that the ground for their position is a religious conviction. Reasons for deferring to constituency judgment may be especially powerful when citizens conceive of a position as required by justice understood in terms shared broadly by society. Perhaps legislators should give less weight to judgments based on religious convictions than to judgments thought to be derived from broadly shared premises. In practice, as I have said, people's propensity to conclude that what they believe on religious grounds about social issues is also required by secular justice precludes any sharp dichotomy between the two sorts of grounds, but the distinction retains some importance.

When we turn to legislators relying on their own convictions, the place of religion is more controversial. As a public representative in a state that is separated from religious organizations, perhaps the legislator should eschew reliance on religious premises insofar as he can. Everything I have said so far indicates how hard this might be to accomplish, but nonreliance might at least be held up as an ideal.

Imagine first a situation like that I posed at the beginning of Chapter 1.

> Jean, a member of Congress, must decide in a special vote whether to risk extinction of a species of fish. Sne must unavoidably rely on her own judgment, because she is unable to ascertain public opinion or thinks it is evenly divided. She sees the central question as coming down to whether the natural world is to be valued for its own sake. She realizes that her own view that it should be valued in this way is informed by her religious conviction about God's universe. She must make up her mind about how to vote. She is deeply uncertain what she would otherwise think and finds it extremely difficult to think about the political issue without reference to what her religion leads her to believe.

Liberalism does not demand that legislators deny the effect of convictions about which they feel deeply and which lead to positions also held by many who do not share their convictions. If a model of liberal democracy has nominal regard for the wholeness and integrity of religious persons, it cannot expect legislators, any more than private individuals, systematically to expunge all religious conviction as a guide to action.

It is more debatable what a legislator should do when he decides whether to rely on his own judgment or those of constituents, and he recognizes that his own judgment is determined by religious convictions that do more than set broad perspectives for his assessment of publicly accessible reasons. On these occasions, subject to qualifications, I believe the legislator should be very hesitant to override contrary constituent judgments, that is, he should be very hesitant to proceed on his religious convictions when he believes that constituent views are opposed to the political position his convictions yield.

The main complicating factors that lead to qualifications are intensity of conviction about an issue and notions of serious wrong. Perhaps when legislators reach the point of perceiving the religious roots of their own positions, the issues will typically be ones about which they feel very strongly and they may think that to act contrary to their convictions would be to fall into very serious wrongs. In deciding when to defer to constituent opinion and when to rely on his own, a legislator is properly guided by the strength of his own conviction; he will understandably be less willing to vote for a policy he is sure is deeply immoral than one he thinks is probably wrong or only unwise.

I want to imagine issues as to which this variable is eliminated, and the legislator has equal strength of conviction.

> Jean thinks that preferential treatment for minorities and saving endangered species are about equally important, but she thinks she can ground her view on preferences in shared premises and common reasons, whereas her view on the endangered species is based on religious premises. On both issues constituency opinions are opposed to her own.

Jean has been elected as a representative of the entire population, chosen for qualities that relate to political judgment rather than religious insight. If her views on preferential treatment start from common and shared grounds that do not implicate her special religious perspectives, she has more reason to rely on them than if her disagreement with her constituents is finally explicable in terms of a divergence between her particular religious insights and their personal judgments or religious convictions.

In sum, both constituent views and those of legislators themselves are entitled to greater weight when they are based on shared premises and common reasons than when they are self-consciously rooted in "personal" attitudes or religious convictions, but views of the latter sorts are ones that legislators can reasonably take into account.

I need say relatively little about the nature of a legislator's political discourse. He is a public figure, representing people of all religious hues and in a government that is separate from any church. Usually he is speaking to and for a general audience, and his discourse should be in nonreligious terms. The country is so generally religious that vague invocations of religion and the deity may be within the realm of acceptability: "God willing, we shall do our best" "We are a religious people unlike the atheist Communists." And legislators, like citizens, may call on imagery and ethical concepts that derive from our religious tradition. There is also room in the public discourse of legislators for some expressions of personal outlook and feeling, and these may include references to one's own religious convictions. But the serious urging of policies on the basis of particularistic religious premises is not proper.

A public official need not wholly eschew discourse directed at coreligionists; when he speaks to church groups he may urge that the tenets of the religion support the policy he adopts. He may also admit, when asked, the degree that his own conscience is informed by religion. But during the period of his office, when he is undeniably a political leader, he should probably not also hold himself out as a religious leader, making original arguments about the implications of religious doctrine for public policy and urging the acceptance of these arguments by members of the faith. His public character cannot be completely divorced from any action he takes in relation to public policy, and as the last chapter suggests, the mixing of the religious and official roles is not healthy.

The Judiciary

Whatever anyone else may do, judges, we might initially suppose, should not rely on religious conviction in making their decisions. Certainly we do not expect to see such arguments in judicial opinions, so there is a strong presumption that in a liberal society judicial discourse should not include them. Nevertheless, occasional reliance by judges on religious convictions is not improper. A full discussion of this topic would require a lengthy examination of judicial interpretation, but I shall content myself with a few summary comments.

Judicial opinions are formalized justifications for decisions. Opinions are supposed to refer only to what is legally relevant. If a distinction, however blurred, exists between decisions that are required by the existing law and decisions that reflect a kind of judicial legislation, the "legislative" decisions are not fully revealed in the opinions themselves, which tend to mount up the legal sources in favor of a result. What is legally relevant is generally conceived to be the same for all judges, so neither personal religious convictions nor any other idiosyncratic convictions are legally relevant. Given this understanding about judicial opinions, it follows that opinions should not contain direct references to the religious premises of judges.

References in opinions to the religious convictions of people more generally is trickier. By and large what people think about an issue is not legally relevant, but there are exceptions. How the clauses of the First Amendment that protect the free exercise of religion and forbid establishment of religion are properly interpreted and applied depends partly on the religious heritage of the country and may also depend on present attitudes about religion and about the religious significance of certain practices. For example, whether crèches in public parks constitute a forbidden establishment of religion has been thought to rest partly on whether people understand the crèche in that context in a religious way, and therefore view the crèche as amounting to state sponsorship of religion.[14] Thus, the religious convictions of the public could figure in this narrow domain to a limited extent.

Of greater interest are the areas in which present community morality might influence the development of common law or the interpretation of a statute. If a judge tries to discern community morality, say, in deciding what is "good moral character" under the naturalization statute, should he disregard all views based on religious premises? Here, we must draw a distinction between good moral character as it affects others and good moral character in some other sense. A popular view that someone's activities are sinful though they do not affect others should not count as relevant to what is "good moral character"; if under liberal principles, the state should not prohibit or inhibit those activities, neither should it use them to bar people from membership in the community.[15] But if many people understand the activities as inflicting direct and unjustifiable harm on others who deserve protection, then the fact that their religious convictions lead them to believe that the humans or other entities victimized deserve protection should not be a bar to taking their views into account.

Can judges reasonably avoid reliance on their own religious convictions? There is a model of judicial decision in which judges are always seeking to determine which result would fit best with existing legal materials. If judges *could* always decide cases in this way, then they would never be in the position of having to rely on personal convictions of any sort. But such a model is implausible. Some legal terms, such as "cruel and unusual punishment" or "good moral character," seem to refer the judge outward to nonlegal domains. Many people believe that in a much broader class of difficult cases, judges must, in a sense, legislate, since no determinate answer can be derived from existing legal materials. Even the most prominent modern spokesman for the law as discovery model, Ronald Dworkin, has made clear in recent writings that in choosing a theory that will best explain existing materials, a judge typically will have to make *independent* judgments of political morality, independent in the sense of not determined by the legal materials themselves.[16] So, a wide spectrum of opinion agrees that on some occasions judges cannot ultimately rely exclusively on legal materials for answers, but must make independent judgments.

That judges will have to make such judgments does not necessarily mean that they will realize they are doing so. In actual cases it is very hard to say where the law runs out. But I am going to imagine the stark case in which the judge is fully aware that an independent judgment is needed. Now, one might claim that in all those situations, judges should simply refer to community morality, but community morality will often be nonexistent or undiscoverable. Further, though the matter is certainly not free from controversy, there are probably at least some occasions when judges should be deciding what is actually right, not what the community thinks is right.

Both because of the indeterminacy of community opinion and because their task is sometimes to decide by themselves what is right, judges will occasionally have to decide what is a correct answer to an issue of moral and political philosophy. Let us suppose, for example, that the judge is interpreting an environmental statute and the statutory language is unilluminating for the problem at hand. Resolution of the issue seems finally to turn on how much respect is owed by humans to the natural world, with no clear guidance from the statute itself or legislative history. I see no escape from the proposition that the judge, like the legislator, may in such settings find it necessary to rely on his religiously informed answers to what is right, though the caution I offered about legislators' reliance applies even more strongly here. Each is a representative of a larger public, but the legislator is one of many and can be voted out of office. In some cases an individual judge will have the final say;[17] in others his voice will be proportionately much more influential than that of an individual legislator. Therefore, the judge should be extremely wary of relying on religious convictions, especially when he recognizes that his premises or the positions they yield are not widely shared. When a choice is available between standards of decision, a judge who understands that his own preferred resolution rests on a particularistic religious premise should look carefully for some other basis to resolve the case. But when such judgments are genuinely unavoidable, the judge within the constraints of the judicial role, should be able to rely on religious premises in the same manner as the citizen and the legislator.

Notes

1. But see infra note 11 for the possibility that as a delegate a legislator should carry out constituency wishes that are inappropriately formed.

2. The point is discussed in J.R. Pennock, "Political Representation: An Overview," in J.R. Pennock and J. Chapman, eds., *Representation: Nomos VIII*, pp. 19–20 (N.Y., Atherton Pr. 1968).

3. See M. Sobolewski, "Electors and Representatives: A Contribution to the

Theory of Representation," in J.R. Pennock and J. Chapman, eds., supra note 2, at p. 95.

4. See generally H. Pitkin, *The Concept of Representation* (Berkeley, Univ. of California Pr. 1972); J.R. Pennock and J. Chapman, supra note 2.

5. See, B. Bailyn, *The Ideological Origins of the American Revolution*, pp. 170–73 (Cambridge, Mass., Harvard Univ. Pr. 1967).

6. See E. Burke, "Speech to the Electors of Bristol," in 2 *The Works of Edmund Burke*, pp. 89, 3d. ed. (1869); H. Mansfield, Jr., "Rationality and Representation in Burke's 'Bristol' Speech," in C.J. Friedrich, ed., *Rational Decision: Nomos VII*, pp. 197–216 (N.Y., Atherton Pr. 1967).

7. I have put aside possible divergences in interests between the constituency and the public at large, but it is worth mentioning that the delegate theory fits most comfortably with the idea that a legislator's first duty is to his constituents, the trustee theory correlates well, as Burke's speech reflects, with a larger range of duty.

8. See Hastings Center Report, *The Ethics of Legislative Life* pp. 29–33 (Hastings-on-Hudson, N.Y., Hastings Center 1984).

9. If deference is due to what constituents now think, possibly some weight should also be given to what they *would* think if they were aware of the issue and alternative choices.

10. In respect to individual adoption of political positions and voting, we needed much less reference to ideal models of individual behavior. There, as the last chapter indicates, the crucial divergence in theories is between the idea that analysis of a political system should suppose (either because such behavior is desirable or inevitable) that individuals make claims and formulate positions basically in terms of self-interest, with compromises between competing interests to be worked out in the political process itself, and the normative idea that citizens should act on their best assessment of what is in the general welfare. If one's religious convictions lead one to think a policy is bad, almost always one thinks the policy is bad for the whole society if its interests are correctly understood; generally that person will also think the policy is not consonant with his own long-term self-interest, though sometimes he may think the policy itself (if not his attitude toward it) is indifferent from that perspective. (A religious person may not suppose his long-term personal interest is affected by policy toward a remote country, but he may think that his leading a proper religious and political life requires him to contend for the policy that is more just.) In most situations in which a person supports a political policy based on his religious convictions, he will not perceive an important difference between public and self-interest.

The critical difference between legislative choice and individual choice for our purposes is the possibility that legislators should vote on the basis of perceptions and values other than their own, namely those of their constituents or a larger part of the citizenry.

11. One could conceivably support an extreme form of the delegate theory, under which legislators should act on constituency views as they are, performing no

screening function. In that event, whatever limits would be appropriately understood by citizens would not be the business of the legislator deciding what political choice to make. Those limits would be relegated exclusively to self-monitoring. Given the legislator's much more active involvement in the political process and his sophistication about it, such a passive response to citizen preferences that are at odds with liberal democratic premises is clearly not called for.

12. This worry would be met to some extent if the only programs citizens could adopt would be ones also approved by legislators.

13. I here pass over the very real possibility that relatively full protection is constitutionally entrenched in the Fifth and Fourteenth Amendments, which protect persons from a deprivation of life without due process of law.

14. See the opinion in *Lynch v. Donnelly*, 465 U.S. 668 (1984); Marshall, "'We Know It When We See It': The Supreme Court and Establishment," 59 *Southern California Law Review*, pp. 514–37 (1986).

15. It might be argued that a community can circumscribe the admission of newcomers to membership on grounds that would not be an appropriate basis to restrict the activities of present members. If this argument had force, it would apply more plausibly to admission to permanent residence than to citizenship. At least as to activities that many people within the community regard as harmless and as matters of moral right, people should not be excluded from membership because they engage in them.

16. See, e.g., R. Dworkin, *Law's Empire* (Cambridge, Mass., Harvard Univ. Pr. 1985); "'Natural' Law Revisited," 34 *Univ. of Florida Law Review*, pp. 165–88 (1982). The point is developed in somewhat greater detail in a book review of mine, "Ronald Dworkin: *A Matter of Principle* and *Law's Empire*," 84 *Journal of Philosophy*, pp. 284–91 (1987).

17. In this respect executives resemble judges rather than legislators.

14

The Boundaries of Unconstitutionality

This final chapter considers the problem of constitutional law I have put to the side for the main part of the analysis: what reliance on religious convictions in lawmaking amounts to an impermissible establishment of religion? I need to begin with some important disclaimers and clarifications.

What I mainly discuss here is a narrow slice of all of establishment clause law. Typical church-state issues, such as financial assistance to religiously connected groups, religious exercises in public settings, state sponsorship of religious ideas, and accommodations to religious conscience, present serious constitutional questions quite independent of the particular premises that underlie adoption of some piece of legislation. In order to focus clearly on the connection between religious convictions and legislative choice, I shall not deal here with such typical church-state issues. Rather, I shall concentrate on laws that forbid, require, or authorize acts when the reason why a law treats an act in the way it does is traceable to someone's religious convictions. Obvious examples are laws forbidding consensual sexual acts, abortions, or particular forms of harm to animals, if religious convictions constitute a critical part of the grounds for believing these acts are wrongful.

As in Chapter 1, I must be careful about what I mean by unconstitutionality, given the difference between legislative and judicial roles and all the complexities of judicial appraisal of legislative action. Though this particular setting nicely illustrates those complexities, my aim is not to pursue them in depth. I begin with the assumption that if every legislator votes for a bill on grounds that are at odds with constitutional premises, the act is in some sense unconstitutional even if alternative permissible grounds could have supported the same legislation. Thus, if all members of a zoning board vote to permit a small factory in a black neighborhood because they hope its location there will help drive blacks from the community, their action would be unconstitutional even if other acceptable reasons might have led to the same decision. In a more extended sense, a single legislator who votes on improper grounds may be acting unconstitutionally, whatever the grounds that determine the votes of other legislators. Whether the "purpose" that is relevant to possible judicial invalidation of legislation involves the actual motives of legislators or only some more "objective" standard of the dominant import and effect of the legislation is itself both murky and controversial, but I believe that present establishment clause jurisprudence indicates that a dominant motive to impose or promote a particular religious view could be relied upon by courts to invalidate a statute if that motive were readily apparent. This is the most straightforward rendering of the Supreme Court's decision declaring unconstitutional a particular "moment of silence" statute evidently designed to encourage silent prayer in school; in that case, the majority of the Court strongly suggested that, absent such powerful evidence of impermissible motive, laws authorizing moments of silence would be acceptable.[1]

How far courts may investigate the actual motives of legislators is another troubling problem, and of course in typical settings, legislative motives will be mixed. Different legislators will vote for a bill for different reasons and even individual legislators will have a variety of reasons for their actions. The bare presence of an impermissible aim to impose or promote a particular religion does not render legislation unconstitutional, but I am assuming that if an impermissible motive is dominant and readily apparent, that is a basis on which courts can strike down a law.[2]

In what follows, I shall imagine that an unambiguous connection can be traced between religious convictions and resulting legislation. Because I do not think it matters for purposes of constitutional law[3] whether the connection involves the legislator's own convictions or his simple deference to convictions of his constituents, I shall disregard that distinction here.

Any comments on how constitutional provisions should be construed must employ some theory of constitutional interpretation. An appropriate place must be assigned to the relevant constitutional language, the intentions of these who framed and adopted the provisions, judicial decisions that have interpreted the provisions, the overall import of our constitutional scheme, and modern notions of what is just and socially desirable. Differences in strategies of constitutional interpretation correlate with sharp disagreements over what are deemed to be correct decisions. A thoroughgoing effort to assess the import of the main claims of this book for sound principles of constitutional law would require defending a general theory of a constitutional interpretation and making an extended examination of the history and scope of the First Amendment's religion clauses and the clauses of the Fifth and Fourteenth Amendments that forbid deprivations of life, liberty, and property without due process of law. In respect to a general theory, I shall simply state my own view that all the factors I have enumerated in this paragraph count significantly and that courts should develop discrete constitutional doctrines in light of judicial capacities and limitations and the overall premises of our liberal democracy. As to the particular place of the religion clauses, the critical element for our purposes is the principle of nonsponsorship, which has been an important theme throughout the book; the possible relevance of the due process clauses concerns limitations on arbitrary choice. The force of these clauses may now appear to be limited to requiring fair procedures, to safeguarding certain fundamental substantive rights (such as the right to have an abortion), and to establishing barely minimal standards of rationality in legislation. I shall consider, however, whether more forceful principles limiting legislative purposes may be warranted, without assuming that some expansion along these lines is foreclosed by existing law.

With some subtle variations, my conclusions about constitutional law bear close resemblance to my conclusions about the implications of the underlying premises of our liberal democracy. Part of the exercise of this chapter is to defend, albeit summarily, those conclusions as principles of constitutional law. Part of the exercise is to explain why some more encompassing principles are rejected. If the discussion is sound, its practical import for courts is decidedly limited, because rarely will a dominant and unambiguous connection between religious conviction and political choice be ascertainable. The discussion has considerable importance, however, for legislators (and for executives involved in legislative decisions), because it suggests that motives that are improper in terms of political philosophy may also be unconstitutional in some legal sense, even when judicial enforcement is highly unlikely.

Permissible and Impermissible Reliances on Religious Convictions

My thoughts about constitutionality parallel fairly closely the conclusions of Chapters 5 through 11. In Chapter 5, I argued that it is improper in a liberal democracy to forbid behavior just because it offends religious notions of wrong, and in Chapter 11, I suggested that people should not try to implement in the political process positions derived from religious beliefs that were clearly contrary to positions people would reach on the basis of shared premises and commonly accessible reasons. Here, I claim that the Constitution can be understood to embody similar constraints. In Chapters 6 through 10 I urged that it is proper to rely on religious convictions to define which entities deserve protection and to resolve difficult questions involving uncertain facts and conflicts of values. Not surprisingly, I conclude that such reliance on religious convictions presents no constitutional problem.

"Pure" Notions of Wrong

If legislation is adopted on the basis that behavior is bad, judged from a religious perspective, but without belief that that bad behavior causes secular harm to entities deserving protection, then the legislation should be held to violate the establishment clause. The basic claim, developed in Chapter 5, is that to demand that other people act in accord with dominant religious beliefs is to promote or impose those beliefs in an impermissible way. Though the religious beliefs themselves are not being directly imposed, requiring other people to live their lives as the beliefs prescribe is to impose the practical consequences of the beliefs. When the acts that the law forbids cause no ascertainable harm, this kind of imposition should be regarded as amounting to their establishment in a constitutional sense. The structure of this argument was suggested more than two decades ago by Louis Henkin, who argued that laws suppressing obscenity might be viewed as upholding a religious conception of sin and might therefore be declared invalid under the establishment clause.[4] A similar attack might be made against laws that forbid deviant sexual behavior among adults. Of course, plausible secular objectives might be used to defeat such attacks, and it may even be true that in few or no cases could the requisite connection to religious beliefs be found. But if the unambiguous connection to religion can be shown to be the main basis for the legislation, the establishment argument should succeed in the courts.

A closely related argument can be made under the due process clauses. The claim can be that unless some harm to secular interests can be shown or imagined, the rational basis that must underlie legislation is lacking. Were such a principle to be accepted, someone challenging prohibitory legislation would have to persuade a court that the grounds for the prohibition were unconnected to notions of secular harm, but would not have to establish that the driving force was religious ideas of wrong. The due process argument, in other words, would reach personal and traditional assumptions about wrongful acts as well as explicitly religious assumptions. Were the due process claim to have practical significance in courts, mere satisfaction over suppression could not itself count as a legitimate secular interest; otherwise, whenever people wished to enforce notions of wrong, their own satisfaction would establish the requisite secular interest in a prohibition.

The due process version of the argument against enforcing pure notions of wrong is somewhat more vulnerable than the establishment clause version. Many scholars and some judges think the exclusive province of due process is procedural or that the scope of substantive due process should be very limited. Nonetheless, setting some limits on what kinds of reasons can count in favor of legislation is much more a matter of "process" than establishing categories of fundamental rights, as recent due process cases have done for use of contraceptive devices,[5] abortion,[6] and family living arrangements.[7] It takes only a slight extension of the traditional principle that legislation must not rest on arbitrary grounds to bar reasons that are unconnected to claims of harm to secular interests, an extension I believe is appropriate.

In 1986, the Supreme Court faced the problem of legitimate reasons for legislation in *Bowers* v. *Hardwick*, a challenge to Georgia's statute prohibiting homosexual sodomy (and other sodomy).[8] By a narrow 5–4 decision, the Court upheld the constitutional validity of the statute. Most of the language in the opinions was addressed to whether earlier cases proclaiming a fundamental constitutional right to privacy should be taken to include a right to engage in homosexual relations in private, but some attention was given to the reasons underlying the prohibition. Justice White wrote for the majority:

> [R]espondent asserts that there must be a rational basis for the law and that there is none in this case other than the presumed belief of a majority of the electorate in Georgia that homosexual sodomy is immoral and unacceptable. This is said to be an inadequate rationale to support the law. . . . We do not agree, and are unpersuaded that the sodomy laws of some 25 states should be invalidated on this basis.[9]

In this rather unilluminating passage, the Court plainly rejected the due process argument that simple judgments of wrongness are not an appropriate basis of legislation, and very probably it meant to reject the analogous establishment argument as well.

In a dissent joined by three other Justices, Justice Blackmun said:

> The assertion that "traditional Judeo-Christian values proscribe" the conduct involved . . . cannot provide an adequate justification for [the law].

That certain, but by no means all, religious groups condemn the behavior at issue gives the State no license to impose their judgments on the entire citizenry. The legitimacy of secular legislation depends instead on whether the State can advance some justification for its law beyond its conformity to religious doctrine. . . .

This case involves no real interference with the rights of others, for the mere knowledge that other individuals do not adhere to one's value system cannot be a legally cognizable interest . . . .[10]

The dissenters plainly accept the claim that religious notions of wrong, standing alone, cannot support legislation, and the last passage also indicates approval of a due process principle that some harm to secular interests must underlie prohibitions. The burden of my discussion is that, whatever their proper application to homosexual sodomy, the principles that the dissent accepts and the majority rejects in these passages are sound principles of constitutional law.

Conclusions Contrary to Those Reachable by Common Forms of Reasoning

I turn now to laws based on religious convictions that are actually at odds with the conclusions of common forms of reason, laws that afford a protection opposed to any possible assessment that is consistent with rational thought as our society understands it. Suppose, for example, that gray cats were accorded a protection not given to other cats because of their claimed religious importance. If we put aside the possible claim of permissible accommodation to deeply held religious feelings, that kind of protective legislation should be viewed as an establishment of religion, and perhaps a violation of due process, since treating a cat's fur color as relevant to its moral status is patently unjustified from the standpoint of shared bases for normative appraisal. A similar conclusion would obtain if a critical factual judgment on which legislation was based was actually irrational. Instances of this sort of legislation are predictably nonexistent, or very rare, in a culture such as ours, where it is recognized that the law must govern people of diverse religious views and religious perspectives themselves are constantly reexamined in light of scientific knowledge and secular morality.

Chapter 11 makes the suggestion that a person properly relies upon religious convictions in the political process only when he or she remains open to the force of publicly accessible reasons. The difficult determination whether such openness exists in citizens or legislators is not an appropriate one for courts passing on legislation. Even if one focuses on legislators who are considering constituency opinion or deciding whether to rely on their own convictions, the requirement of openness to accessible reasons is too subtle in its impact to be cast as a standard of constitutional law. Thus, my claims about unconstitutionality based on lack of coherence with publicly accessible reasons are considerably more modest, and have much less practical significance, than my analogous claims about what liberal democratic premises imply for political action.

Appropriate Uses of Religious Convictions

A law should not be treated as unconstitutional if the place of religious convictions or personl intuitions is to define the entities that warrant protection or to help resolve questions of fact or conflicts of value when the critical problem is not one that shared premises and common forms of reasoning can resolve. A law protecting animals or fetuses is not an establishment of religion, even if it is religious convictions that largely persuade people that animals or fetuses warrant protection. I have already indicated why reliance on such views by citizens does not constitute an imposition of religion in the ordinary sense and further why such reliance not only is unavoidable and constitutionally protected, but is proper for a good citizen in a liberal society. These same reasons indicate why a law that embodies such reliance does not rest on a constitutionally invalid religious purpose, constitute an establishment of religion, or violate the due process requirement of a valid purpose.

Why Other Constitutional Approaches to Reliance on Religious Convictions Are Rejected

I now turn to other possible constitutional positions and explain my rejection of them. Since many of these bear resemblance to what I have discussed in Chapter 8 as some possible principles of proper behavior for liberal citizens, some of my responses here largely echo what is said there.

A More Restricted Notion of Religious Sponsorship

One possible position is that the constitutional idea of a forbidden religious purpose refers only to the promotion of religious belief or practices themselves and does not at all concern the prohibition of behavior as immoral. In this view, not only is abortion a moral rather than a religious question, the same may be said about consenting sexual acts and obscenity. The establishment clause would then have nothing to do with those subjects if all that was involved was a religiously informed view of what behavior was immoral. Though Chapter 5 is not addressed to constitutional interpretation, I have implicitly tried to meet this view there, as well as in brief comments in this chapter. The same values that foreclose establishment of religious opinions also foreclose the prohibition of acts simply because they constitute a religious sin. If that theoretical point is sound, the language and the boundaries of proper interpretation of the establishment clause are broad enough to treat prohibitions based on concepts of sin in this narrow sense as unconstitutional.

Treating Active Involvement by Religious Groups as Generating Establishments

A second possibility is that active involvement by religious organizations in the adoption of legislation would render a resulting statute unconstitutional. Though rhetoric about the gross threat posed by political activities of religious organizations occasionally may suggest such a constitutional principle, I am not aware of anyone who has seriously proposed and defended it. Three objections are conclusive. One is the unworkability of any test of degree here. How much activity and influence, in comparison with the activity and influence of others, would be needed to make legislation unconstitutional? It is hard to imagine how the requisite degrees of political effort and of success with legislators would be measured. The second objection concerns the disturbing implications for the political activity of religious groups. Not only are political efforts by these groups as well as other private organizations constitutionally protected, they should be deemed a healthy part of a liberal democracy. It would, of course, be a conceivable position that religious political activities are permitted but not favored, the view being that a liberal society would be better if religious organizations were not at all active. But at least with the plurality of religious organizations in the United States, their political involvement does not pose a threat to liberal government. Though the political involvement of religious groups is sometimes divisive, churches and related organizations represent both particular interests that warrant advocacy and deep strains of conscience. The constitution should not be interpreted to render legislation suspect whenever the activity of these organizations has helped to promote it. The third, and related, objection concerns the sorts of laws and policies that churches support. Very often the relevant laws or policies are strongly supportable on secular grounds; the involvement of religious organizations is mainly to call people to take a "longer view" based on justice and the permanent interests of the society. This might be said both about the misguided attempt to impose prohibition on society (the dreadful evils of alcohol misuse are real enough) and about efforts to have civil rights laws adopted and to have the country extract itself from the Vietnam War. If laws are otherwise justified and the grounds for their passage unobjectionable, the laws cannot reasonably be rendered unconstitutional because many of the people and organizations who make the arguments for these grounds are moved by religious conviction as well.[11]

A Priority for Values Fully Rooted in Publicly Accessible Reasons

A third possible approach to constitutionality corresponds to an approach discussed in Chapter 8, that in a conflict between a value rooted in common forms of reason and a value grounded significantly in personal attitudes or religious convictions, the value grounded in common reasons should take priority. In the context of an illustration I offered there, the idea is roughly this: that given basic concepts of personal liberty, a woman's strong interest in control of her body cannot rationally be denied, but that the interest of an early fetus in the preservation of its life is supportable only on the basis of some judgment beyond reason;[12] therefore the woman's interest should be given priority in political choice. Were this idea turned into a principle of constitutional law, the principle would be that when a legislature gives priority to a value based on a judgment beyond reason over a value that cannot reasonably be denied, it acts unconstitutionally. A straightforward reading of *Roe* v. *Wade*[13] (the Supreme Court decision establishing the constitutional right to have an abortion with the consent of one's doctor through the second trimester of pregnancy) suggests that the woman's interest is simply stronger than that of the fetus prior to viability, but the decision might be reconceptualized to rest on the proposition that because the woman's interest is squarely grounded in common forms of reason, it must prevail for purposes of constitutional law.

A general constitutional priority for judgments fully grounded in common reasons would presumably be an aspect of a due process requirement that legislation have a reasonable basis. The priority would then operate against all "personal" judgments of value, not just religiously based judgments.[14]

In response to various challenges to any expansive substantive due process, I shall assume that a priority for values based on publicly accessible reasons is within an appropriate range of what due process might include if the priority is otherwise sound. If the priority is to have judicial significance, the boundaries it would mark between legislative choice and judicial scrutiny must be appropriate ones for a liberal democracy with judicial review.

At the simplest level, the priority would certainly not be sound. As I have suggested, our social morality is shot through with judgments beyond common reason, among them that human infants deserve the protection of mature human beings and that we should make substantial efforts to preserve dying species. Holding unconstitutional every legislative decision to implement one of those values at the expense of some other interest or value that could not reasonably be rejected would be absurd. Often the conflict will be between a widely shared and strongly held judgment that reaches beyond reason and an undeniably rational but very weak value, such as the economic benefits of killing members of a particular endangered species.

To be plausible, the principle of priority for judgments based on common reasons would have to be qualified. Priority might be given only if the value based on reason met some test of importance or if the competing value failed some such test. One might insist that a value beyond reason be relied on only if it serves a compelling interest. That test, however, would be too severe, since a moderately substantial value of this sort should be able to outweigh a weak value based on reason. One might instead allow a value based on personal attitudes or religious convictions to hold sway only if it were more powerful than the value based on common reasons, but that standard would have no practical import. Laws that interfere with rationally undeniable values will rarely be adopted unless many people believe the competing value is more powerful. Abortion is a perfect illustration: those who favor a restrictive law regard the right to life as more important than the woman's control over her body. Thus, comparing the strength of the two values will rarely be helpful if the aim is to develop a test that will sometimes give priority to values supportable on common reasons alone. One might require priority for the value based on common reasons so long as the value is an important one. This hurdle is one that the woman's interest in her body could pass but that the hunter's ordinary economic interest in killing members of a nearly extinct species could not.[15] Under this approach the result in *Roe* v. *Wade* could be justified.

My basic objections to such a principle are, first, that it demands a distinction between values based on common reasons and those that are not that would be exceedingly difficult for legislators and courts to apply in practice and, second, that by according priority to values based on common reasons, it grants a superiority to rational modes of thought that is inappropriate given the range and complexity of moral judgments that individuals and societies must make. Though I shall not attempt to develop the second objection at this point, I believe that a good deal of the body of this book supports it.

Another possible qualification would be allowing priority for judgments beyond reason only if they are generally shared. My problems with this approach are indicated in a slightly different context in the ensuing discussion on combined attention to sources of values and political actors.

Conceivably, a priority of values grounded in common reasons might be based on the establishment clause instead of the due process clauses. In that event, the priority would apply only against values that are religiously grounded. Such an approach would require legislators and courts not only to distinguish judgments based on religious grounds from those based on common reasons, but also to ascertain when values that receive some support from religious convictions are also embraced on personal nonreligious grounds that would not raise establishment difficulties. Such a determination would be virtually impossible to make, and the distinction it would reflect would create an unfortunate preference for values derived from personal feelings over those rooted in religious convictions.

Combined Attention to Sources of Values and Political Actors

Although subsequently abandoning his main thesis, Lawrence Tribe developed one of the most sophisticated treatments of this general problem.[16] Recognizing the pitfalls of any simple test along the lines suggested, he comes up with a multifaceted test that would support *Roe* v. *Wade* on establishment clause grounds and would conceivably authorize judicial invalidation in some other situations. Tribe is sensitive to the critical role of nonrational judgments of value and does not suppose they can properly be extirpated from the legislative process. He recognizes that the widespread support of particular moral notions by religious convictions cannot alone make legislation of those notions unconstitutional, and he also recognizes that extensive church involvement on behalf of legislation cannot itself be a basis for invalidation. Tribe manages to arrive at a set of much more plausible and circumscribed principles that he claims are responsive to the danger of religious involvement in political decisions and that happen to be neatly tailored to support a constitutional right to abortion.

Tribe begins by asserting that at this point in history, the only theories that claim the status of personhood for the nonviable fetus are "unmistakably religious."[17] He argues that an establishment clause issue is raised "whenever the views of organized religious groups have come to play a pervasive role in an entire subject's legislative consideration for reasons intrinsic to the subject matter itself."[18] When these conditions are met, the government's regulation in an area will be unconstitutional unless an affirmative demonstration can be made "that a particular control is needed to serve a compelling purpose that can be defined, and defended as applicable, in terms generally regarded to be wholly secular."[19]

Finely nuanced as it is, Tribe's approach has grave difficulties, some revealed by the uncertain application of the approach to abortion. Despite Tribe's claim that theories that assign the early fetus the status of a human being are unmistakably religious, many people, religious and not, believe that science and rational moral thought strongly support such a status, and some other people believe that status is self-evident without regard to transcendent premises. I agree with Tribe that people who believe either of these things are mistaken, but suppose, as is true, that such claims are honestly made by those who support restrictive laws, and that legislators either accept their arguments or decide to defer to the opinions of constituents who hold them. Judicial determination that the roots of the legislative decision were religious would be exceptionally difficult.

Another troublesome aspect of Tribe's analysis is his consideration of whether any secular compelling interest supports a restrictive abortion law. He claims that such an interest can be found for the viable fetus but not for the previable fetus. This combination of conclusions is hard to sustain.

To deny a secular compelling interest in protecting the previable fetus, Tribe must not only make the dubious claim that only a religious premise can support the personhood of the fetus, he must also argue that the *potentiality* of the fetus is not enough to warrant protection. Here Tribe describes the state's interest as providing a more "detached" determination of the pros and cons of a new life than the pregnant woman may make, and he concludes that the interest in a more detached determination is not strong enough to override the establishment concern.[20] But Tribe omits the more powerful account of the state's interest: protecting the *right* of the fetus to realize its potentialities. That interest sounds much stronger than any vague interest in a more detached determination. My discussion in Chapter 7 indicates how difficult it is to say whether an entity has interests or rights based largely on potentiality, but the view that it does is not unreasonable. Tribe might respond that, so put, the argument based on potentiality falls into the trap of being inevitably religious, but I have indicated the unpersuasiveness of that response.

If the force of Tribe's argument were granted for the previable fetus, what of the status of the fetus after viability? Tribe does not suppose that viability marks some obvious threshold regarding the intrinsic status of the fetus, but he contends that restrictive laws after viability are warranted on rational secular grounds, grounds that do not rely either on present inherent status or on potentiality. His position is that abortion of the viable fetus is essentially indistinguishable from infanticide, because the woman at that stage should not be able to ensure the death of the fetus as well as ensure its removal.[21] Since not all viable fetuses are actually "deliverable," this position does not seem applicable to the early stages of viability in which virtually no fetuses could be induced to be born and to survive. But even if the assumption is made that the viable fetus is deliverable and has a chance to survive, the position is flawed. It is flawed because if a woman retains absolute control over her body at that stage, she should be able to choose delivery (even if not destruction of the fetus) whenever she wants, however markedly reduced the chances of survival of the fetus may be. Tribe, however, acknowledges that the government may interfere with the woman's choice to deliver if her choice would significantly reduce the changes of survival of the fetus.[22]

Is this concession warranted given what else Tribe says? *If* potentiality is not crucial and the status of the fetus has not altered, the death of the fetus is still not a worry of the state; *if* delivery occurs in a manner that tries to preserve the fetus upon birth, no one is guilty of infanticide. One might talk about medical expenses and severe retardation that may occur from premature birth, but these hardly seem at the root of the protection of the viable fetus. Conceivably it might be argued that if a woman decides to free her body of the fetus *either* in a way that kills in a womb an entity that might be born alive or in a way that *risks* death after a live birth, she is guilty of a culpable homicide. But such subtleties seem inadequate to ground any sharp distinction of the nonviable and viable fetus from a rational secular point of view. Tribe's inability to justify this distinction further compromises the persuasiveness of his approach as it applies to abortion.

These difficulties in application help reveal some deeper and more general problems with Tribe's proposal. Tribe seem to assume that when moral principles are widely shared and not perceived to rest on religious bases, legislative reliance on these principles does not render a resulting statute vulnerable, even if religious groups have been active in promoting the statute. Thus at this stage of history, the judgment that newborns deserve full protection, even if originally rooted in religious conviction and even if essentially nonrational, is a proper basis for legislative action. However, if a prior consensus starts to erode and the religious roots of a view are starkly exposed, it might cease, on Tribe's theory, to be a proper basis for legislation.

We may imagine, for example, that opponents of specism begin to claim that no newborn human should get protection greater than is given to mature animals that have the maximum capacities which the particular human baby may possibly develop. On this approach, the law should not give to newborn human babies who predictably will be incapable of developing further than an ordinary six-month-old any greater protection than it gives to animals with the capacities of a six-month-old human being. Even though a relatively small part of the population, say 15 percent, agrees with this challenge to specism, we may suppose that the majority now realizes that its contrary judgment rests on religious premises. At that point, as I understand Tribe, the previously, "taken for granted" position is no longer an acceptable basis for legislation, though still accepted by the vast majority of the population.[23] That such shifts of minority view over time can bring things within the prohibition of the establishment clause is more than a little disturbing. As this book has suggested many times, making the legitimacy of political reliance turn on the extent to which views are presently shared and their religious roots obscured is not a sound principle of liberal democracy. It is also not a sound principle of constitutional law.

This example illuminates another subsidiary problem with Tribe's position. His recommendation for areas infected with establishment difficulties is that the government stay out, leaving choice to the private individuals. But in respect to gravely retarded human infants the government must not only decide whether to leave a range of parental choice but also determine how far public resources will be spent to preserve these tragic human lives that will never develop in capacity beyond those of higher animals. Given the necessity of that choice, the government cannot simple remove itself, leaving everything up to private decision, unless Tribe supposes that it is illegimate for the government even to spend money when the reason for counting the lives as valuable is irreducibly religious.

Both Tribe's analysis and his proposed constitutional position have warranted our attention, because they reinforce our understanding of how complicated is the interrelationship of religious conviction and legal policy. If his initially attractive position is shown to have substantial flaws, ones now acknowledged by him, that lends some support to the more modest constitutional standards I have suggested. Though I believe there is a great need for further and deeper analysis of this constitutional problem, I do not now see practically feasible and theoretically supportable limits on legislative choice that go beyond those proposed here.

Conclusion

Like most issues, the question of religion and politics proves much more complex than appears at first sight and than many people would like to believe. This issue is peculiarly subject to oversimplification because it is obfuscated by rhetoric serving particular political objectives and because many intellectuals who think that religious convictions are foolish superstitions want to minimize their legitimate position in social life without confronting them head on.

I began my investigation of this subject with a belief that the claim that citizens and legislators should rely exclusively on secular grounds was definitely wrong. I have found it more difficult than I initially supposed to show that the claim is *definitely* wrong, but increasing familiarity has persuaded me that at the deepest level the claim is not only wrong but absurd. It invites religious persons to displace their most firmly rooted convictions about values and about the nature of humanity and the universe in a quest for common bases of judgment that is inevitably unavailing when virtually everyone must rely on personal perspectives. The product of serious efforts by religious people to be model liberal citizens of the sort recommended would necessitate a frustrating alienation of their whole persons from their political characters. Rather than asserting any exclusivity for nonreligious reasoned judgment, sensible thought about a model of liberal democracy focuses mainly on domains of liberty and a more constrained commitment to shared premises and forms of reason.

Perhaps the most important lesson of this entire exercise is that liberalism demands a high degree of tolerance, not the tolerance of indifference, but the tolerance of a sympathetic mutual understanding of the place that religious premises occupy in the life of serious believers and of the dangers to those of different beliefs if religious convictions and discourse overwhelm the common dialogue of rational secular morality.

Notes

1. Wallace v. Jaffree 105 S. Ct. 2479 (1985). An alternative reading is possible. One might say that because of the way the new statutory language altered the old the only possible purpose for the new was to promote prayer, or that the main proponent's stated objective would affect the actual impact of the statute. So understood the case is consistent with a more objective understanding of purpose.

2. Id. For long-standing legislation, one might need to distinguish initial purposes from the purposes that underlie continuance of the law. See McGowan v. Maryland, 366 U.S. 420 (1961) (upholding law that requires businesses to close on Sunday).

3. Matters may be more complex if a legislator defers to constituents because of fear of serious social disruption or discontent, but I assume that even in that event

the purpose would be religious if the constituency opinion would be regarded as religious in the relevant sense.

4. L. Henkin, "Morals and the Constitution: The Sin of Obscenity," 63 *Columbia Law Review*, pp. 391–414 (1963).

5. Griswold v. Connecticut, 381 U.S. 479 (1965).

6. Roe v. Wade, 410 U.S. 113 (1973).

7. Moore v. East Cleveland, 431 U.S. 494 (1977).

8. 106 S. Ct. 2841 (1986).

9. Id. at p. 2846. In an omitted sentence Justice White comments that "if all laws representing essentially moral choices are to be invalidated under the Due Process Clause, the courts will be very busy indeed." What this comment does not acknowledge is that most moral choices embodied in restrictive laws involve protecting people from undoubted harms.

10. Id. at pp. 2854–56.

11. In the unlikely event that virtually the *only* support for legislation came from religious groups (and the legislation did not concern how the groups themselves were to be treated), that might properly constitute a kind of evidence that the position taken was one at odds with shared premises and common forms of reason.

12. This apparently is Justice Steven's position, concurring in *Thornburgh v. American College of Obstetricians and Gynecologists*, 106 S. Ct. at 2188. He suggests that only a theological argument can support the idea that the state's interest in protecting the fetus is equally compelling from the moment of conception. He confusingly implies that if the argument is theological, the interest protected is not secular (see especially his footnote 7), missing the point that the role of the theological argument may be to indicate what entities deserve protection of ordinary future secular interests.

13. 410 U.S. 113 (1973).

14. Of course, one might, contrary to what I have assumed up to now in the book, say that all judgments beyond reason are irreducibly religious; but, given the making of "personal" judgments by those who are agnostic about or disbelieving of any transcendent reality and the making of such judgments by religious persons who perceive no connection between the judgments and their religious convictions, that position is implausible. The outer range of "religion" for constitutional purposes is a difficult and complex question that I do not address here, but I have throughout the book implicitly rejected the idea that every matter of ultimate concern is religious and the idea that every religious judgment involves ultimate concern. See K. Greenawalt, "Religion as a Concept in Constitutional Law," 72 *Calif. Law Review*, pp. 753–816 (1984).

15. I put aside situations in which the survival of the hunters or of their native style of life depends on their hunting members of the species.

16. L. Tribe, "The Supreme Court, 1972 Term, Foreword: Toward A Model of Roles in the Due Process of Life and Law," 87 *Harvard Law Review*, pp. 1–53 (1973). Professor Tribe does not develop this analysis in the chapter on religion in his influential text on constitutional law (L. Tribe *American Constitutional Law*,

pp. 812–85 [Mineola, N.Y., Foundation Pr. 1978]), and in the discussion of *Roe v. Wade* (id. at 928) indicates that he has changed his mind.

17. *Harvard Law Review* at p. 21. See also supra note 12.

18. *Harvard Law Review* at p. 23.

19. Id. at p. 24.

20. Id. at p. 26.

21. Id. at pp. 26–29.

22. Id. at p. 29, note 131.

23. I am putting to one side the possible argument that the Constitution's protection of persons reaches severely defective human beings and does not reach animals of greater capacity.

Index